Lecture Notes in Computer Science   12866

More information about this subseries at http://www.springer.com/series/7409

Gerd Berget · Mark Michael Hall ·
Daniel Brenn · Sanna Kumpulainen (Eds.)

Linking Theory and Practice of Digital Libraries

25th International Conference on Theory and Practice
of Digital Libraries, TPDL 2021
Virtual Event, September 13–17, 2021
Proceedings

 Springer

Editors
Gerd Berget ⓘ
OsloMet – Oslo Metropolitan University
Oslo, Norway

Mark Michael Hall ⓘ
The Open University
Milton Keynes, UK

Daniel Brenn
Martin Luther University Halle-Wittenberg
Halle, Germany

Sanna Kumpulainen ⓘ
Tampere University
Tampere, Finland

ISSN 0302-9743   ISSN 1611-3349 (electronic)
Lecture Notes in Computer Science
ISBN 978-3-030-86323-4   ISBN 978-3-030-86324-1 (eBook)
https://doi.org/10.1007/978-3-030-86324-1

LNCS Sublibrary: SL3 – Information Systems and Applications, incl. Internet/Web, and HCI

This Springer imprint is published by the registered company Springer Nature Switzerland AG
The registered company address is: Gewerbestrasse 11, 6330 Cham, Switzerland

Preface

We are happy and proud to present this volume of proceedings, which contains the accepted papers presented at the 25th International Conference on Theory and Practice of Digital Libraries (TPDL 2021), which was held online at The Open University, UK, during September 13–17, 2021.

This year TPDL celebrated its 25th edition as a leading scientific forum that brings together both practitioners and researchers in the field of digital libraries and related fields. This edition of TPDL was held under the general theme of "Linking Theory and Practice", to highlight TPDL's emphasis on including both researchers and practitioners and on providing a forum for productive exchange between the groups. To further strengthen this, this year's edition introduced the full-length practitioner paper aimed at allowing the presentation of high-quality, applied work. The interest in and success of this category was clearly shown by its uptake: 27% of the full-length submissions and 30% of the accepted full-length papers were practitioner papers. We hope that this strengthens links between the groups and leads to the inclusion of more applied research in future editions of TPDL.

TPDL 2021 received a total of 53 submissions, divided into 27 research, 10 practitioner, 9 short, 3 poster, and 4 demo papers. The reviewing process was double-blind, with at least three reviews per paper, combined with a meta-review step. Based on the outcome of this process a total of 16 papers were accepted (30%), divided into 7 research (26%), 3 practitioner (30%), 3 short (33%), 1 poster (33%), and 2 demo papers (50%). Additionally, based on the reviewers' suggestions, we offered 10 papers the opportunity to submit a shortened poster paper, increasing the overall number of accepted papers to 26 (49%). In this respect, the overall acceptance rate is in line with past editions (generally around 45%).

The conference welcomed one keynote speaker: Ulrike Wuttke from the University of Applied Sciences Potsdam, Germany. In keeping with the general theme of "Linking Theory and Practice", her work on digital humanities methods and tools, research infrastructures, eResearch and research data management, open access and open science, and book and library history perfectly encapsulated the conference's collaborative and interdisciplinary focus.

In addition to the main conference, the program included a pre-conference workshop on "LinkedArchives – International Workshop on Archives and Linked Data" and a Doctoral Consortium. To enable the conference's social aspect, making links between researchers and practitioners, between disciplines, and between new and experienced participants, the conference used a technical solution to allow for dynamic, between-session chats and discussions amongst participants.

This conference was only possible because of all the work put in by many people. First, we want to thank all researchers for submitting their work and the members of our Program Committee for their reviews. Thank you also to our Workshop chairs, Dana McKay and Philipp Mayr-Schlegel, and to our Doctoral Consortium chairs,

Morgan Harvey and Helena Francke, for running their tracks so smoothly. Finally, we also express our gratitude to the TPDL Steering Committee, who supported us in experimenting with the online format.

September 2021

Gerd Berget
Mark Michael Hall
Daniel Brenn
Sanna Kumpulainen

Organization

General Chair

Mark Michael Hall   The Open University, UK

Program Committee Chairs

Gerd Berget   Oslo Metropolitan University, Norway
Daniel Brenn   Martin-Luther-Universität Halle-Wittenberg, Germany
Sanna Kumpulainen   Tampere University, Finland

Workshop/Tutorial Chairs

Dana McKay   University of Melbourne, Australia
Philipp Mayr-Schlegel   GESIS - Leibniz Institute for the Social Sciences, Germany

Doctoral Consortium Chairs

Morgan Harvey   Sheffield University, UK
Helena Francke   University of Gothenburg, Sweden

Steering Committee Chair

Trond Aalberg   OsloMet, Norway

Steering Committee

Trond Aalberg   OsloMet, Norway
Bolette Ammitzboll   Jurik State and University Library, Denmark
George Buchanan   The University of Melbourne, Australia
Fabien Duchateau   Université Lyon 1, France
Vittore Casarosa   ISTI-CNR, Italy
Milena Dobreva   University of Malta, Malta
Mark Michael Hall   The Open University, UK
Lazaros Iliadis   Democritus University of Thrace, Greece
Jaap Kamps   University of Amsterdam, The Netherlands
Sarantos Kapidakis   Ionian University, Greece
Laszlo Kovacs   MTA SZTAKI, Hungary
Tanja Merčun   University of Ljubljana, Slovenia
Wolfgang Neidl   L3S Research Center, Germany
Yannis Manolopoulos   Aristotle University of Thessaloniki, Greece

Cezary Mazurek	Poznań Supercomputing and Networking Center, Poland
Christos Papatheodorou	Ionian University, Greece
Edie Rasmussen	University of British Columbia, Canada
Andreas Rauber	Technical University of Wien, Austria
Thomas Risse	Goethe University Frankfurt - University Library J. C. Senckenberg, Germany
Heiko Schuldt	University of Basel, Switzerland
Ingeborg Solvberg	Norwegian University of Technology and Science, Norway
Marcin Werla	Qatar National Library, Qatar

Program Committee

Maristella Agosti	University of Padua, Italy
Hamed Alhoori	Northern Illinois University, USA
Robert Allen	Independent Researcher
Vangelis Banos	Aristotle University of Thessaloniki, Greece
José Borbinha	Universidade de Lisboa, Portugal
Maria Manuel Borges	University of Coimbra, Portugal
George Buchanan	The University of Melbourne, Australia
Ricardo Campos	Ci2 - Polytechnic Institute of Tomar, Portugal
Vittore Casarosa	ISTI-CNR, Italy
Songphan Choemprayong	Culanlongkorn University, Thailand
Mickaël Coustaty	University of La Rochelle, France
Theodore Dalmagas	ATHENA Research Centre, Greece
Tahereh Dehdarirad	Chalmers University of Technology, Sweden
Elena Demidova	Bonn University, Germany
Boris Dobrov	Moscow State University, Russia
Shyamala Doraisamy	University Putra, Malaysia
Antoine Doucet	University of La Rochelle, France
Fabien Duchateau	Université Claude Bernard Lyon 1, France
Ralph Ewerth	Leibniz Universität Hannover, Germany
Edward Fox	Virginia Tech, USA
Nuno Freire	INESC-ID, Portugal
Ingo Frommholz	University of Wolverhampton, UK
Maria Gäde	Humboldt-Universität zu Berlin, Germany
Manolis Gergatsoulis	Ionian University, Greece
C. Lee Giles	Pennsylvania State University, USA
Koraljka Golub	Linnaeus University, Sweden
Sergiu Gordea	Austrian Institue of Technology, Austria
Matthias Hagen	Martin-Luther-Universität Halle-Wittenberg, Germany
Andreas Henrich	University of Bamberg, Germany
Nikos Housos	IRI, Greece
Antoine Isaac	Europeana and VU University Amsterdam, The Netherlands

Robert Jäschke	Humboldt-Universität zu Berlin, Germany
Roman Kern	Graz University of Technology, Austria
Heikki Keskustalo	Tampere University, Finland
Martin Klein	Los Alamos National Laboratory, USA
Petr Knoth	The Open University, UK
Stefanos Kollias	Independent Researcher, Greece
Marijn Koolen	Royal Netherlands Academy of Arts and Sciences, The Netherlands
Laura Korkeamäki	Tampere University, Finland
Laszlo Kovacs	Institute for Computer Science and Control, Hungary
Elina Late	Tampere University, Finland
Suzanne Little	Dublin City University, Ireland
Ying-Hsang Liu	Oslo Metropolitan University, Norway
Clifford Lynch	CNI, USA
Elena Maceviciute	University of Boras, Sweden
Yannis Manolopoulos	Open University of Cyprus, Cyprus
Bruno Martins	University of Lisbon, Portugal
Cezary Mazurek	Poznan Supercomputing and Networking Center, Poland
Robert H. McDonald	University of Colorado Boulder, USA
Tanja Merčun	University of Ljubljana, Slovenia
András Micsik	Institute for Computer Science and Control, Hungary
Jean-Philippe Moreux	Bibliothèque nationale de France, France
Agnieszka Mykowiecka	IPI PAN, Poland
Michael Nelson	Old Dominion University, USA
Erich Neuhold	University of Vienna, Austria
David Nichols	University of Waikato, New Zealand
Kjetil Nørvåg	Norwegian University of Science and Technology, Norway
Christos Papatheodorou	Ionian University, Greece
Vivien Petras	Humboldt Universität zu Berlin, Germany
Nils Pharo	Olso Metropolitan University, Norway
Dimitris Plexousakis	FORTH, Greece
Edie Rasmussen	University of British Columbia, Canada
Andreas Rauber	Vienna University of Technology, Austria
Christina Ribeiro	University of Porto, Portugal
Thomas Risse	Goethe University Frankfurt, Germany
João Rocha Da Silva	University of Porto, Portugal
Irene Rodrigues	Universidade de Evora, Portugal
Heiko Schuldt	University of Basel, Switzerland
Michalis Sfakakis	Ionian University, Greece
Marc Spaniol	Université de Caen Normandie, France
Shigeo Sugimoto	University of Tsukuba, Japan
Cyrille Suire	Université Paris-Saclay, France
Hussein Suleman	University of Cape Town, South Africa
Atsuhiro Takasu	National Institute of Informatics, Japan

Keynote Speaker

Ulrike Wuttke ⓘ

University of Applied Sciences Potsdam
https://ulrikewuttke.wordpress.com/

Ulrike Wuttke has been the Interim Professor for "Library and Information Technology and Digital Services" at the Department of Information Sciences at the University of Applied Sciences Potsdam (FHP), Germany, since 2020. She received her PhD (Doctor of Literature) from Ghent University in 2012. Her teaching and research interests include digital research infrastructures, research data management, digital humanities, scholarly communication, and open science. She contributes to various (inter-)national networks and working groups in these areas. She has been task leader within the PARTHENOS project (FHP), scientific coordinator of the AGATE-project (Union of the German Academies of Sciences and Humanities), worked for the Humanities Data Center (Göttingen Academy of Sciences and Humanities) and the Göttingen eResearch Alliance (Göttingen State and University Library).

Contents

Linked Data and Open Data

User Interfaces and Experience

Document and Text Analysis

FETD²: A Framework for Enabling Textual Data Denoising via Robust Contextual Embeddings

Govind, Céline Alec, Jean-Luc Manguin, and Marc Spaniol[✉]

Department of Computer Science, Université de Caen Normandie,
Campus Côte de Nacre, 14032 Caen Cedex, France
{govind,celine.alec,jean-luc.manguin,marc.spaniol}@unicaen.fr

Abstract. Efforts by national libraries, institutions, and (inter-) national projects have led to an increased effort in preserving textual contents - including non-digitally born data - for future generations. These activities have resulted in novel initiatives in preserving the cultural heritage by digitization. However, a systematic approach toward Textual Data Denoising (TD²) is still in its infancy and commonly limited to a primarily dominant language (mostly English). However, digital preservation requires a universal approach. To this end, we introduce a "Framework for Enabling Textual Data Denoising via robust contextual embeddings" (FETD²). FETD² improves data quality by training language-specific data denoising models based on a small number of language-specific training data. Our approach employs a bi-directional language modeling in order to produce noise-resilient deep contextualized embeddings. In experiments we show the superiority compared with the state-of-the-art.

Keywords: Textual Data Denoising · AI · Contextual representations

1 Introduction

1.1 Motivation and Problem

In recent years, natural language processing (NLP) has seen major improvements by the application of machine learning ranging from "low-level" text (pre-) processing up to "high-level" semantic enrichment. Each component is an important asset ensuring data quality along the entire value chain, e.g., when preserving the cultural heritage by digitization of textual documents. Despite all recent achievements in document digitization, the overall process is still in its infancy. In particular, studies have been primarily conducted on English language text. While the approaches are - in general - conceptually transferable to other languages, there are several drawbacks to be considered. First, models of contextual as well as non-contextual word representations have been predominantly developed for English language text. Second, these models provide dense representation for the vocabulary tokens but broadly make an assumption that tasks in NLP do not have to deal with noisy textual data, which is more prevalent in real-world or digitized documents. Last, but not least, adapting data (pre-) processing for

© Springer Nature Switzerland AG 2021
G. Berget et al. (Eds.): TPDL 2021, LNCS 12866, pp. 3–16, 2021.
https://doi.org/10.1007/978-3-030-86324-1_1

less commonly used languages requires a generalized approach in order to overcome performance drain caused by data scarcity.

1.2 Approach and Contribution

In this paper, we present FETD^2: "a $\underline{F}$ramework for $\underline{E}$nabling $\underline{T}$extual $\underline{D}$ata $\underline{D}$enoising". FETD^2 employs a noise-resilient deep contextualized embedding model based on bi-directional language modeling. Further, language adaptability is supported by emulating language-specific patterns of spelling-errors (referred to as "Confusion Matrix++") by systematically injecting them into high-quality contents for training the model. Finally, in extensive intrinsic and extrinsic evaluations we demonstrate the superiority of FETD^2.

2 Related Work

2.1 Pre-trained Language Representation Models

Pre-trained language representation models aim at encoding the syntactic and semantic knowledge about tokens by building their continuous representations in a high dimensional space. Popular context-insensitive models such as Word2Vec [18] and GloVe [20] learn fixed embeddings of words based on their co-occurrence in large corpora. Although, these models are prone to out-of-vocabulary (OOV) problem caused by spelling errors/variations as well as fail to build unique representations of homonyms. To address this, the idea of deep contextualized representation aims at producing separate representations of a token when used in different contexts. ELMo [21] uses multiple stacked Long Short-Term Memory (LSTM) [9] layers to produce a high-level contextual representation of words with respect to their use in a sentence. BERT [6] proposes the use of masked language modeling with Transformers [26] to process the natural language text in a truly bidirectional way. ELMo and BERT work on sub-word level and thus have the ability to produce representations for misspelled/OOV tokens. Although, it has been widely reported that the model performance suffers significantly as representations of these noisy tokens degrade in quality [12,24]. Recently, there have been several advancements in LMs via transformers such as XLNet [29], ALBERT [13], Character-BERT [3] and ELECTRA [5]. Even these approaches have not adequately focused on dealing with noisy data and the resilient language representation needs further exploration.

2.2 Handling Noise in Textual Data

Real world text often contains noise of various nature such as misspellings, optical character recognition (OCR) errors, typographical errors, etc. Models trained on clean data are prone to fail already in the presence of little noise, although being relatively easily decodeable for a human [2,23]. Multiple studies [12,24,28] have reported that pre-trained language representation models (e.g. BERT, ELMo) suffer in domains such as social media and noisy data in general. Further, [15] show the effects of OCR noise on named entity linking resulting in a considerable drop in performance. Persuaded by the ubiquity of noisy text, there have been growing interest in building robust word representations recently. [7] propose a fastText based model to learn robust embeddings for misspellings by mapping the representation of misspelled words closer to their respective original words in the embedding space. On the other hand, [17] have introduced a context-informed embeddings model based on RNNs. In [1] embedding subspaces are exploited to learn word representation in scarce and noisy data, whereas [25] use a masked language model for denoising. Also, [16] introduce the use of noise-contrastive estimation to improve language modeling and a data augmentation framework Telephonetic to deal with misspellings is introduced by [14]. Adversarial machine learning has also received growing attention in the NLP domain recently [8,27], such as training with adversarial examples in order to build more robust machine learning models [22,24,30]. It has been noted in aforementioned works that having robust word embeddings in-turn helps in building robust models for multiple downstream NLP tasks. To the best of our knowledge, none of the prior approaches tackle data denoising by systematically building a deep contextualized bi-directional language model that is implicitly noise-resilient.

3   Noise-Resilient Contextual Representations

3.1   Bi-Directional Language Models for Contextual Representation

The task of language modeling aims at assigning probability values to future tokens given a history of previous tokens. To this end, a forward language model can be utilized to compute the probability of observing a sequence of tokens as formalized in Eq. 1 and similarly a backward language model in the backward direction as can be seen in Eq. 2. Given a sequence of tokens $t_1, t_2, \ldots, t_N$, a bi-directional language model tries to jointly maximize the log-likelihood in the forward as well as in the backward direction as formalized in Eq. 3.

$$p(t_1, t_2, \ldots, t_N) = \prod_{i=1}^{N} p(t_i | t_1, t_2, \ldots, t_{i-1}) \tag{1}$$

$$p(t_1, t_2, \ldots, t_N) = \prod_{i=1}^{N} p(t_i | t_{i+1}, t_{i+2}, \ldots, t_N) \tag{2}$$

$$\sum_{i=1}^{N} \left(log\big(p(t_i | t_1, t_2, \ldots, t_{i-1}; \overrightarrow{\theta})\big) + log\big(p(t_i | t_{i+1}, t_{i+2}, \ldots, t_N; \overleftarrow{\theta})\big) \right) \tag{3}$$

3.2   Noise-Resilient Bi-Directional Language Modeling

In order to make language modeling and the underlying token representation robust towards noise, we propose a novel language modeling objective where the tokens' history is perturbed via realistic noise patterns. To achieve this, we introduce a noise function Γ, which imparts noise in the sequence of history tokens in a controlled manner as seen in Eq. 4 (cf. Sect. 4.1 for details on the noise generation algorithm). Given a sequence of tokens $T = (t_1, t_2, \ldots, t_j)$, the noise function Γ produces a noisy sequence

$\widetilde{T} = (\widetilde{t_1}, \widetilde{t_2}, \ldots, \widetilde{t_j})$ with ratio of noisy tokens controlled by the parameter η. To this end, the new forward and backward language models assign probability to future tokens based on noisy histories (cf. Eqs. 5 and 6). Now, the bi-directional language model tries to optimize the joint log-likelihood in the forward and backward direction given the noise in history tokens. The intuition behind preserving the noisy tokens as a history is that the model will have to learn the representation of noisy tokens close to their original versions in order to improve the correct prediction of future tokens.

$$\widetilde{T} = \Gamma(T, \eta) \tag{4}$$

$$p(t_1, t_2, \ldots, t_N) = \prod_{i=1}^{N} p(t_i | \widetilde{t_1}, \widetilde{t_2}, \ldots, \widetilde{t_{i-1}}) \tag{5}$$

$$p(t_1, t_2, \ldots, t_N) = \prod_{i=1}^{N} p(t_i | \widetilde{t_{i+1}}, \widetilde{t_{i+2}}, \ldots, \widetilde{t_N}) \tag{6}$$

$$\sum_{i=1}^{N} \left(log\big(p(t_i | \widetilde{t_1}, \widetilde{t_2}, \ldots, \widetilde{t_{i-1}}; \overrightarrow{\theta})\big) + log\big(p(t_i | \widetilde{t_{i+1}}, \widetilde{t_{i+2}}, \ldots, \widetilde{t_N}; \overleftarrow{\theta})\big) \right) \tag{7}$$

Note that this language modeling objective is not simply building a LM on noisy data. Here, the model has to predict correct future token given the noise in previous tokens. In this way, the model does not intend to generate the noisy text but to recover from the noise in tokens as it aims to always predict the next correct token. In contrast, if a LM is trained on noisy text in a brute fashion then it will aim to generate the noisy text where the goal of predicting noisy future tokens will inadvertently penalize the learning of quality representations. To this end, the noise-resilient LM objective implicitly encodes the task of being robust towards noise in tokens and map them closer to their original version in embedding space (empirically evaluated in experiments, cf. Sect. 5).

3.3   Character-Aware Word Representation

Traditionally, a fixed vocabulary of tokens has been often employed for the language modeling without any sub-word level knowledge to build token representations. This might lead to vocabulary explosion because of noise and thus, a character-aware processing is required. Large-scale transformer-based language models such as BERT have popularized the Byte-Pair Encoding (BPE) tokenization of words into smaller sub-word units. On the other hand, models like ELMo use convolutional neural network based kernels in order to extract character level features of a token. Sub-word units based tokenization itself can be sensitive to the noise in tokens [3,19], which adds further complexity in building a robust LM. In the scope of this paper, we consider a simple yet effective setup to process words as a whole on char-level. We employ an "ELMo-like" character level processing on individual words aiming at capturing sub-word features.

3.4   Language Model Architecture

Concerning the underlying architecture, we employ a bi-directional language model architecture adopted and modified from the ELMo architecture proposed by

Peters et al. [21]. The ELMo model extends the ideas from [10] and [11] by introducing a residual connection between the LSTM layers and building bi-directional language model. In broad specification, the model has two bi-directional LSTM layers with 4096 units and the residual connection. A character level input processing module is utilized with 2048 character n-grams convolutional filters and 2 highway layers. It processes tokens in the input sequence on character level and aims to extract the low-level syntactical features for each of the tokens independently. We modify the model in order to adjust it to the requirements of our noise-resilient language modeling objective. To this end, we integrate a noise generation module at the char-level processing layer (Layer 0 in ELMo terminology) to impart desired level of noise in history tokens during the pre-training process. We discuss the noise generation mechanism in the subsequent section.

4 Noisy Data Generation

4.1 Noise Generation Model

Different noise occurs in texts, e.g. misspellings or erroneous OCR. We focus on noise induced by the OCR process (but is also applicable to other kind of orthographic noise). In order to synthetically generate OCR-inspired noisy text, we introduce a noise generation model in Algorithm 1 based on four parameters: input token sequence T, desired noise ratio η, the number of transformations per token K, and our transformation matrix called Confusion Matrix++ (the core of our noise generation model). In our experiments, we keep $K = 1$ constant whereas varying η over several values between 0 and 0.99.

Algorithm 1. Noise Generation Model (Γ)

Input: Token sequence T; Noise ratio η; Confusion Matrix++ $\mathcal{M}$; # transformations per token K
Output: Noisy tokens sequence $\widetilde{T}$

```
 1:  seq_len ← len(T)
 2:  noise_indices ← random_sample(T, ⌈seq_len * η⌉)
 3:  for each index i, token t in T do
 4:      if noise_indices contains i then
 5:          // get character unigrams and bigrams
 6:          chars_unigrams ← unigrams(t)
 7:          chars_bigrams ← bigrams(t)
 8:          ngrams = chars_unigrams + chars_bigrams
 9:          // filter non-existing noise transformation
10:          initialize transforms
11:          for each ngram ng in ngrams do
12:              if M contains ng then
13:                  insert ng into transforms
14:          // sample K transformations randomly
15:          transforms ← random_sample(transforms, K)
16:          n_token ← apply_transforms(t, transforms, M)
17:          insert n_token into T̃
18:      else
19:          insert token into T̃
```

4.2 Confusion Matrix++

In order to overcome data-scarcity we introduce the Confusion Matrix++. It differs from a standard confusion matrix as it goes beyond unigram transformations and aims at generating synthetically OCR inspired noise. To this end, we construct it from manually corrected ground truth pairs by obtaining the probability values of different possible erroneous character n-gram transformations (i.e. substitution, deletion, insertion) as well as no error. We consider unigrams and bigrams (which are extremely sparse) by extracting the statistics from the ICDAR2017 Competition on Post-OCR Text Correction [4] ground truth data in English and French (cf. Table 1 for examples). The Confusion Matrix++ is then used to inject the OCR inspired noise in any presumably clean text.

Table 1. Noisy text generated corresponding to clean sentences for English and French

Language	Noise (η)	Text
English	0	Europe had been hit by the virus shortly before the Americas , although recently some countries are beginning to announce more positive steps .
English	0.25	Europe had been hit b? the virus shorly before the Americas , altbough recently some countries ate beginning to announce more positive stes .
French	0	Antoine Meillet devait diriger la thèse de Jean Paulhan sur la sémantique de le proverbe et c' est lui qui découvrit Gustave Guillaume .
French	0.25	Antoine Meillet devail diriger la thêse de Jean Paulhan sur la semantique de le proverbe et cf est lui qut découvrit Gustave Cuillaume .

5   Experimental Evaluation

5.1   Experimental Datasets

Language-Specific Datasets
In order to demonstrate the language adaptability of the FETD[2] framework, we perform extensive experiments on English and French by employing Wikipedia dumps[1] (February 2020 for English and March 2019 for French). We train the models on around 5 million sentences from the English dataset by randomly sampling 2M paragraphs and 2.5M paragraphs for French in order to keep the same ratio. As a result, we obtain 121M tokens for English and 130M tokens for French. We put aside 10% data for model testing while keeping a separate validation set. The intrinsic evaluation is performed on 534K sentences for English and on 540K sentences for French. Further, we construct the vocabulary by discarding single occurring tokens. As a result, the English and French dataset vocabulary contain 735K and 759K tokens.

Document Classification Datasets
We perform an extrinsic evaluation on the task of document classification. For that purpose, we use the 20 Newsgroups[2] dataset for English, which contains of 18K documents categorized in 20 classes. We perform a random split of 80:10:10 (training, validation, test) by keeping the same percentage of articles from individual categories in each split. For French, we crawled the L'Express[3] newspaper and created a dataset of 2,207 news articles annotated with five different categories maintaining the same split ratio as before.

---

[1] Wikipedia Dumps https://dumps.wikimedia.org/.
[2] 20 Newsgroups dataset http://qwone.com/~jason/20Newsgroups/.
[3] L'Express https://www.lexpress.fr/.

5.2 Model Configurations

Assessing the sensitivity of FETD^2, we train three different models. They differ in the strategy of importing noise and the amount of noise while performing the training. Moreover, demonstrating the applicability across different languages, we train these models for English and French. To this end, we use two models with noise ratio of $\eta = 0.10$ and $\eta = 0.50$ in all of the training sentences, denoted by FETD^2(0.1) and FETD^2(0.5). Further, we introduce an additional model, namely FETD^2(0.1H), which is trained with noise ratio of $\eta = 0.10$, but only in a random selection of half of the training sentences while keeping the remaining half clean. For the sake of providing an extensive comparative analysis of our models, we also train an original ELMo based model, simply denoted by ELMo. All of the models are trained for 10 epochs and implemented in TensorFlow[4] by extending the open source bi-directional LM library bilm-tf[5] by AllenAI. FETD^2 pre-trained models and evaluation data are publicly available here[6].

In addition to evaluating the models performance on clean texts, we perform experiments at various level of synthetic noise (ranging from minor to extreme), specifically at 0.01, 0.05, 0.10, 0.40, 0.55, 0.70, 0.85, and 0.99. Smaller intervals near the initial boundary value have been chosen in order to analyze the sensitivity on minor perturbations already. At the same time, we analyze the models' sensitivity towards higher level of noise stretching to the extent when almost all the tokens contain noise in some form.

5.3 Noise Sensitivity Study

Embeddings Divergence
We assess the divergence of embedding vectors with respect to the noise imparted in tokens of the input sequence by using cosine similarity (cf. Eq. 8) and Euclidean distance (cf. 9). We report the results in Tables 2 and 3. The scores are aggregated by utilizing micro-averaging as well as macro-averaging. The test sets contain around 500,000 sentences for each language. The original and noisy versions of individual sentence are passed through the concerned model in order to obtain the contextual embeddings

Table 2. Results on model noise sensitivity evaluation at Layer 2 for English

Models	ELMo				FETD^2(0.1H)				FETD^2(0.1)				FETD^2(0.5)			
Test	Micro-Avg		Macro-Avg		Micro-Avg		Macro-Avg		Micro-Avg		Macro-Avg		Micro-Avg		Macro-Avg	
Noise (η)	CosSim	Euclidean	CosSim	Euclidean	CosSim	Euclidean	CosSim	Euclidean	CosSim	Euclidean	CosSim	Euclidean	CosSim	Euclidean	CosSim	Euclidean
0.01	0.967	7.189	0.948	9.304	0.992	3.017	0.985	4.326	0.994	2.689	0.987	3.914	**0.997**	**1.795**	**0.992**	**2.692**
0.05	0.948	10.089	0.934	11.223	0.988	4.314	0.982	5.190	0.991	3.831	0.985	4.699	**0.995**	**2.571**	**0.991**	**3.228**
0.10	0.911	14.219	0.901	14.870	0.980	6.216	0.975	6.885	0.984	5.519	0.979	6.208	**0.991**	**3.731**	**0.988**	**4.265**
0.25	0.800	23.018	0.798	22.863	0.957	10.388	0.952	10.726	0.965	9.236	0.961	9.632	**0.981**	**6.314**	**0.978**	**6.640**
0.40	0.681	29.763	0.688	29.135	0.932	13.680	0.927	13.886	0.945	12.195	0.941	12.471	**0.971**	**8.381**	**0.968**	**8.628**
0.55	0.558	35.526	0.569	34.782	0.905	16.512	0.899	16.826	0.924	14.745	0.918	15.114	**0.960**	**10.163**	**0.955**	**10.499**
0.70	0.441	40.464	0.463	39.302	0.879	18.941	0.873	19.135	0.903	16.948	0.897	17.208	**0.949**	**11.691**	**0.945**	**11.966**
0.85	0.332	45.023	0.363	43.461	0.850	21.197	0.846	21.263	0.880	19.002	0.875	19.145	**0.938**	**13.096**	**0.934**	**13.294**
0.99	0.251	48.566	0.292	46.497	0.825	23.011	0.824	22.832	0.860	20.655	0.858	20.577	**0.928**	**14.211**	**0.925**	**14.268**

---

[4] TensorFlow https://www.tensorflow.org/.
[5] AllenAI bilm-tf https://github.com/allenai/bilm-tf.
[6] FETD^2 data https://spaniol.users.greyc.fr/research/FETD%5e2/.

Table 3. Results on model noise sensitivity evaluation at Layer 2 for French

Models	ELMo				FETD²(0.1H)				FETD²(0.1)				FETD²(0.5)			
Test	Micro-Avg		Macro-Avg		Micro-Avg		Macro-Avg		Micro-Avg		Macro-Avg		Micro-Avg		Macro-Avg	
Noise (η)	CosSim	Euclidean	CosSim	Euclidean	CosSim	Euclidean	CosSim	Euclidean	CosSim	Euclidean	CosSim	Euclidean	CosSim	Euclidean	CosSim	Euclidean
0.01	0.969	7.409	0.950	9.688	0.993	3.151	0.985	4.614	0.994	2.766	0.987	4.096	**0.997**	**1.915**	**0.992**	**2.940**
0.05	0.948	10.740	0.935	11.916	0.988	4.676	0.982	5.638	0.991	4.097	0.985	4.993	**0.995**	**2.818**	**0.991**	**3.554**
0.10	0.911	15.121	0.902	15.730	0.980	6.772	0.974	7.480	0.984	5.939	0.979	6.610	**0.991**	**4.068**	**0.988**	**4.648**
0.25	0.799	24.343	0.799	24.024	0.955	11.301	0.951	11.623	0.965	9.945	0.961	10.266	**0.981**	**6.875**	**0.978**	**7.205**
0.40	0.681	31.334	0.690	30.502	0.930	14.828	0.926	14.994	0.944	13.084	0.941	13.265	**0.970**	**9.087**	**0.968**	**9.327**
0.55	0.559	37.297	0.574	36.288	0.902	17.865	0.897	18.126	0.923	15.794	0.918	16.057	**0.959**	**10.994**	**0.955**	**11.303**
0.70	0.443	42.404	0.469	40.953	0.875	20.462	0.871	20.581	0.901	18.121	0.897	18.257	**0.948**	**12.625**	**0.945**	**12.855**
0.85	0.336	47.052	0.370	45.202	0.846	22.884	0.843	22.866	0.878	20.298	0.875	20.306	**0.937**	**14.123**	**0.934**	**14.272**
0.99	0.256	50.619	0.302	48.250	0.820	24.850	0.820	24.548	0.858	22.060	0.857	21.812	**0.927**	**15.320**	**0.925**	**15.307**

of tokens before and after adding noise in the sentence. Micro-averaging computes an average over similarity values for individual token versions (i.e. clean and noisy). Macro-averaging first averages the similarity scores for tokens within a sentence and subsequently averaging over all the sentences. We perform macro-averaging in order to capture the influence of sentence lengths stemming from different languages.

$$CosSim(\overrightarrow{emb_t}, \overrightarrow{emb_{\tilde{t}}}) = \frac{\overrightarrow{emb_t} \cdot \overrightarrow{emb_{\tilde{t}}}}{||\overrightarrow{emb_t}|| \cdot ||\overrightarrow{emb_{\tilde{t}}}||} \tag{8}$$

$$Euclidean(\overrightarrow{emb_t}, \overrightarrow{emb_{\tilde{t}}}) = \sqrt{\sum_{i=1}^{n}(emb_t^i - emb_{\tilde{t}}^i)^2} \tag{9}$$

Cosine Similarity: Table 2 and 3 highlight similarity of embedding vectors where a higher value quantifies the lesser divergence and demonstrates a higher robustness towards noise. In Table 2 values vary heavily for the baseline ELMo model. It is worth noting, that even with as little as 1% (i.e. $\eta = 0.01$) of noise, the baseline model embeddings diverge quickly. In contrast, FETD² models perform fairly robust as there is comparatively low variance in similarity values. Among the FETD² models $\eta = 0.5$ shows the highest resiliency. Thus, FETD² models recover from noise at diverse scale by mapping the contextual embeddings of noisy tokens closer to their original versions, while keeping contextual embeddings of clean tokens fairly unaffected.

Euclidean Distance: Table 2 and 3 show the divergence of contextual embeddings where the higher the distance value is, the lower the robustness of the concerned model is. As before, we observe a similar pattern of performance degeneration while FETD² remain stable mostly on noisy input. In addition, findings are consistent across languages.

Perplexity

We assess Perplexity (PP) by quantifying "how well a language model predicts the next token if the history tokens contains noise". Equation 10 defines the modified robust perplexity (RPP) measure for token sequence T of length N. We perform the perplexity evaluation at different levels of noise for ELMo and FETD² models (cf. Table 4). ELMo performs best without noise in the token history and decreases rapidly with increasing noise-levels. Perplexity values for the English ELMo model differ by over 4,000 as well

Table 4. Evolution of perplexity values with respect to noise in test set sequences

	Test Noise (η)	ELMo	FETD^2(0.1H)	FETD^2(0.1)	FETD^2(0.5)		Test Noise (η)	ELMo	FETD^2(0.1H)	FETD^2(0.1)	FETD^2(0.5)
English	0.00	**65.217**	66.846	66.186	69.941	French	0.00	**42.073**	43.272	43.636	45.189
	0.01	75.383	68.445	**67.347**	70.606		0.01	48.544	**44.257**	44.374	45.606
	0.05	81.933	69.387	**68.063**	70.974		0.05	53.526	44.945	**44.907**	45.886
	0.10	96.598	71.241	**69.426**	71.685		0.10	64.027	46.205	**45.863**	46.380
	0.25	161.221	77.223	**73.833**	73.892		0.25	112.207	50.330	48.982	**47.929**
	0.40	285.483	84.330	79.001	**76.326**		0.40	207.603	55.276	52.629	**49.625**
	0.55	416.297	89.250	82.522	**77.914**		0.55	312.278	58.780	55.179	**50.748**
	0.70	1303.862	105.626	93.967	**82.686**		0.70	1043.002	70.460	63.416	**54.076**
	0.85	2177.934	113.727	99.462	**84.795**		0.85	1769.731	76.375	67.492	**55.566**
	0.99	4174.887	125.227	107.231	**87.519**		0.99	3473.314	85.047	73.293	**57.546**

as over 3,000 for French. Even at low noise levels such as 10% the perplexity of ELMo increases rapidly. In contrast, FETD^2 models remain considerably stable with increasing noise while achieving comparable performance on the clean test set. In addition, we observe that models trained with lower η perform better at lower noise level whereas the models with higher η remain more consistent towards higher noise level.

$$RPP(T) = \sqrt[N]{\prod_{i=1}^{N} \frac{1}{p(t_i|\widetilde{t_1}, \widetilde{t_2}, \ldots, \widetilde{t_{i-1}})}} \tag{10}$$

5.4 Document Classification

Classification Model

We employ a plain document classification model to study the effect of noise on the classification performance. The intuition is to observe and demonstrate the robustness of the contextual embeddings produced by different bi-directional language models on a higher level NLP task. To this end, we represent a document by averaging the embedding vectors of the tokens it contains. Each of the tokens in a document is represented by concatenating the token context-insensitive embedding from Layer 0 along with the contextualized representations from Layer 1 and 2 of LSTMs. We first run the concerned bi-directional language model on individual sentences of the document. Then, we average over the embeddings of tokens in individual sentences. This way, we first compute the sentence representations and then average over the representation vectors of sentences to produce the document representation. By means of macro-averaging the influence of sentence lengths in the overall representation of the document is incorporated.

Subsequently, the document representations are fed into the perceptron-based classification model, which basically consists of a single hidden layer of size 512 with ReLU activation function. The hidden layer is connected to the softmax output layer. The number of units in softmax are equal to the class labels in datasets. The English dataset has 20 output class labels whereas the French dataset has 5 classes. Further, we do not fine-tune the pre-trained contextual embedding models as part of our document classification model training process. The model is trained using the Adam optimizer

Table 5. English documents classification results with model noise sensitivity

Models	ELMo			FETD^2(0.1H)			FETD^2(0.1)			FETD^2(0.5)		
Test Noise (η)	Precision	Recall	F1	Precision	Recall	F1	Precision	Recall	F1	Precision	Recall	F1
0	0.769	0.765	0.766	**0.777**	**0.772**	**0.773**	0.767	0.765	0.763	0.772	0.770	0.769
0.01	0.738	0.734	0.735	0.758	0.752	0.753	**0.760**	**0.756**	**0.755**	0.758	0.754	0.753
0.05	0.743	0.736	0.737	**0.766**	**0.760**	**0.761**	0.759	0.756	0.754	0.761	0.756	0.756
0.10	0.729	0.721	0.722	0.756	0.749	0.750	**0.757**	**0.752**	**0.752**	0.751	0.746	0.746
0.25	0.680	0.654	0.652	0.744	0.735	0.736	0.745	0.737	0.736	**0.754**	**0.750**	**0.748**
0.40	0.621	0.562	0.555	0.716	0.703	0.704	0.723	0.715	0.714	**0.753**	**0.747**	**0.747**
0.55	0.577	0.465	0.442	0.684	0.665	0.664	0.702	0.686	0.686	**0.723**	**0.716**	**0.714**
0.70	0.491	0.342	0.312	0.661	0.628	0.627	0.684	0.656	0.655	**0.718**	**0.706**	**0.705**
0.85	0.299	0.220	0.192	0.623	0.575	0.571	0.667	0.613	0.615	**0.705**	**0.689**	**0.687**
0.99	0.221	0.150	0.116	0.575	0.521	0.515	0.618	0.570	0.568	**0.700**	**0.680**	**0.678**

Table 6. French documents classification results with model noise sensitivity

Models	ELMo			FETD^2(0.1H)			FETD^2(0.1)			FETD^2(0.5)		
Test Noise (η)	Precision	Recall	F1	Precision	Recall	F1	Precision	Recall	F1	Precision	Recall	F1
0	0.906	0.841	0.855	**0.926**	**0.843**	**0.868**	0.897	0.839	0.858	0.884	0.785	0.817
0.01	0.909	0.844	0.858	**0.938**	**0.860**	**0.884**	0.900	0.843	0.861	0.907	0.793	0.833
0.05	0.910	0.843	0.855	**0.935**	**0.858**	**0.882**	0.893	0.833	0.851	0.885	0.778	0.811
0.10	0.903	0.840	0.854	**0.911**	**0.853**	**0.872**	0.894	0.837	0.855	0.882	0.782	0.814
0.25	0.870	0.826	0.827	0.904	0.842	0.864	**0.921**	**0.858**	**0.872**	0.885	0.786	0.818
0.40	0.795	0.736	0.718	**0.914**	**0.852**	**0.874**	0.904	0.833	0.852	0.889	0.789	0.821
0.55	0.703	0.643	0.542	**0.912**	**0.855**	**0.875**	0.910	0.828	0.851	0.883	0.787	0.818
0.70	0.659	0.517	0.375	**0.913**	**0.846**	**0.875**	0.890	0.820	0.837	0.887	0.788	0.820
0.85	0.289	0.495	0.316	0.881	0.820	**0.842**	**0.889**	**0.821**	0.838	0.883	0.784	0.816
0.99	0.261	0.352	0.223	**0.905**	**0.816**	**0.852**	0.874	0.793	0.809	0.884	0.789	0.819

with a learning rate of 0.0001 and betas of (0.99, 0.999) for 50 epochs. We use a step learning rate scheduler with step size of 1 and decay coefficient gamma of 0.95. As we do not train the pre-trained contextual embeddings model as part of classification model training, the document representations are pre-computed.

Classification Results

We report the results on the document classification task in Table 5 and 6. Precision, recall, and F1 measures are macro-averaged in order to give equal weight to each of the output class labels and avoid a biasing towards more populated classes. Findings are in-line with the observations from the intrinsic evaluation. From experiments in English we notice that all of the models have almost similar performance on the clean text (i.e. $\eta = 0$) with FETD^2(0.1H) being slightly better than others. The performance of the baseline ELMo classification model is fragile in nature and, thus, the F1 score drops from 0.766 for clean text to 0.116 at $\eta = 0.99$ noise level. However, the F1 score of the FETD^2(0.5) model performance remains quite robust as it only drops by less than 10%. Similar to the perplexity, the FETD^2 models trained with lower noise level perform better on test sets with low(er) noise-level, while models trained with higher η are more robust towards high noise without compromising too much performance for low(er) noise levels. In experiments on the French dataset a clear dominance of the FETD^2 models can be observed. Scores are overall higher for French than for English. This can be attributed to the fact that there are fewer classes in the French dataset, which makes the problem less complex. In addition, the FETD$^2(0.1H)$ model performs best, although performance differences with other FETD^2 models are less compared to the English dataset.

In summary, extensive experiments on intrinsic evaluation (language-specific data denoising) along with extrinsic evaluation (document classification in different languages) confirm our hypothesis that noise robustness can be added to the bi-directional contextual embedding models without compromising their performance on clean data.

5.5 Success and Error Analysis

Figure 1 depicts the effect of noise on the contextual embeddings of tokens at different layers in an example English sequence by comparing the cosine similarity between embeddings of token pairs from clean and noisy versions of an English sentence with 50% noise. The heatmap color-encodes the scores (yellow $\hat{=}$ lowest and blue $\hat{=}$ highest). At the context-insensitive Layer 0, it can be seen that the effects of noisy tokens are isolated. Further, Fig. 1a and 1d show that Layer 0 embeddings of noisy tokens diverge for both models but the effect is more visible in ELMo than FETD^2. On Layer 1, noisy tokens degrade their own embeddings and neighboring tokens in case of ELMo (cf. Fig. 1b). In contrast, a dark blue colored diagonal in Fig. 1e for FETD$^2(0.1)$ can be observed, while some of the light colored diagonal boxes from layer 0 have already become darker. This means that FETD$^2(0.1)$ recovers from noise in contrast to ELMo, which becomes even more evident at Layer 2 (cf. Fig. 1f and 1c).

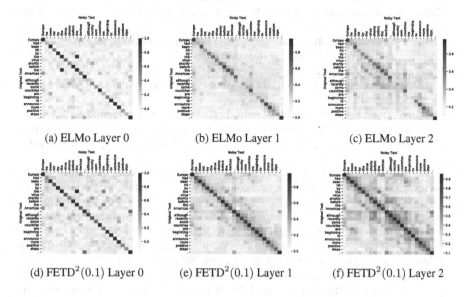

(a) ELMo Layer 0   (b) ELMo Layer 1   (c) ELMo Layer 2

(d) FETD$^2(0.1)$ Layer 0   (e) FETD$^2(0.1)$ Layer 1   (f) FETD$^2(0.1)$ Layer 2

Fig. 1. Cosine similarity of token pairs between a clean and noisy (50%) sentence

6 Conclusion and Outlook

We presented FETD^2, mitigating noisy input data (e.g., from digitization) by utilizing robust contextual embeddings. FETD^2 tackles two aspects of digital preservation at the same time: improving the data quality of digitally and non-digitally born data as well as by providing a language-adaptable framework. While deep neural networks, suffer from performance drop for languages with less ample resources, our Confusion Matrix++ overcomes sparsity issues. In our extensive experiments on English and French datasets, we prove the superiority of FETD^2 compared with the state-of-the-art implementations.

In future, we intend to apply FETD^2 as part of a content semantification pipeline for digitized documents by employing it on OCRed data of historical texts with a subsequent step of named entity recognition and disambiguation utilized for semantic retrieval afterwards. In addition, we consider further adaptations of our noise-resilient bi-directional deep contextualized embeddings framework in the context of other language modeling objectives such as masked or autoregressive language modeling.

Acknowledgements. This work was supported by the RIN RECHERCHE Normandie Digitale research project ASTURIAS contract no. 18E01661. We thank our colleagues for the inspiring discussions.

References

1. Astudillo, R., Amir, S., Ling, W., Silva, M., Trancoso, I.: Learning word Representations from scarce and noisy data with embedding subspaces. In: Proceedings of the 53rd Annual Meeting of the Association for Computational Linguistics and the 7th International Joint Conference on Natural Language Processing (Volume 1: Long Papers), pp. 1074–1084. Association for Computational Linguistics, Beijing, China, July 2015. https://www.aclweb.org/anthology/P15-1104
2. Belinkov, Y., Bisk, Y.: Synthetic and natural noise both break neural machine translation. In: International Conference on Learning Representations (2018)
3. Boukkouri, H.E., Ferret, O., Lavergne, T., Noji, H., Zweigenbaum, P., Tsujii, J.: CharacterBERT: Reconciling ELMo and BERT for Word-Level Open-Vocabulary Representations From Characters (2020)
4. Chiron, G., Doucet, A., Coustaty, M., Moreux, J.: ICDAR2017 competition on post-OCR text correction. In: 2017 14th IAPR International Conference on Document Analysis and Recognition (ICDAR). vol. 01, pp. 1423–1428, November 2017. https://doi.org/10.1109/ICDAR.2017.232
5. Clark, K., Luong, M.T., Le, Q.V., Manning, C.D.: ELECTRA: pre-training text encoders as discriminators rather than generators. In: ICLR (2020). https://openreview.net/pdf?id=r1xMH1BtvB
6. Devlin, J., Chang, M., Lee, K., Toutanova, K.: BERT: pre-training of deep bidirectional transformers for language understanding. CoRR abs/1810.04805 (2018)
7. Edizel, B., Piktus, A., Bojanowski, P., Ferreira, R., Grave, E., Silvestri, F.: Misspelling oblivious word embeddings. In: Proceedings of the 2019 Conference of the North American Chapter of the Association for Computational Linguistics: Human Language Technologies (NAACL-HLT 2019), Minneapolis, MN, USA, June 2–7 2019, Vol. 1 (Long and Short Papers), pp. 3226–3234 (2019). https://aclweb.org/anthology/papers/N/N19/N19-1326/

8. Eger, S., et al.: Text processing like humans do: visually attacking and shielding NLP systems. In: Proceedings of the 2019 Conference of the North American Chapter of the Association for Computational Linguistics: Human Language Technologies, vol. 1 (Long and Short Papers), pp. 1634–1647. Association for Computational Linguistics, Minneapolis, Minnesota, June 2019. https://www.aclweb.org/anthology/N19-1165

9. Hochreiter, S., Schmidhuber, J.: Long short-term memory. Neural Comput. **9**(8), 1735–1780 (1997), http://dx.doi.org/10.1162/neco.1997.9.8.1735

10. Józefowicz, R., Vinyals, O., Schuster, M., Shazeer, N., Wu, Y.: Exploring the limits of language modeling. CoRR abs/1602.02410 (2016). http://arxiv.org/abs/1602.02410

11. Kim, Y., Jernite, Y., Sontag, D., Rush, A.M.: Character-aware neural language models. In: Proceedings of the Thirtieth AAAI Conference on Artificial Intelligence (AAAI 2016), pp. 2741–2749. AAAI Press (2016)

12. Kumar, A., Makhija, P., Gupta, A.: noisy text data: achilles' heel of BERT. In: Proceedings of the Sixth Workshop on Noisy User-generated Text (W-NUT 2020), pp. 16–21. Association for Computational Linguistics, November 2020. https://doi.org/10.18653/v1/2020.wnut-1.3, https://www.aclweb.org/anthology/2020.wnut-1.3

13. Lan, Z., Chen, M., Goodman, S., Gimpel, K., Sharma, P., Soricut, R.: ALBERT: a lite BERT for self-supervised learning of language representations. In: International Conference on Learning Representations (2020). https://openreview.net/forum?id=H1eA7AEtvS

14. Larson, C., Lahlou, T., Mingels, D., Kulis, Z., Mueller, E.: Telephonetic: making neural language models robust to ASR and semantic noise. ArXiv abs/1906.05678 (2019)

15. Linhares Pontes, E., Hamdi, A., Sidere, N., Doucet, A.: Impact of OCR quality on named entity linking. In: Proceedings of 21st International Conference on Asia-Pacific Digital Libraries (ICADL 2019) (2019)

16. Liza, F.F., Grzes, M.: Improving language modelling with noise-contrastive estimation. In: AAAI (2018)

17. Malykh, V., Logacheva, V., Khakhulin, T.: Robust word vectors: context-informed embeddings for noisy texts. In: Proceedings of the 2018 EMNLP Workshop W-NUT: The 4th Workshop on Noisy User-generated Text, pp. 54–63. Association for Computational Linguistics, Brussels, Belgium, November 2018. https://www.aclweb.org/anthology/W18-6108

18. Mikolov, T., Sutskever, I., Chen, K., Corrado, G.S., Dean, J.: Distributed representations of words and phrases and their compositionality. In: Advances in Neural Information Processing Systems, pp. 3111–3119 (2013)

19. Nayak, A., Timmapathini, H., Ponnalagu, K., Venkoparao, V.G.: Domain adaptation challenges of BERT in tokenization and sub-word representations of out-of-vocabulary words. In: Rogers, A., Sedoc, J., Rumshisky, A. (eds.) Proceedings of the 1st Workshop on Insights from Negative Results in NLP, Insights 2020, pp. 1–5. ACL (2020)

20. Pennington, J., Socher, R., Manning, C.D.: GloVe: global vectors for word representation. In: Empirical Methods in Natural Language Processing (EMNLP), pp. 1532–1543 (2014)

21. Peters, M.E., Neumann, M., Iyyer, M., Gardner, M., Clark, C., Lee, K., Zettlemoyer, L.: Deep contextualized word representations. In: Proceedings of NAACL (2018)

22. Ren, S., Deng, Y., He, K., Che, W.: Generating natural language adversarial examples through probability weighted word saliency. In: Proceedings of the 57th Annual Meeting of the Association for Computational Linguistics, pp. 1085–1097. Association for Computational Linguistics, Florence, Italy, July 2019. https://www.aclweb.org/anthology/P19-1103

23. Subramaniam, L., Roy, S., Faruquie, T., Negi, S.: A survey of types of text noise and techniques to handle noisy text. In: ACM International Conference Proceeding Serie, pp. 115–122, January 2009. https://doi.org/10.1145/1568296.1568315

24. Sun, L., et al.: Adv-BERT: BERT is not robust on misspellings! Generating nature adversarial samples on BERT. arXiv preprint arXiv:2003.04985 (2020)

25. Sun, Y., Jiang, H.: Contextual text denoising with masked language model. In: Proceedings of the 5th Workshop on Noisy User-generated Text (W-NUT 2019), pp. 286–290. Association for Computational Linguistics, Hong Kong, China, November 2019
26. Vaswani, A., et al.: Attention is all you need. In: Advances in Neural Information Processing Systems 30, pp. 5998–6008. Curran Associates, Inc., Red Hook (2017)
27. Wang, W., Tang, B., Wang, R., Wang, L., Ye, A.: A survey on adversarial attacks and defenses in text. arXiv preprint arXiv:1902.07285 (2019)
28. Xiong, W., et al.: TweetQA: a social media focused question answering dataset. In: Proceedings of the 57th Annual Meeting of the Association for Computational Linguistics (2019)
29. Yang, Z., Dai, Z., Yang, Y., Carbonell, J.G., Salakhutdinov, R., Le, Q.V.: XLNet: generalized autoregressive pretraining for language understanding. CoRR abs/1906.08237 (2019). http://arxiv.org/abs/1906.08237
30. Zhang, W.E., Sheng, Q.Z., Alhazmi, A.A.F.: Generating textual adversarial examples for deep learning models: a survey. arXiv preprint arXiv:1901.06796 (2019)

Minimalist Fitted Bayesian Classifier-Based on Likelihood Estimations and Bag-of-Words

Jean-Rémi Bourguet[1]([✉])[iD], Wesley Silva[2][iD], and Elias de Oliveira[2][iD]

[1] Vila Velha University, Av. Comissário José Dantas de Melo,
21 - 29102-920, Vila Velha, ES, Brazil
`jean-remi.bourguet@uvv.br`
[2] Federal University of Esprito Santo, Av. Fernando Ferrari,
514 - 29075-910 - Goiabeiras, Vitória, ES, Brazil
`{wpsilva,elias.oliveira}@lcad.inf.ufes.br`

Abstract. The expansion of institutional repositories involves new challenges for autonomous agents that control the quality of semantic annotations in large amounts of scholarly knowledge. While evaluating metadata integrity in documents was already widely tackled in the literature, a majority of the frameworks are intractable when confronted with a big data environment. In this paper, we propose an optimal strategy based on feature engineering to identify spurious objects in large academic repositories. Through an application case dealing with a Brazilian institutional repository containing objects like PhD theses and MSc dissertations, we use maximum likelihood estimations and bag-of-words techniques to fit a minimalist Bayesian classifier that can quickly detect inconsistencies in class assertions guaranteeing approximately 94% of accuracy.

Keywords: Semantic metadata · Institutional repository · Spurious objects · Bayesian classifier · Statistical inference · Bag-of-words

1 Introduction

Classification is an old concern that dates back to ancient times. The issue of classifying is consubstantial with the approach of many sciences because a good classification allows not only the summarization of knowledge but also their enrichment by revealing similarities and differences. Aristotle was one of the first to systematically classify knowledge and concepts by observing criteria of resemblance about living beings [29]. Since then, classifying represents a common abstraction for human knowledge and an informational consolidation for various repositories. For example, during the early modern period marked by the invention of moveable type printing, institutions were overwhelmed with information. Thus, clerks invented new ways to index and catalog such an expanding world by archiving both probative and administrative materials [11]. The classification became an autonomous agent-based challenge with the industrial revolution.

© Springer Nature Switzerland AG 2021
G. Berget et al. (Eds.): TPDL 2021, LNCS 12866, pp. 17–28, 2021.
https://doi.org/10.1007/978-3-030-86324-1_2

For instance, on a conveyer belt, robots inspect and classify parts by accepting or rejecting them [26]. When confronted with textual corpus, autonomous classifiers assume constructions of *a priori metadata* for retrieving objects stored in digital libraries [see 33]. From the statistics maintained by the *Directory of Open Access Repositories*[1] of the University of Nottingham, it is possible to monitor the expansion of the academic repositories around the world, between the years 2005 and 2018. In 2015, there were 2,989 repositories, while in 2017, this number reached 3,633 and in 2018, 3,783 repositories were counted. Within this perspective, an important challenge appeared in order to tractably identify spurious objects in digital repositories. The integrity of a semantics-based repository ensures that the contents are accurately represented through its metadata [19]. It is commonly recognized that manual annotations often result in a highly qualitative description [25]. Nevertheless, in order to be able to ensure trustable and quantitative semantic annotations, the frameworks usually require manual annotations to build training datasets and supervise machine learnings in a semi-automatic way. In the literature, a common challenge is to release systems performing fair trade-offs with human efforts resulting in acceptable accuracies in the classification tasks [see for example 22]. While the majority of the machine learning techniques parse whole documents to perform the prediction slowing the computational time, some feature engineering-based strategies can considerably alleviate the classification task by minimizing the inputs during the learning and the predictions tasks. In this paper, we propose a trade-off by selecting optimal features of a document that will fit a minimalist classifier. Our approach is illustrated through the institutional repository of the Federal University of Espírito Santo called RiUfes[2]. A recurrent issue for this repository concerns the imperfections in the information retrieval process due to an unfair usage of the metadata. Here, we will focus on the classification inconsistencies of two kinds of digital objects: MSc thesis and PhD thesis. While only two classes (MSc and PhD) were used in this work, it is worth noting that the methodology is scalable to a larger number of classes. For this, statistical inferences and Bayesian modeling techniques were used, both applied to the development of an autonomous agent which pointed out the spurious objects in the institutional repository. In our multi-agent system, specialists are called to classify object's samples in order to train and fit a classifier. Naturally, a naive proposal for solving this problem requires an exhaustive procedure in which one or more specialists go through each object of the collection to examine their natures. As the repository contains 4.723 objects, such a manual scan would require approximately 158 h leaving a time gap of at least 2 min per object. By applying our minimalist classifier such a task can be reduced to less than 1 h, identifying 1.847 spurious items and guaranteeing approximately 94% of accuracy.

The organization of this paper is structured as follows. In Sect. 2, we detail some works which have some similarities with our approach in this paper.

---

[1] https://v2.sherpa.ac.uk/opendoar/.
[2] http://repositorio.ufes.br/.

In Sect. 3, we describe our methodology. In Sect. 4, we present our results. Finally, we put our closing remarks in Sect. 5.

2   Related Works

Digital repositories store, systematize, display and support retrieval of digital objects, allowing for efficient dissemination of knowledge. Metadata are commonly employed as crucial markers for such infrastructures. However, a lack of information about repositories, doubts and insecurities in self-archiving operations are the main factors that inhibit the academic publication of data [5].

Neither a manual nor an automated approach alone is sufficient to effectively assess and address issues of metadata quality and repository integrity [21]. Associating meta information to learning objects by humans is a labour intensive activity. The manual annotation often results in a very high quality metadata but is a very time consuming activity [25]. For a complete review regarding semi-automatic metadata generations, the authors in [23] examine a range of 39 tools while providing an analysis of their techniques. In [10], the authors complete the aforementioned review by highlighting research initiatives from the *Metadata Generation Research Projects.*

In terms of evaluation, there exist different frameworks that support fundamental principles for assessing semantic metadata such that *SemRef* [18]. In [13], the authors measure the level of metadata integrity being produced from textual documents in order to ascertain whether the data contained in the original document are represented with an accurate reflection. Feature engineering represents the act of extracting features from raw data and transforming them into formats that are suitable for fitting the machine learning models [34]. Feature engineering promotes features as first-class objects throughout data processing [32]. The key idea behind feature selections is to identify a feasible subset of features by evaluating them, through some indicators [28].

In bag-of-words representation, documents can occupy a maximum feature space with one dimension for each term, posing a problem for many machine learning algorithms that suffer from overfitting when the number of features greatly exceeds the number of training examples [14]. To address this issue, a subset of relevant features must be selected. A relevant feature is one that increases the performance when included in the set of features utilized by a particular machine learning algorithm [4]. In [7], different feature-sets can be used in conjunction with each other to improve performance and reduce the number of documents that need to be labeled.

A large part of features reduction are based on hotspots selecting inputs that maximize the information gain in relation to a specified cut-off value [see for example 8]. A method called *Combined Feature Selection* supports effective categorizations of web pages by selecting the optimum number of attribute features to improve the classification accuracy [28]. In [9], a document is classified by extracting one feature vector per page and by computing one score per page per class before aggregating the page-level scores into document-level scores for each document class. In [20], a novel technique called *Learning Feature Engineering* is released for automating feature engineering in classification tasks by applying changes to numerical features from past feature engineering experiences. In relation to the Bayesian inferences, different approaches exist to classify or annotate documents. In [31], *Paper-Base* predicts likely keywords for the preprints based on a controlled vocabulary of keywords. In [27], the authors propose an automatic Bayesian classification of learning resources on a given taxonomic organization of the knowledge. In [6], *JADE* was released as a platform to semi-automatically classify learning contents through Bayesian methods in the virtual e-learning environment *Moodle*.

Finally, to the best of our knowledge, the most similar approach to our proposal was proposed in [15]. The system proposed in this work performs extractions from the first page of 100 scientific papers in PDF formats that contain all available metadata in the majority of the cases. Then, the features serve to evaluate classifiers by using cross validations on a manually annotated corpus.

3   Methodology

In a context of massive production of information contained in digital objects, the use of statistical inferences and machine learning allows for the treatment of data storage, description, representation and preservation [see for example 3].

3.1   Repository

Until RiUfes came online in 2010, our central library servers were publishing data to the *Brazilian Digital Library for Theses and Dissertations* (BDTD)[3] containing approximately 1,500 objects. In 2016, data migrated from BDTD to RiUfes, a period in which duplications of records and usage of various description standards generated inconsistencies. Even with an insufficient staff to keep the integrity constant, RiUfes has continued to register strong growth in the past decade. Currently the repository contains 5.686 items, namely: 116 books, 183 scientific articles, 450 theses and 4,920 dissertations. Our first intention was to build a probability distribution representing the chance of finding a certain type of object according to its number of pages. To obtain such a distribution, we first automatically extracted from the metadata of the objects both their numbers of pages and the type of document registered as *thesis* and *dissertations*. This initial inspection of RiUfes generated the distributions illustrated in Fig. 1. In the center of the aforementioned graph, there is an overlap of the bell curves, occupying a significant area in relation to the one another. Thus, we detected the existence of some objects of both natures with numbers of pages in the same range of values (above 100 and below 200 pages).

---

[3] http://bdtd.ibict.br/vufind/.

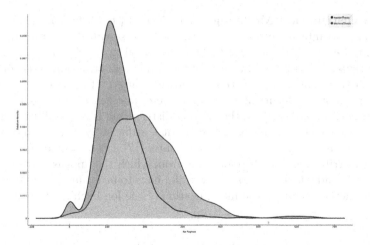

Fig. 1. Distributions in RiUfes: *Dissertations* in blue and *Theses* in red. (Color figure online)

3.2 Maximum Likelihood Estimations Based on Metadata

The Maximum Likelihood Estimation (MLE) is a statistical estimator used to infer the parameters of a given probability distribution by searching for the values of the parameters and by maximizing a likelihood function in relation to a given sample. This method is largely used when the objective is to estimate the parameters of a distribution modeling a statistical phenomenon.

Normal Distribution Modeling. The normal distribution is a well-known representation of situations in which there are several independent, non-trivial and realistic factors, which together generate randomly distributed data [30]. Let a sample $(x_1, ..., x_n)$ of a normal $\mathcal{N}(\mu, \sigma)$ population from which the approximate values of parameters μ and σ have to be evaluated, its maximum likelihood method requires the maximization of the log-likelihood function[4]:

$$\ln \mathcal{L}^{\mathcal{N}}(\mu, \sigma \mid x_1, ..., x_n) = \ln \prod_{i=1}^{n} f^{\mathcal{N}}(\mu, \sigma \mid x_i) = \sum_{i=1}^{n} \ln \frac{1}{\sigma\sqrt{2\pi}} e^{-\frac{1}{2}\left(\frac{x_i - \mu}{\sigma}\right)^2}$$

Taking derivatives with respect to μ and σ the maximum likelihood estimates:

$$\mu = \frac{1}{n}\sum_{i=1}^{n} x_i \qquad\qquad \sigma = \sqrt{\frac{1}{n}\sum_{i=1}^{n}(x_i - \mu)^2}$$

---

[4] the likelihood function and the log of the likelihood function both peak at the same values for σ and μ.

Gamma Distribution Modeling. In 1755, Euler published a treatise about differential and integral calculus and released the so-called Eulerian functions containing the so-called function Γ. Many probability distributions are defined by using the gamma function, naturally the Gamma distribution is one of them. Gamma distributions are used to model a wide variety of phenomena, and particularly phenomena occurring over time where, in essence, the elapsed time is a positive real quantity. Thus, the gamma distribution is a distribution used in reliability work to fit failure data, because it is sufficiently flexible to deal with decreasing, constant and increasing failure rates [17]. Let a sample $(x_1, ..., x_n)$ of a gamma distribution $\mathcal{G}(\kappa, \theta)$ population from which the approximate values of parameters κ and θ (the shape and the scale) have to be evaluated, its maximum likelihood method requires the maximization of the log-likelihood function:

$$\ln \mathcal{L}^{\mathcal{G}}(\kappa, \theta \mid x_1, ..., x_n) = \ln \prod_{i=1}^{n} f^{\mathcal{G}}(\kappa, \theta \mid x_i) = \sum_{i=1}^{n} \ln \frac{x_i^{\kappa-1}}{\theta^\kappa \Gamma(\kappa)} e^{-\frac{x_i}{\theta}} \quad with \; \kappa, \theta > 0$$

where $\Gamma(\alpha)$ is the gamma function $\Gamma(\alpha) = (\alpha - 1)!$.

Taking derivatives with respect to κ and θ the maximum likelihood estimates:

$$\kappa \approx \frac{1}{2(\ln \frac{1}{n} \sum_{i=1}^{n} x_i - \frac{1}{n} \sum_{i=1}^{n} \ln x_i)} \qquad \theta = \frac{1}{n\kappa} \sum_{i=1}^{n} x_i$$

3.3 Bag-Of-Words

A bag-of-words strategy generally tries to map a document to a vector using a dictionary of words [16]. A document is represented by a vector of the same size as the dictionary. The i-th component of a vector indicates the number of occurrences of the i-th word of the dictionary and can be standardized in different ways: reduced to a unitary norm by dividing each component by the norm of the vector, binarized by indicating only the presence or absence of a word from the dictionary or weighted according to a different strategy. It is generally necessary to pre-process words in order to normalize them by means of lemmatization and stemming and removing words from a stop words list. It is also possible to consider combinations of words, called n-grams. Naturally, such combinations increase the size of the dictionary. Let a document d be a finite sequences of words $d = \langle w_1^d, \ldots, w_N^d \rangle$ $w_i^d \in V$ where V represents a vocabulary which is represented as a set of integers $V = \{1, \ldots, |V|\} = \{1, \ldots, V\}$, $x \in \mathbb{R}^{V^n}$ is defined by:

$$x_{(w_1,...,w_n)} = \frac{1}{N - n + 1} \sum_{i=1}^{N-n+1} \prod_{k=1}^{n} \delta(w_{i+k-1}^d, w_k)$$

where $\delta(a, b) = 1$ if $a = b$ and 0 otherwise. In the case of 1-g the above representation is reduced to $x_{(w_j)} = \frac{1}{N} \sum_{i=1}^{N} \delta(w_i^d, w_j)$ which is simply the relative frequencies of the different words in the document. Smoothed versions can also be considered. For example, a smoothed 1-g representation is:

$$x_{(w_j)} = \frac{1}{Z} \sum_{i=1}^{N} c + \delta(w_i^d, w_j) \qquad c \leqslant 0$$

where Z is a normalization constant such that $\sum x_{(w_j)} = 1$.

A representation of a document based on bags-of-words employs parsimonious vectors, because each document frequently contains only a tiny part of the possible words in the dictionary. In practice, n is chosen to be smaller than N, often taking the values 1, 2, or 3. The specific case of $n = 1$ is a classical bag-of-words representation. Frequently occurring word patterns being considered, such practices allow word-sense disambiguations. For the sequence of words that are greater than to n, the information is lost.

3.4 Bayesian Classifier

The classification of data deals with the task of stipulating labels for unclassi-fied items from a set of predefined classes [2]. Naive Bayes Classifiers (NBCs) have been remarkably successful in information retrieval as powerful probabilis-tic model used to classify objects in relation with predefined categories. Usually the parameters of the classifier are learnt from a sample of labeled objects, and support the classification of new objects. Naturally, we consider our issue here as a classification problem based on statistical and computational techniques allow-ing to identify spurious elements and increase the integrity of the repository.

Let a document $d_i \in D$, a class $c_j \in C$ and a function F returning the features of a given document, the document-conditioned class probability is defined as follows:

$$p(c_j \mid F(d_i)) = \frac{p(c_j)\, p(F(d_i) \mid c_j)}{p(F(d_i))}$$

In practice, the interest stands only on the numerator, because the denom-inator does not depend on any class and only depends on the values of the features. Such denominators denoted Z are constant within the class. The *naive* conditional independence assumptions assuming that all the features in $F(d_i)$ are mutually independent aims to apply a joint probability model as described below:

$$p(c_j \mid F(d_i)) = \frac{1}{Z}\, p(c_j) \prod_{f_k \in F(d_i)} p(f_k \mid c_j)$$

The use of *a priori* information from data is an important conviction of NBC [1]. The training of the model is performed applying the so called Bayes' theorem based on the information available about a given phenomenon representing a *priori* knowledge. New data can appear and modify the learning deriving new logical consequences from the model and the data. NBCs pick the hypothesis that is most probable [24], i.e. for a document d_i, it is the maximum *a posteriori* probability assigning a given class label $\hat{y}_i$ such that:

$$\hat{y}_i = \operatorname*{argmax}_{c_j \in C} \; p(c_j) \prod_{f_k \in \mathsf{F}(d_i)} p(f_k \mid c_j)$$

4 Experiments

In this section, we will present our attempts to fit a minimalist Bayesian classifier through the different feature engineerings employed to support the machine learnings. We will also present the evaluations of these different approaches. We asked students to observe and classify objects from a sample of the repository RiUfes. The interface used is available at http://rii.lcad.inf.ufes.br/wpsilva/ repo-meia/. The reported experiment was carried out on 500 human observations and classifications. We built a training dataset containing 80% of the objects and a test dataset containing 20% of the objects.

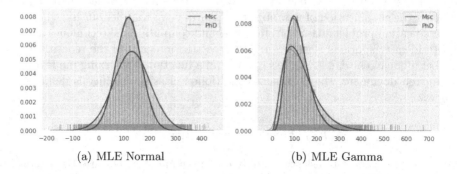

(a) MLE Normal   (b) MLE Gamma

Fig. 2. MLE Normal and Gamma distributions (500 observations)

In a first trial, we used only one feature namely the number of pages such that $\mathsf{F}^{\mathtt{PAG}}(d_i) = (\mathtt{pages}(d_i))$ where $\mathtt{pages}$ is a function returning the number of pages of a given document. We proceeded to MLEs based on Gaussian and Gamma distributions for each type. Figure 2(a) presents the MLE based on Gaussian distribution while Fig. 2(b) presents the MLE based on Gamma distribution. The both figures present the models generated from a sample of 500 observations. The X axis of the graph symbolizes the scale of the number of pages for each item and the Y axis symbolizes the relative density of the distributions. In both figures, we note the overlapping tails of the bell curves. This informs us that analysis of a single feature is not sufficient to accurately characterize the objects in RiUfes. Table 1 refers to the sum of squared residuals scaled between 0 and 1 for each MLE. It represents the likelihoods between the distribution models and the observations. The metrics clearly show that the best distribution in terms of likelihood is the distribution Gamma for both kinds.

Table 1. Scores of the MLE based on Normal and Gamma distributions

	$\mathcal{N}$	$\mathcal{G}$
MSc	103.397708	65.301993
PhD	100.848804	72.411722

In a second trial, we used a reduced set of features through a bag-of-words technique allowing us to obtain the best possible tradeoff between a fair accuracy, a minimum number of features and retrieval range. To define a vocabulary we used three parameters as thresholds: the α first words will be considered in the construction of the vocabulary; the β most frequent n-grams (in the α first words) will constitute the vocabulary; γ the maximum values n for the n-grams that have to be considered as possible occurrence of the vocabulary.

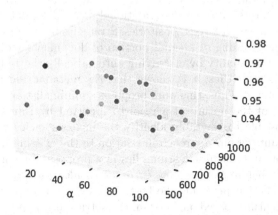

Fig. 3. Evolution of the accuracy in function of (α_i, β_j)

Figure 3 describes the level of accuracy in relation with different pairs of values (α_i, β_j) for $\gamma_o = 3$ (identified as the optimum value for γ). We obtained an optimum pair value $(\alpha_o, \beta_o) = (25, 500)$ for the parameters α and β such that:

$$F^{BOW}(d_i) = (x_1^{d_i}, \dots, x_{\beta_o}^{d_i}) \text{ with } x_j^{d_i} = x_{(w_{k_j}^{d_i}, \dots, w_{k_j+n_j-1}^{d_i})}, \ x_j^{d_i} \in \mathbb{R} \text{ and } n_j \in [\![1, \gamma_o]\!].$$

Building the two previous sets of features through the documents from riUfes, a natural trial is to combine them in a minimalist features-based approach such that: $\mathtt{F}^{\mathtt{MIN}}(d_i) = \mathtt{F}^{\mathtt{PAG}}(d_i) \cup \mathtt{F}^{\mathtt{BOW}}(d_i)$. Table 2 presents the evaluation metrics values obtained by the aforementioned strategies. We can observe that our minimalist features approach outperforms the others. The dataset and code for replicating our experiments are accessible at https://gitlab.com/rii_lcad/riufes.

Table 2. Evaluation metrics values of the different fitted Bayesian classifiers

	PAG	BOW	MIN
ACCURACY	0.865072	0.867609	0.939928
PRECISION	0.832952	0.838721	0.938310
F1	0.827319	0.836224	0.935511

5 Conclusion

Automated text classification has been considered to be a keystone when processing a large amount of digital documents [12]. When used improperly, *metadata* can cause problems for the integrity of a digital repository. The *metadata* are essential elements for information retrieval systems because they are used to support the interoperability. Thus, the quality of the repository depends on the data maintained, as well as the correct use of the *metadata* over the contents. For delivering accurate information, traditional methods of data processing are no longer compatible with large repositories. Strategies based on statistical inferences through the training of a small portion of documents reduce the human effort in maintaining quality by classifying automatically the rest of the base.

In the repository RiUfes, it is known that the metadata do not adequately represent the contents. Thus, this work proposes a minimalist approach for automatic indication of the nature of a record supported by Bayesian inferences, which makes possible to tractably identify the inconsistencies with high accuracy. The originality of our approach in relation to the existing literature about text classification and machine learning lies in a proposal for performing a preprocessing phase before the training in order to identify a set of features in which the classification performs the best. Moreover, our approach proposes a hybrid usage of features based on a document metrics (e.g. number of pages) and bag-of-words. The repository containing 4.723 objects, a manually scan would require approximately 158 h by requiring 2 min from a human to analyze the item. By applying our minimalist classifier such task can be reduced to less than 1 h, identifying 1.847 spurious items and guaranteeing approximately 94% of accuracy. Our solution is able to support identifications in large volumes of items by helping experts to classify exhaustive sets of documents, rationalizing their efforts and reducing the time needed to complete such tasks.

References

1. Albert, J.: Bayesian Computation with R. Springer-Verlag, New York (2009)
2. Baeza-Yates, R.A., Ribeiro-Neto, B.: Modern Information Retrieval. Addison-Wesley Longman Publishing Co., Inc., Boston, MA, USA (1999)
3. Biehl, M., Hammer, B., Villmann, T.: Prototype-based models in machine learning. Wiley Interdiscip. Rev. Cogn. Sci. **7**(2), 92–111 (2016)
4. Blum, A., Langley, P.: Selection of relevant features and examples in machine learning. Artif. Intell. **97**(1–2), 245–271 (1997)
5. Chapman, J.W., Reynolds, D., Shreeves, S.A.: Repository metadata: approaches and challenges. Cat. Classif. Q. **47**(3–4), 309–325 (2009)
6. Chellatamilan, T., Suresh, R.: Automatic classification of learning objects through dimensionality reduction and feature subset selections in an e-learning system. In: International Conference on Technology Enhanced Education, pp. 1–6 (2012)
7. Finn, A., Kushmerick, N.: Learning to classify documents according to genre. J. Assoc. Inf. Sci. Technol. **57**(11), 1506–1518 (2006)
8. Garla, V., Brandt, C.: Ontology-guided feature engineering for clinical text classification. J. Biomed. Inform. **45**(5), 992–998 (2012)
9. Gordo, A., Perronnin, F.: A bag-of-pages approach to unordered multi-page document classification. In: 20th International Conference on Pattern Recognition, Istanbul, Turkey, 23–26 August 2010, pp. 1920–1923. IEEE (2010)
10. Greenberg, J.: Metadata generation: processes, people and tools. Bull. Am. Soc. Inf. Sci. Technol. **29**(2), 16–19 (2003)
11. Head, R.C.: Making Archives in Early Modern Europe: Proof, Information, and Political Record-Keeping, 1400–1700. Cambridge University Press, Cambridge (2019)
12. Ikonomakis, M., Kotsiantis, S., Tampakas, V.: Text classification using machine learning techniques. WSEAS Trans. Comput. **4**(8), 966–974 (2005)
13. Isinkaye, F., Robert, A., Ojokoh, B.: An evaluation of metadata integrity in textual documents. J. Libr. Metadata **12**(1), 1–14 (2012)
14. Joachims, T.: Text categorization with support vector machines: learning with many relevant features. In: Nédellec, C., Rouveirol, C. (eds.) ECML 1998. LNCS, vol. 1398, pp. 137–142. Springer, Heidelberg (1998). https://doi.org/10.1007/BFb0026683
15. Kovacevic, A., Ivanovic, D., Milosavljevic, B., Konjovic, Z., Surla, D.: Automatic extraction of metadata from scientific publications for CRIS systems. Program **45**(4), 376–396 (2011)
16. Lebanon, G., Mao, Y., Dillon, J.: The locally weighted bag of words framework for document representation. J. Mach. Learn. Res. **8**(10), 2405–2441 (2007)
17. Lees, F.: Lees' Loss Prevention in the Process Industries: Hazard Identification, Assessment and Control. Butterworth-Heinemann, Oxford (2012)
18. Lei, Y., Uren, V., Motta, E.: A framework for evaluating semantic metadata. In: Proceedings of the 4th International Conference on Knowledge Capture, pp. 135–142 (2007)
19. Marco, D.: Building and managing the meta data repository: a full lifecycle guide, vol. 1. Wiley, New York (2000)
20. Nargesian, F., Samulowitz, H., Khurana, U., Khalil, E.B., Turaga, D.S.: Learning feature engineering for classification. In: Sierra, C. (ed.) Proceedings of the Twenty-Sixth International Joint Conference on Artificial Intelligence, IJCAI 2017, Melbourne, Australia, 19–25 August 2017, pp. 2529–2535. ijcai.org (2017)

21. Nichols, D.M., et al.: Experiences in deploying metadata analysis tools for institutional repositories. Cat. Classif. Q. **47**(3–4), 229–248 (2009)

22. Oliveira, E., Roatti, H., de Araujo Nogueira, M., Basoni, H.G., Ciarelli, P.M.: Using the cluster-based tree structure of k-nearest neighbor to reduce the effort required to classify unlabeled large datasets. In: Fred, A.L.N., Dietz, J.L.G., Aveiro, D., Liu, K., Filipe, J. (eds.) Proceedings of the International Conference on Knowledge Discovery, Lisbon, Portugal, pp. 567–576. SciTePress (2015)

23. Park, J.r., Brenza, A.: Evaluation of semi-automatic metadata generation tools: a survey of the current state of the art. Inf. Technol. Libr. **34**(3), 22–42 (2015)

24. Pfeffer, A.: Practical Probabilistic Programming, 1st edn. Manning Publications Co., Greenwich, CT, USA (2016)

25. Roy, D., Sarkar, S., Ghose, S.: A comparative study of learning object metadata, learning material repositories, metadata annotation & an automatic metadata annotation tool. Adv. Semant. Comput. **2**(2010), 103–126 (2010)

26. Russell, S.J., Norvig, P.: Artificial Intelligence: A Modern Approach. Pearson Education Limited, Malaysia (2016)

27. Saini, P.S., Ronchetti, M., Sona, D.: Automatic generation of metadata for learning objects. In: Proceedings of the 6th International Conference on Advanced Learning Technologies, Kerkrade, The Netherlands, 5–7 July 2006, pp. 275–279. IEEE (2006)

28. Selvakuberan, K., Indradevi, M., Rajaram, R.: Combined feature selection and classification-a novel approach for the categorization of web pages. J. Inf. Comput. Sci. **3**(2), 083–089 (2008)

29. Smith, R.: Aristotle's logic. Stanford Encyclopedia of Philosophy (2000)

30. Spatz, C.: Basic Statistics: Tales of Distributions. Cengage Learning, Boston (2007)

31. Tonkin, E., Muller, H.L.: Semi automated metadata extraction for preprints archives. In: Larsen, R.L., Paepcke, A., Borbinha, J.L., Naaman, M. (eds.) ACM/IEEE Joint Conference on Digital Libraries, JCDL 2008, Pittsburgh, PA, USA, 16–20 June 2008, pp. 157–166. ACM (2008)

32. Turner, C.R., Fuggetta, A., Lavazza, L., Wolf, A.L.: A conceptual basis for feature engineering. J. Syst. Softw. **49**(1), 3–15 (1999)

33. Weinstein, P.C., Birmingham, W.P.: Creating ontological metadata for digital library content and services. Int. J. Digit. Libr. **2**(1), 20–37 (1998). https://doi.org/10.1007/s007990050034

34. Zheng, A., Casari, A.: Feature Engineering for Machine Learning: Principles and Techniques for Data Scientists. O'Reilly Media, Inc., Sebastopol (2018)

Inventory and Content Separation in Grammatical Descriptions of Languages of the World

Harald Hammarström[✉][iD]

Department of Linguistics and Philology, Uppsala University,
Box 635, 751 26 Uppsala, Sweden
harald.hammarstrom@lingfil.uu.se

Abstract. Grammatical descriptions of languages of the world form a sub-genre of scholarly documents in the field of linguistics. A document of this genre may be modeled as a concatenation of table of contents, sociolinguistic description, phonological description, morphosyntactic description, comparative remarks, lexicon, text, bibliography and index (where morphosyntactic description is the only mandatory section). Separation of these parts is useful for information extraction, bibliometrics and information content analysis. Using a collection of over 10 000 digitized grammatical descriptions and an associated bibliography with document-level categorizations, we show that standard techniques from text classification can be adapted to classify individual pages. Assuming that the divisions of interest form continuous page ranges, we can achieve the sought after division in a transparent way. In contrast to previous work on similar tasks in other domains, no use is made of formatting cues, no additional annotated data is needed, high-quality OCR is not required, and the document collection is highly multilingual.

Keywords: Scholarly document processing · Text classification · Bibliography identification

1 Introduction

Grammatical descriptions are documents written in some (meta-)language (typically a major European languages) describing the grammatical make-up of some (object-)language—typically one of the approximately 7 000 minority languages of the world. They form a sub-genre of scholarly documents in the field of linguistics. Some example of works in this genre are:

- Evans, Nicholas D. (1995) *A Grammar of Kayardild: With Historical-Comparative Notes on Tangkic* (Mouton Grammar Library 15). Berlin: Mouton de Gruyter. xxiv+837 pp.
- Krumm, Bernhard. (1912) *Grundriß einer Grammatik des Kimatuumbi*. Mittheilungen des Seminars für Orientalische Sprachen XV. 1–63.

© Springer Nature Switzerland AG 2021
G. Berget et al. (Eds.): TPDL 2021, LNCS 12866, pp. 29–40, 2021.
https://doi.org/10.1007/978-3-030-86324-1_3

- Yu, Cuirong 喻翠容. (1980) *Buyiyu jianzhi* 布依语简志 [A brief description of the Buyi language]. Beijing: Minzu Chubanshe. 113 pp.
- Grasserie, Raoul de la & Nicolas Léon. (1896) *Langue Tarasque: Grammaire, dictionnaire, textes traduits et analysés* (Bibliothèque Linguistique Américaine XIX). Paris: Librairie-Éditeur J. Maisonneuve. 293 pp.

The defining characteristic of this genre is a substantial section on morphosyntax [8]. Grammatical descriptions may also include (and often do) longer or shorter sections on sociolinguistic-ethnographic description, phonological description, comparative remarks, lexicon and texts [24]. Like other scholarly documents they may also include a table of contents, bibliography and index.

The separation of the sections mentioned is useful for a number of downstream tasks. In Information Retrieval/Extraction [7,12,20,22,23], noise can be reduced by only searching in the appropriate section. Bibliometric studies—which promise interesting historical trends to be discovered in this domain [1,10]—naturally need the bibliography section separated, but can also be sharpened by knowing in which section(s) the citations occur. For automated analysis of the amount and type of grammatical description [16,17] that is contained in a document, section segmentation is the starting point.

In this paper we focus on distinguishing only the sections lexicon, text, bibliography and grammar (subsuming the remaining prose-based categories) since these are the most important divisions for information extraction and are the ones most readily distinguished by text type. Table-of-contents and index sections are most probably also distinguishable by similar techniques, but are not targeted due to lack of training data and their lesser importance.

2   Related Work

We are not aware of any previous work on content-analysis of the specific domain of grammatical descriptions. Within the large body of work targeting scientific texts more generally, at least two lines of work are relevant for our task [13].

The first line of work seeks to extract the bibliography and metadata (such as title, year, author etc.) from a given document, typically an article. Disregarding metadata-extraction (which is not needed in our case), a large variety of cues and supervised Machine Learning techniques have been brought forward to isolate and parse the bibliography (see [2,13,19] and references therein). These methods are typically used for source documents which are richer in terms of layout, OCR quality and training data. The subproblem tangential to the present study is much simpler—to isolate the pages of the bibliography—and, we argue, can be solved with simpler means. However, the existing bibliography parsing tools can, with high probability, be used also for the present collection when the turn comes to actually parse the bibliography.

The second line of work (see [3,4,11,15] and references therein) indeed seeks to divide scientific articles into different segments using supervised Machine Learning techniques. So far these approaches have sought to address the type of discourse in various segments (title, experiment, conclusion, etc.) and have therefore chosen the sentence as the basic unit. For the present task, we rather address the text type (prose, dictionary, vernacular text—one could even say genre) of a larger unit (such as a paragraph or page) which makes frequency-intense techniques such as TF-IDF available. Again, most extant techniques require richer layout, OCR quality and foremostly training data to work well. In our setting, however, it is possible to use document-level annotation to bootstrap page-level classification, and thus to short-cut the need for page-level annotated data. Nevertheless, extant work on article segmentation is similar in spirit to the approach in the present paper in that the problem is modeled as a sequence classification problem over smaller units amenable to text-classification. The difference is that we are targeting a simpler problem which can be addressed with simpler machinery on poorer data.

3   Data

The data for the experiments in this paper consists of a collection of over 10 000 raw text grammatical descriptions digitally available for computational processing [21]. A listing of the collection can be enumerated via the open-access bibliography Glottolog (glottolog.org, [6]). For each reference pertaining to the present study, this catalogue features manually curated annotations of

(i) the language it is written in (the meta-language, usually English, French, German, Spanish, Russian or Mandarin Chinese, see Table 1),

(ii) the language(s) described in it (the vernacular, typically one of the thousands of minority languages throughout the world), and

(iii) the type of description (comparative study, description of a specific feature, phonological description, grammar sketch, full grammar etc., see Table 2 and Table 3 for examples).

The typology of description types was devised with the goal of measuring the description of minority languages in mind, before the prospect of computational content division appeared on the horizon [8]. It is important to understand that the description type labels the qualified majority content of the document, and thus does not exclude some amount of other content. For example, a grammar typically also contains some lexicon, text and a bibliography. Dictionaries and text collections often have introductions with a phonological outline. If there is roughly equal content, the document may carry several labels, such as the Usila Chinantec dictionary and grammar sketch in Table 3. What we wish to achieve leveraging these document-level labels for majority type (that have already been manually curated) is a finer labelling of the contents which distinguishes different sections of the same documents.

   The collection has been OCRed using ABBYY Finereader 14 using the meta-language as recognition language. The original digital documents are of quality varying from barely legible typescript copies to high-quality scans and even born-digital documents. In essence, the OCR correctly recognizes most tokens of the meta-language but is hopelessly inaccurate on most tokens of the vernacular being described. This is completely expected from the typical,

Table 1. Meta-languages of the grammatical descriptions in the present collection.

Meta-language		# languages	# documents
English	eng	3 497	7 284
French	fra	826	1 323
German	deu	620	813
Spanish	spa	394	808
Russian	rus	288	498
Mandarin	cmn	180	234
Portuguese	por	141	274
Indonesian	ind	130	210
Dutch	nld	113	171
Italian	ita	92	141
...	...	...	...

Table 2. Description types in the Glottolog bibliography and content types used in the present study.

Content type	Description type		# docs in digital collection	
GRAM	Grammar	A description of most elements of the grammar (≈150 pages and beyond)	5 129	10.0%
GRAM	Grammar sketch	A less extensive description of many elements of the grammar (≈50 pages)	7 975	15.6%
GRAM	Specific feature	Description of some element of grammar (i.e., noun class system, verb morphology, etc.)	3 486	6.8%
PHON	Phonology	A description of the sound inventory utilizing minimal pairs	1 977	3.8%
LEX	Dictionary	≈75 pages and beyond	2765	5.4%
LEX	Wordlist	≈100–200 words	4 216	8.2%
TEXT	Text	Text material	1 024	2.0%
CMP	Comparative	A comparative-historical study	6 546	12.8%
CMP	Dialectological	Dialectological study	254	0.4%
BIB	Bibliographical	Bibliography	619	1.2%
MIN	Minimal	A small number of morphemes	2 107	4.1%
MIN	Socling	Sociolinguistic information	1 646	3.2%
MIN	Overview	Meta-information about the language (i.e., where spoken, non-intelligibility to other languages, etc.)	8 420	16.5%
ETHNO	Ethnographic	Ethnographic description	4 859	9.5%
			38 675	

Table 3. Examples of description types and associated languages in Glottolog.

Language	Description Type	Bibliographic Reference
Bolon [bof]	grammar	Zoungrana, Ambroise. (1987) *Esquisse phonologique et grammaticale du Bolon (Burkina-Faso)- contribution à la dialectologie mandé.* Université de la Sorbonne Nouvelle (Paris 3) doctoral dissertation. 336pp.
Usila Chinantec [cuc]	grammar sketch, dictionary	Skinner, Leonard E. & Marlene B. Skinner. (2000) *Diccionario Chinanteco de San Felipe Usila, Oaxaca* (Serie de vocabularios y diccionarios indígenas Mariano Silva y Aceves 43). Coyoacán, México: Instituto Lingüístico de Verano. xxix+602.
Norwegian Sign Language [nsl]	specific feature	Slowikowska Schröder, Bogumila. (2010) *Imperativ i norsk tegnspråk — en eksplorerende studie av et fenomen innen et visuelt-gestuelt språk [Imperative in Norwegian sign language an explorating study of a phenomenon in a visual-gestural language].* University of Oslo MA thesis.
Sobei [sob]	phonology	Sterner, Joyce K. (1975) Sobei phonology. Oceanic Linguistics 14. 146–167.
Northern Tujia [tji]	dictionary	Zhang, Weiquan. (2006) *Hàn yǔ tǔjiā yǔ cídiǎn* 汉语土家语词典*[Chinese-Tujia dictionary].* Guiyang Shi: Guizhou Minzu Chubanshe. 6+20+3+436pp.
Nisga'a [ncg]	text	Boas, Franz. (1902) *Tsimshian Texts* (Bulletin of American Ethnology 27). Washington: Government Printing Office. 254pp.
Asháninka [cni], Yine [pib], Shipibo-Conibo [shp]	wordlist	Carrasco, Francisco. (1901) *Principales palabras del idioma de las tribus de infieles antis, piros, conibos, sipibos.* Boletín de la Sociedad Geográfica de Lima 11. 204–211.
Dizin [mdx]	minimal	Conti Rossini, Carlo. (1937) *Il Popolo dei Magi nell'Etiopia Meridionale e il suo linguaggio.* In V Sezione: Etnografica-Filologica-Sociologica (Atti del Terzo congresso di Studi Coloniali VI), 108–118. Firenze: Centro di Studi Coloniali, Instituto Coloniale Fascista.
Busuu [bju], Bikya [byb], Akum [aku], Kutep [kub], Beezen [bnz], Naki [mff], Bishuo [bwh], Yukuben [ybl]	overview	Breton, Roland. (1995) *Les Furu et leurs Voisins: Découverte et essai de classification d'un groupe de langues en voie d'extinction au Cameroun.* Cahiers des Sciences Humaines 31(1). 17–48.

dictionary/training-heavy, contemporary techniques for OCR, and cannot easily be improved on the scale relevant for the present collection. However, some post-correction of OCR output very relevant for the genre of linguistics is possible (see [9]). Given the variable amounts of vernacular tokens in any given document, we know of no automatic way to determine the OCR quality of an individual document. Hence, the bottom line is that, for this collection as a whole, we cannot rely on headings, page numbers, layout, specific keywords, vernacular dictionaries or other OCR-sensitive single items to anchor a division into sections.

4   Method

To divide grammatical descriptions into sections, we propose the following simple strategy:

1. Train a page-level text classifier using the document-level labels (available from an external database) projected onto all pages as training data
2. Group labeled pages into continuous sections using a naive maximum likelihood divider

   To motivate the first step, we note again that the document-level labels do not correctly describe every single page, but they are designed to do so for a qualified majority of pages. Some references have multiple labels, reflecting roughly equal content, and for them an assumption of a qualified majority does not hold. Hence, to train a page-level text classifier, we take only the references with a single label and project that label to all pages for training, assuming that the vast majority are correct. For the categories lexicon, text, grammar and bibliography, there are documents with this single label. But, of course, there are no documents labeled entirely as table-of-contents or index, so training data for such sections cannot be obtained the same way.

   To motivate the second step, we need only note that the section types as defined nearly always come in one coherent sequence. This very strong assumption leaves only the matter of possible overlap to resolve. Since each possible label C has a probability of misclassification m_C from the text classifier, the natural solution is to choose the section division which maximizes the probability of the observed classifications. Formally, if l_k is the label predicted for page k and C_i, C_j are the start and end pages of text type $C \in \{LEX, GRAM, BIB, TEXT\}$, we seek the non-overlapping (possibly empty) page ranges that maximize $\prod_{C_i \leq k \leq C_j, l_k \neq C} m_{l_k} \prod_{\neg(C_i \leq k \leq C_j), l_k = C} m_C$ for all C.

5   Experiments

As described above, we trained a Naive Bayes classifier over word token[1] TF-IDF vectors of dimension 5 000 for each page of 200 references of each text type[2].

---

[1] For Chinese characters, the Jieba tokenizer https://github.com/fxsjy/jieba was employed, otherwise tokens were split simply by whitespace.

[2] Essentially equivalent variations is to include punctuation tokens and capitalization, use Doc2Vec vector embeddings, another classifier (e.g. Logistic Regression) or different size vectors (e.g., 500, 10000). No interesting variations in accuracy was found across these variations, although no exhaustive search with significance tests were carried out. We stay with Naive Bayes and TD-IDF vectors since they have no additional parameters and have no convergence issues.

The experiments were implemented and carried out in Python 3.8 using the scikit-learn package [14]. The accuracy was tested on each page of a fresh set of 100 references of each text type. All experiments were done separately for each meta-language.

A confusion matrix using the full set of labels for English is shown in Fig. 1. We should not expect close to full accuracy on this test set since it carries the document-level label for each page of the document. In particular, grammars contain bits of lexicon, text and bibliography which is readily reflected in the confusion matrix. In addition, it shows that the other descriptive prose categories are difficult to distinguish from grammatical description. Better prospects, while retaining the most important distinctions, are therefore to be expected with only the text, lexicon, dictionary and grammar categories. Figure 2 shows the corresponding confusion matrix for only these categories. Again, we observe the expected overlap between grammar and the other categories since they are typically contained in grammars. (Even if the test set were perfect we should still not expect total correspondence in this matrix since many pages of a grammar contain text examples and a good dictionary has many example sentences.)

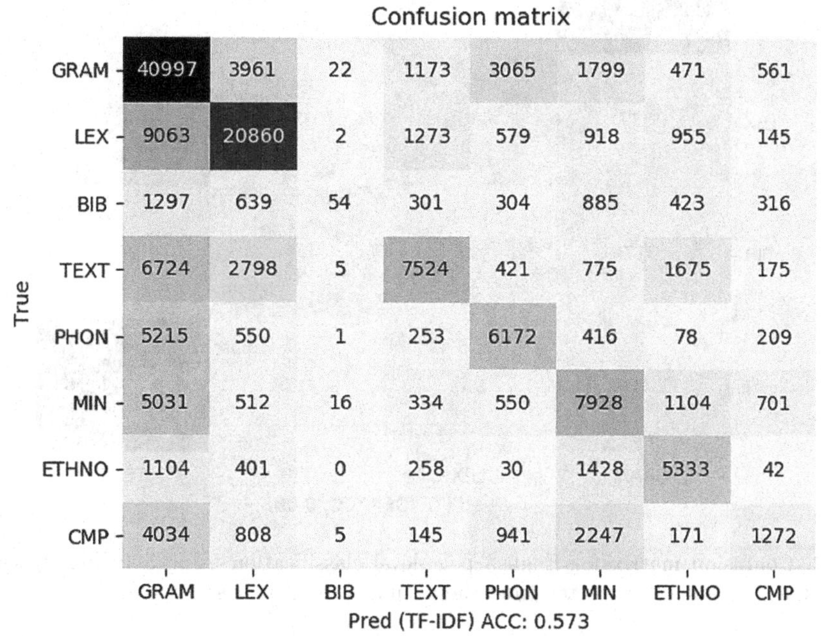

Confusion matrix

True \ Pred	GRAM	LEX	BIB	TEXT	PHON	MIN	ETHNO	CMP
GRAM	40997	3961	22	1173	3065	1799	471	561
LEX	9063	20860	2	1273	579	918	955	145
BIB	1297	639	54	301	304	885	423	316
TEXT	6724	2798	5	7524	421	775	1675	175
PHON	5215	550	1	253	6172	416	78	209
MIN	5031	512	16	334	550	7928	1104	701
ETHNO	1104	401	0	258	30	1428	5333	42
CMP	4034	808	5	145	941	2247	171	1272

Pred (TF-IDF) ACC: 0.573

Fig. 1. Confusion matrix for English page-level classification using the full set of labels. The "True" labels are projected from the document-level labels.

Now, for the actual task, Appendix A shows the predicted labels for the pages of Evans' grammar of Kayardild [5]. Given the assumption of up to four single continuous sections, there will be maximally only four transitions between sections, so an HMM or CRF sequence labeling approach looks unnecessary. From the confusion matrix of Fig. 2 we can gauge probabilities of mislabeling in either direction. To obtain the final section-division we simply search for the start-end page pairs for each category that maximize the probability of the predicted labels. In principle, this search is quadratic in the number of pages, but only endpoints of different blocks actually need to be checked, which yields an effective speed-up in practice. With only four labels, a full check of all possibilities is tractable, but in practice an order of precedence (bibliography, grammar, dictionary, text) can be imposed without loss towards the ultimate goal. In the example of [5], the resulting divisions are shown in Table 4, which match up quite well (97.1%) with the actual content.

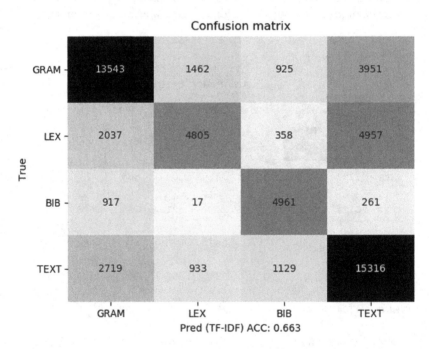

Fig. 2. Confusion matrix for English page-level classification using only four labels. The "True" labels are projected from the document-level labels.

As a formal evaluation, we annotated the sections of 10 grammars each for the 10 languages with the most training data. The resulting accuracies, with caveats on training data sizes, are shown in Table 5. The differences in accuracies across these meta-languages, not surprisingly, relate to differences in category-balanced training data at hand.

Table 4. Actual and predicted sections of [5].

Pages	Actual content	Predicted section
1–10	Title pages	–
11–19	Table-of-contents	
20–27	Abbreviations	
27–76	Sociolinguistics	9-595 GRAM
77–109	Phonology	
110–595	Grammar	
596–661	Text	596-660 TEXT
662–826	Dictionary	665-824 LEX
827–845	Bibliography	826-844 BIB
846–851	Plates	–
852–864	Indices	–

Table 5. Training data sizes (number of items, number of pages) and accuracy of section division of grammars across meta-languages.

Language		Training								Test	
		GRAM	# Pgs	TEXT	# Pgs	DICT	# Pgs	BIB	# Pgs	# Pgs	% Acc
English	eng	100	19470	100	20373	100	11497	100	6078	1244	**93.1%**
Russian	rus	100	19262	20	4043	100	49234	3	90	1152	**88.9%**
Indonesian	ind	100	16079	5	491	84	15121	3	844	1553	**76.4%**
Spanish	spa	100	19730	41	5933	100	15511	65	4238	1489	**80.0%**
Portuguese	por	100	17886	13	2833	100	13606	29	2275	2394	**83.8%**
French	fra	100	25007	48	8856	100	19951	71	5200	1230	**84.3%**
German	deu	100	20705	59	10818	100	12445	35	1892	1557	**74.7%**
Dutch	nld	100	15911	23	4286	100	17539	4	395	2097	**89.5%**
Italian	ita	100	20657	4	347	57	16116	6	582	1631	**93.7%**
Chinese	cmn	100	21423	11	3410	41	21175	1	4	1768	**60.4%**

6   Conclusion

We have presented the first section division method for the domain of grammatical descriptions. The task is narrowed down to the tractable division of lexicon, text, bibliography and grammar ("rest") sections for which we can obtain high accuracy scores with only light machinery and impoverished input data. The task may be generalized to other domains of scholarly text as well as sharpened to distinguish more section types.

A   Appendix: Pages and Predicted Labels for Evans' Grammar of Kayardild [5]

Page	Label	Page	Label	Page	Label	Page	Label	Page	Label	Page	Label	Page	Label	Page	Label	Page	Label	Page	Label
0	TEXT	87	GRAM	174	GRAM	261	GRAM	348	GRAM	435	GRAM	522	GRAM	609	TEXT	696	TEXT	783	LEX
1	TEXT	88	GRAM	175	GRAM	262	GRAM	349	GRAM	436	GRAM	523	GRAM	610	TEXT	697	TEXT	784	LEX
2	TEXT	89	GRAM	176	GRAM	263	GRAM	350	GRAM	437	GRAM	524	GRAM	611	TEXT	698	TEXT	785	LEX
3	BIB	90	GRAM	177	GRAM	264	GRAM	351	GRAM	438	GRAM	525	GRAM	612	TEXT	699	TEXT	786	LEX
4	TEXT	91	GRAM	178	GRAM	265	GRAM	352	GRAM	439	GRAM	526	GRAM	613	TEXT	700	LEX	787	LEX
5	TEXT	92	GRAM	179	GRAM	266	TEXT	353	GRAM	440	GRAM	527	GRAM	614	TEXT	701	LEX	788	LEX
6	BIB	93	GRAM	180	GRAM	267	GRAM	354	GRAM	441	GRAM	528	GRAM	615	TEXT	702	LEX	789	TEXT
7	BIB	94	GRAM	181	GRAM	268	GRAM	355	GRAM	442	GRAM	529	GRAM	616	TEXT	703	LEX	790	LEX
8	BIB	95	GRAM	182	GRAM	269	GRAM	356	GRAM	443	GRAM	530	GRAM	617	TEXT	704	LEX	791	TEXT
9	GRAM	96	GRAM	183	GRAM	270	GRAM	357	GRAM	444	GRAM	531	GRAM	618	TEXT	705	LEX	792	LEX
10	BIB	97	GRAM	184	GRAM	271	GRAM	358	GRAM	445	GRAM	532	GRAM	619	TEXT	706	TEXT	793	TEXT
11	GRAM	98	GRAM	185	GRAM	272	GRAM	359	GRAM	446	GRAM	533	GRAM	620	TEXT	707	LEX	794	TEXT
12	GRAM	99	GRAM	186	GRAM	273	GRAM	360	TEXT	447	GRAM	534	GRAM	621	GRAM	708	LEX	795	LEX
13	GRAM	100	GRAM	187	GRAM	274	GRAM	361	TEXT	448	GRAM	535	GRAM	622	TEXT	709	LEX	796	LEX
14	GRAM	101	GRAM	188	GRAM	275	GRAM	362	GRAM	449	GRAM	536	GRAM	623	TEXT	710	LEX	797	LEX
15	GRAM	102	GRAM	189	GRAM	276	GRAM	363	GRAM	450	GRAM	537	GRAM	624	TEXT	711	LEX	798	LEX
16	GRAM	103	GRAM	190	GRAM	277	GRAM	364	GRAM	451	GRAM	538	GRAM	625	TEXT	712	TEXT	799	LEX
17	GRAM	104	GRAM	191	GRAM	278	GRAM	365	GRAM	452	GRAM	539	GRAM	626	TEXT	713	TEXT	800	LEX
18	TEXT	105	GRAM	192	GRAM	279	GRAM	366	GRAM	453	GRAM	540	GRAM	627	TEXT	714	LEX	801	LEX
19	GRAM	106	GRAM	193	GRAM	280	GRAM	367	GRAM	454	GRAM	541	GRAM	628	TEXT	715	LEX	802	LEX
20	GRAM	107	GRAM	194	GRAM	281	GRAM	368	GRAM	455	GRAM	542	GRAM	629	TEXT	716	LEX	803	LEX
21	GRAM	108	GRAM	195	GRAM	282	GRAM	369	GRAM	456	GRAM	543	GRAM	630	TEXT	717	LEX	804	LEX
22	GRAM	109	GRAM	196	GRAM	283	GRAM	370	GRAM	457	GRAM	544	GRAM	631	TEXT	718	LEX	805	LEX
23	GRAM	110	GRAM	197	GRAM	284	GRAM	371	GRAM	458	GRAM	545	GRAM	632	TEXT	719	TEXT	806	LEX
24	TEXT	111	GRAM	198	GRAM	285	GRAM	372	GRAM	459	GRAM	546	GRAM	633	TEXT	720	LEX	807	LEX
25	TEXT	112	GRAM	199	TEXT	286	GRAM	373	GRAM	460	GRAM	547	GRAM	634	TEXT	721	LEX	808	TEXT
26	GRAM	113	GRAM	200	GRAM	287	GRAM	374	GRAM	461	GRAM	548	GRAM	635	TEXT	722	LEX	809	TEXT
27	GRAM	114	GRAM	201	GRAM	288	TEXT	375	GRAM	462	GRAM	549	GRAM	636	TEXT	723	LEX	810	LEX
28	GRAM	115	GRAM	202	GRAM	289	TEXT	376	GRAM	463	GRAM	550	TEXT	637	TEXT	724	TEXT	811	TEXT
29	GRAM	116	GRAM	203	GRAM	290	GRAM	377	GRAM	464	GRAM	551	GRAM	638	TEXT	725	TEXT	812	TEXT
30	GRAM	117	GRAM	204	GRAM	291	GRAM	378	GRAM	465	GRAM	552	GRAM	639	TEXT	726	LEX	813	LEX
31	GRAM	118	GRAM	205	GRAM	292	GRAM	379	TEXT	466	GRAM	553	GRAM	640	TEXT	727	LEX	814	LEX
32	GRAM	119	TEXT	206	GRAM	293	GRAM	380	GRAM	467	GRAM	554	GRAM	641	TEXT	728	LEX	815	TEXT
33	GRAM	120	GRAM	207	GRAM	294	GRAM	381	GRAM	468	GRAM	555	GRAM	642	TEXT	729	LEX	816	LEX
34	GRAM	121	GRAM	208	GRAM	295	GRAM	382	GRAM	469	GRAM	556	GRAM	643	TEXT	730	LEX	817	LEX
35	TEXT	122	GRAM	209	GRAM	296	GRAM	383	GRAM	470	GRAM	557	GRAM	644	TEXT	731	LEX	818	TEXT
36	GRAM	123	GRAM	210	GRAM	297	GRAM	384	GRAM	471	GRAM	558	GRAM	645	TEXT	732	LEX	819	TEXT
37	GRAM	124	GRAM	211	GRAM	298	GRAM	385	GRAM	472	GRAM	559	GRAM	646	TEXT	733	LEX	820	LEX
38	GRAM	125	GRAM	212	TEXT	299	GRAM	386	GRAM	473	GRAM	560	GRAM	647	TEXT	734	TEXT	821	LEX
39	TEXT	126	GRAM	213	GRAM	300	GRAM	387	GRAM	474	GRAM	561	GRAM	648	TEXT	735	LEX	822	LEX
40	TEXT	127	GRAM	214	GRAM	301	GRAM	388	GRAM	475	GRAM	562	GRAM	649	TEXT	736	LEX	823	TEXT
41	TEXT	128	GRAM	215	GRAM	302	GRAM	389	GRAM	476	GRAM	563	GRAM	650	TEXT	737	LEX	824	LEX
42	TEXT	129	GRAM	216	GRAM	303	GRAM	390	GRAM	477	GRAM	564	GRAM	651	TEXT	738	LEX	825	TEXT
43	TEXT	130	GRAM	217	GRAM	304	GRAM	391	GRAM	478	GRAM	565	GRAM	652	TEXT	739	LEX	826	BIB
44	GRAM	131	GRAM	218	GRAM	305	GRAM	392	TEXT	479	GRAM	566	GRAM	653	TEXT	740	LEX	827	BIB
45	GRAM	132	GRAM	219	GRAM	306	GRAM	393	GRAM	480	GRAM	567	GRAM	654	TEXT	741	LEX	828	BIB
46	TEXT	133	GRAM	220	GRAM	307	GRAM	394	TEXT	481	GRAM	568	GRAM	655	GRAM	742	LEX	829	BIB
47	TEXT	134	GRAM	221	GRAM	308	GRAM	395	GRAM	482	GRAM	569	GRAM	656	TEXT	743	LEX	830	BIB
48	TEXT	135	GRAM	222	GRAM	309	GRAM	396	GRAM	483	GRAM	570	GRAM	657	TEXT	744	LEX	831	BIB
49	GRAM	136	GRAM	223	GRAM	310	TEXT	397	GRAM	484	GRAM	571	GRAM	658	TEXT	745	TEXT	832	BIB
50	BIB	137	GRAM	224	GRAM	311	GRAM	398	GRAM	485	GRAM	572	GRAM	659	TEXT	746	TEXT	833	BIB
51	GRAM	138	GRAM	225	GRAM	312	GRAM	399	GRAM	486	GRAM	573	GRAM	660	TEXT	747	LEX	834	BIB
52	GRAM	139	GRAM	226	GRAM	313	GRAM	400	GRAM	487	GRAM	574	GRAM	661	GRAM	748	LEX	835	BIB
53	GRAM	140	GRAM	227	GRAM	314	GRAM	401	GRAM	488	GRAM	575	GRAM	662	GRAM	749	TEXT	836	BIB
54	TEXT	141	GRAM	228	GRAM	315	GRAM	402	GRAM	489	GRAM	576	TEXT	663	GRAM	750	TEXT	837	BIB
55	GRAM	142	GRAM	229	GRAM	316	GRAM	403	GRAM	490	GRAM	577	TEXT	664	TEXT	751	LEX	838	BIB
56	GRAM	143	GRAM	230	GRAM	317	TEXT	404	GRAM	491	GRAM	578	GRAM	665	LEX	752	LEX	839	BIB
57	GRAM	144	GRAM	231	GRAM	318	GRAM	405	GRAM	492	TEXT	579	GRAM	666	LEX	753	LEX	840	BIB
58	GRAM	145	GRAM	232	GRAM	319	GRAM	406	GRAM	493	GRAM	580	GRAM	667	TEXT	754	LEX	841	BIB
59	GRAM	146	GRAM	233	GRAM	320	GRAM	407	TEXT	494	GRAM	581	GRAM	668	LEX	755	LEX	842	BIB
60	GRAM	147	GRAM	234	GRAM	321	GRAM	408	GRAM	495	GRAM	582	TEXT	669	LEX	756	TEXT	843	BIB
61	GRAM	148	GRAM	235	GRAM	322	GRAM	409	TEXT	496	GRAM	583	GRAM	670	LEX	757	LEX	844	BIB
62	GRAM	149	GRAM	236	GRAM	323	GRAM	410	GRAM	497	GRAM	584	GRAM	671	LEX	758	TEXT	845	TEXT
63	GRAM	150	TEXT	237	TEXT	324	TEXT	411	TEXT	498	GRAM	585	GRAM	672	LEX	759	LEX	846	TEXT
64	BIB	151	GRAM	238	GRAM	325	GRAM	412	TEXT	499	GRAM	586	GRAM	673	LEX	760	LEX	847	TEXT
65	TEXT	152	GRAM	239	GRAM	326	TEXT	413	GRAM	500	GRAM	587	GRAM	674	TEXT	761	LEX	848	TEXT
66	TEXT	153	GRAM	240	GRAM	327	GRAM	414	GRAM	501	GRAM	588	GRAM	675	LEX	762	LEX	849	TEXT
67	TEXT	154	GRAM	241	GRAM	328	GRAM	415	GRAM	502	GRAM	589	GRAM	676	LEX	763	LEX	850	TEXT
68	GRAM	155	GRAM	242	GRAM	329	GRAM	416	TEXT	503	GRAM	590	GRAM	677	LEX	764	LEX	851	TEXT
69	BIB	156	GRAM	243	GRAM	330	GRAM	417	GRAM	504	GRAM	591	GRAM	678	LEX	765	LEX	852	TEXT
70	GRAM	157	GRAM	244	GRAM	331	GRAM	418	GRAM	505	GRAM	592	GRAM	679	LEX	766	LEX	853	BIB
71	GRAM	158	GRAM	245	GRAM	332	GRAM	419	GRAM	506	GRAM	593	GRAM	680	LEX	767	TEXT	854	TEXT
72	GRAM	159	GRAM	246	GRAM	333	GRAM	420	GRAM	507	TEXT	594	GRAM	681	LEX	768	TEXT	855	TEXT
73	GRAM	160	GRAM	247	GRAM	334	TEXT	421	TEXT	508	GRAM	595	GRAM	682	LEX	769	TEXT	856	TEXT
74	BIB	161	GRAM	248	GRAM	335	TEXT	422	TEXT	509	GRAM	596	TEXT	683	TEXT	770	TEXT	857	GRAM
75	TEXT	162	GRAM	249	GRAM	336	GRAM	423	GRAM	510	TEXT	597	TEXT	684	LEX	771	TEXT	858	GRAM
76	GRAM	163	GRAM	250	GRAM	337	TEXT	424	GRAM	511	GRAM	598	TEXT	685	LEX	772	TEXT	859	GRAM
77	GRAM	164	GRAM	251	GRAM	338	GRAM	425	GRAM	512	GRAM	599	TEXT	686	LEX	773	LEX	860	GRAM
78	GRAM	165	GRAM	252	GRAM	339	GRAM	426	GRAM	513	GRAM	600	TEXT	687	LEX	774	TEXT	861	GRAM
79	TEXT	166	GRAM	253	GRAM	340	GRAM	427	GRAM	514	GRAM	601	TEXT	688	TEXT	775	LEX	862	GRAM
80	GRAM	167	GRAM	254	TEXT	341	GRAM	428	GRAM	515	GRAM	602	TEXT	689	LEX	776	TEXT	863	TEXT
81	GRAM	168	GRAM	255	GRAM	342	GRAM	429	GRAM	516	GRAM	603	TEXT	690	LEX	777	TEXT	864	GRAM
82	GRAM	169	GRAM	256	GRAM	343	GRAM	430	GRAM	517	GRAM	604	TEXT	691	LEX	778	LEX		
83	GRAM	170	GRAM	257	TEXT	344	GRAM	431	GRAM	518	GRAM	605	TEXT	692	LEX	779	TEXT		
84	GRAM	171	GRAM	258	GRAM	345	GRAM	432	GRAM	519	GRAM	606	TEXT	693	LEX	780	TEXT		
85	GRAM	172	GRAM	259	GRAM	346	GRAM	433	GRAM	520	GRAM	607	TEXT	694	LEX	781	LEX		
86	TEXT	173	GRAM	260	GRAM	347	GRAM	434	GRAM	521	GRAM	608	TEXT	695	TEXT	782	LEX		

References

1. Chelliah, S.L., de Reuse, W.J.: Handbook of Descriptive Linguistic Fieldwork. Springer, Dordrecht (2011). https://doi.org/10.1007/978-90-481-9026-3
2. Chenet, M.: Identify and extract entities from bibliography references in a free text. Master's thesis, University of Twente (2017)
3. Cuong, N.V., Chandrasekaran, M.K., Kan, M.Y., Lee, W.S.: Scholarly document information extraction using extensible features for efficient higher order semi-CRFs. In: Proceedings of the 15th ACM/IEEE-CS Joint Conference on Digital Libraries, JCDL 2015, pp. 61–64. Association for Computing Machinery, New York (2015). https://doi.org/10.1145/2756406.2756946
4. Dasigi, P., Burns, G.A., Hovy, E., de Waard, A.: Experiment segmentation in scientific discourse as clause level structured prediction using recurrent neural networks, pp. 1–6. arXiv preprint arXiv:1702.05398 (2017)
5. Evans, N.D.: A Grammar of Kayardild: With Historical-Comparative Notes on Tangkic, Mouton Grammar Library, vol. 15. Mouton de Gruyter, Berlin (1995)
6. Hammarström, H., Forkel, R., Haspelmath, M., Bank, S.: Glottolog 4.4. Leipzig: Max Planck Institute for Evolutionary Anthropology (2021). http://glottolog.org. Accessed 05 May 2020
7. Hammarström, H.: Measuring prefixation and suffixation in the languages of the world. In: Proceedings of the 3rd Workshop on Research in Computational Typology and Multilingual NLP, pp. 81–89. Association for Computational Linguistics, Stroudsburg, PA (2021)
8. Hammarström, H., Nordhoff, S.: LangDoc: bibliographic infrastructure for linguistic typology. Oslo Stud. Lang. **3**(2), 31–43 (2011)
9. Hammarström, H., Virk, S.M., Forsberg, M.: Poor man's OCR post-correction: unsupervised recognition of variant spelling applied to a multilingual document collection. In: Proceedings of the Digital Access to Textual Cultural Heritage (DATeCH) Conference, pp. 71–75. ACM, Göttingen (2017)
10. Kelly, B., Lahaussois, A.: Chains of influence in Himalayan grammars: models and interrelations shaping descriptions of Tibeto-Burman languages of Nepal. Linguistics **59**(1), 207–245 (2021)
11. Luong, M.T., Nguyen, T.D., Kan, M.Y.: Logical structure recovery in scholarly articles with rich document features. In: Romary, L., Armbruster, C. (eds.) Multimedia Storage and Retrieval Innovations for Digital Library Systems, pp. 270–292. Hershey, IGI Global (2012)
12. Macklin-Cordes, J.L., et al.: Robots who read grammars. Poster presented at CoEDL Fest 2017, Alexandra Park Conference Centre, Alexandra Headlands, QLD (2017)
13. Nasar, Z., Jaffry, S.W., Malik, M.K.: Information extraction from scientific articles: a survey. Scientometrics **117**(3), 1931–1990 (2018). https://doi.org/10.1007/s11192-018-2921-5
14. Pedregosa, F., et al.: Scikit-learn: machine learning in Python. J. Mach. Learn. Res. **12**, 2825–2830 (2011)
15. Ramesh Kashyap, A., Kan, M.Y.: SciWING- a software toolkit for scientific document processing. In: Proceedings of the First Workshop on Scholarly Document Processing, pp. 113–120. Association for Computational Linguistics, November 2020. https://doi.org/10.18653/v1/2020.sdp-1.13. https://www.aclweb.org/anthology/2020.sdp-1.13

16. Rehg, K.L.: The language documentation and conservation initiative at the University of Hawai'i at Mānoa. In: Rau, D.V., Florey, M. (eds.) Documenting and Revitalizing Austronesian Languages, pp. 13–24. University of Hawaii Press, Honolulu (2007)

17. Rice, K.: A typology of good grammars. Stud. Lang. **30**(2), 385–415 (2005)

18. Summers, K.: Automatic discovery of logical document structure. Ph.D. thesis, Cornell University (1998)

19. Tkaczyk, D., Szostek, P., Fedoryszak, M., Dendek, P.J., Bolikowski, Ł: CERMINE: automatic extraction of structured metadata from scientific literature. Int. J. Doc. Anal. Recogn. (IJDAR) **18**(4), 317–335 (2015). https://doi.org/10.1007/s10032-015-0249-8

20. Virk, S.M., Borin, L., Saxena, A., Hammarström, H.: Automatic extraction of typological linguistic features from descriptive grammars. In: Ekštein, K., Matoušek, V. (eds.) TSD 2017. LNCS (LNAI), vol. 10415, pp. 111–119. Springer, Cham (2017). https://doi.org/10.1007/978-3-319-64206-2_13

21. Virk, S.M., Hammarström, H., Forsberg, M., Wichmann, S.: The DReaM corpus: a multilingual annotated corpus of grammars for the world's languages. In: Proceedings of the 12th Language Resources and Evaluation Conference, pp. 871–877. European Language Resources Association, Marseille, May 2020. https://www.aclweb.org/anthology/2020.lrec-1.109

22. Virk, S.M., Muhammad, A.S., Borin, L., Aslam, M.I., Iqbal, S., Khurram, N.: Exploiting frame-semantics and frame-semantic parsing for automatic extraction of typological information from descriptive grammars of natural languages. In: Proceedings of the International Conference on Recent Advances in Natural Language Processing (RANLP 2019), pp. 1247–1256. NCOMA Ltd., Varna (2019)

23. Wichmann, S., Rama, T.: Towards unsupervised extraction of linguistic typological features from language descriptions. In: First Workshop on Typology for Polyglot NLP, Florence, 1 August 2019 (Co-located with ACL, 28 July–2 August 2019) (2019)

24. Woodbury, A.: Language documentation. In: Austin, P., Sallabank, J. (eds.) The Cambridge Handbook of Endangered Languages, pp. 159–186. Cambridge University Press, Cambridge (2011)

An Empirical Study of Span Modeling in Science NER

Xiaorui Jiang[(✉)] (iD)

Centre for Computational Science and Mathematical Modelling,
Coventry University, Coventry, UK
`xiaorui.jiang@coventry.ac.uk`

Abstract. Little evaluation has been performed on the many modeling options for span-based approaches. This paper investigates the performances of a wide range of span and context representation methods and their combinations with a focus on scientific named entity recognition (science NER). While some most common classical span encodings and their combination prove to be effective, few conclusions can be derived to context representations.

Keywords: Scientific named entity recognition · Span-based model · Span representation · Context representation · SciBERT

1 Span Modeling Options

Span-based models have been proposed for a wide range of natural language processing (NLP) problems such as keyphrase extraction [1], semantic role labeling [2], extractive question answering [3, 4], constituency parsing [5], coreference resolution [6], relation extraction [7], aspect-based sentiment analysis [8], and etc. Recently, span-relation modeling was proposed as a general NLP methodology for these different tasks [9].

This paper focuses on the design options of span modeling and targets at span-based NER [10–15] in science domains. Closest to mine is [16], which investigated span representations on six NLP tasks including NER. I extensively extend the span modeling options compared to [16]. Parallel to this study witness the probing of token embeddings [17], domain transferability [18] and different deep learning architectures [19].

Table 1 summarises the potential span and context representation methods. For a sentence of tokens $t_1, \ldots, t_N$, pretrained token embeddings $\mathbf{e}$ of each token will be encoded by BERT [15] to a token representation vector $\mathbf{h}$. Candidate spans are enumerated. The feature vector for each span $s = [i, j]$ is $\mathbf{f} = [\mathbf{s}; \mathbf{c}^l; \mathbf{c}^r; \mathbf{w}]$, where $\mathbf{s}$ is the span representation for $t_i, \ldots, t_j$, $\mathbf{c}^l$ and $\mathbf{c}^r$ are two optional context representations with regard to $t_1, \ldots, t_{i-1}$, and $t_{j+1}, \ldots, t_N$ respectively, and $\mathbf{w}$ is a learnable vector for span length.

2 Probing Task and Results

Experimental setup is in the Appendix. Below summarises the main findings.

© Springer Nature Switzerland AG 2021
G. Berget et al. (Eds.): TPDL 2021, LNCS 12866, pp. 41–48, 2021.
https://doi.org/10.1007/978-3-030-86324-1_4

Table 1. Span and context representation options tested.

SPAN_ENDS	SPAN_SUMM	END_COMB	CONTEXT
CONCAT [11,14]: $[\mathbf{h}_i, \mathbf{h}_j]$	MAX_POOL	DIFF_SUM [22]: $[\mathbf{h}_i - \mathbf{h}_j, \mathbf{h}_i + \mathbf{h}_j]$	CLS [12]
	SELF_ATT [20]	COHERE* [11, 20]: $\mathbf{h}_i \circ \mathbf{h}_j$	MAX_POOL
		OFFSET_DIFF* [23]: $[\mathbf{h}_i - \mathbf{h}_{j+1}, \mathbf{h}_j - \mathbf{h}_{i-1}]$	SELF_ATT

Note: Max pooling (MAX_POOL) is surprisingly effective and widely adopted [24, 25]. Self attention (SELF_ATT) was also compared in [9]. The encoding of the special BERT symbol "[CLS]" is the only global context tested [12]. Un-common span modelling methods marked by "*" are left to future work

Probing Question 1: Which is the most effective single feature method? From the NONE columns in Table 2, MAX_POOL is a surprisingly strong single feature for span-only representation (c.f. [9] as well). CONCAT is also promising followed by DIFF_SUM. However, the performance of SELF_ATT drops drastically on both datasets, but it seems to complement context encodings well (see Line 13–16 in Table 4).

Probing Question 2: Whether SPAN_ENDS is the most useful feature? Most of the time, CONCAT is a promising feature, either as a span-only representation or used together with context representation (see the CONCAT columns in Table 2 and 3), although more experiments are necessary to derive a conclusive statement on its role. This reasonably justifies the fact that most span-based models only used CONCAT. When combined with DIFF_SUM, however, its impact becomes more random (see the two downward arrows in Table 3 and Line 9–12 in Table 4). In particular, DIFF_SUM does not seem to go perfectly well with CONCAT: no clear trend can be observed.

Probing Question 3: Whether END_COMB helps improve science NER performance? From the DIFF_SUM columns in Table 3, it can be seen that when the span representation is "weak" adding DIFF_SUM also results in a performance boost (see the 10 rows with SPAN_END = NONE). For both datasets, the best performing models (in boldface) appear in the END_COMB = DIFF_SUM category. The best micro F1 value 47.13% on ScienceIE2017 is significantly better than BERT-NER (using SciBERT [26]). This partially justifies that comprehensive span representation, in combination with an appropriate context representation, indeed has significant importance.

Probing Question 4: Whether and how CONTEXT can be promising for science NER? To conclude on CONTEXT is the hardest. However, it seems to be a prominent phenomenon that CONCAT alone usually does not get along well with CONTEXT while MAX_POOL is more agreeable with context representations (see Line 5–8 in Table 4). [CLS] is a surprisingly good CONTEXT feature when combined with CONCAT and MAX_POOL (or SELF_ATT) (see Line 10 and Line18 in Table 4).

Table 2. Performances of Individual Span Representation Methods and the Impact of SPAN_END.

SPAN_SUMM	CONTEXT	END_COMB	SciERC: SPAN_END (micro F1 dev/test)		ScienceIE2017: SPAN_END (micro F1 dev/test)	
			NONE	CONCAT	NONE	CONCAT
MAX_POOL	NONE	NONE	$71.295_{1.709}$ / $68.954_{0.568}$	$71.381_{0.627}$ / $69.099_{1.269}$ ↑	$57.713_{1.709}$ / $45.118_{0.568}$	$57.667_{0.501}$ / $46.194_{0.902}$ ↑
SELF_ATT	NONE	NONE	$62.177_{0.615}$ / $60.613_{0.561}$	$71.212_{0.357}$ / $68.552_{1.067}$ ↑	$49.810_{0.508}$ / $39.625_{0.681}$	$71.212_{0.357}$ / $46.585_{0.353}$ ↑
NONE	NONE	NONE	N/A	$70.757_{0.853}$ / $68.458_{0.779}$	N/A	$55.890_{0.648}$ / $45.833_{0.897}$
NONE	NONE	DIFF_SUM	$71.245_{0.593}$ / $68.186_{1.025}$	--	$56.358_{0.576}$ / $45.711_{0.440}$	--
[18]: BERT NER + char embed (SciBERT [26])				----$_{??}$ / $65.6_{1.0}$		----$_{??}$ / $43.8_{1.0}$
[11]: SciIE (BiLSTM + Glove; +RE/COREF)				$68.1_{??}$ / $64.2_{??}$		----$_{??}$ / $46.0_{??}$
[12]: SpERT (SciBERT; +RE)				----$_{??}$ / 70.33		N/A

Note: Upward (resp. downward) arrows represent performance increase (resp.) decrease using span ends. The shaded blanks are four simplest span representations in [22]. "----" and underscripted "??" indicate unreported figure and standard deviation respectively. It is unclear whether average or the best results were reported in [6, 21, 34]

Table 3. Performances of combinations of span and context representations and the impact of SPAN_END.

SPAN_SUMM	CONTEXT	SciERC: SPAN_END (micro F1 dev/test)		ScienceIE2017: SPAN_END (micro F1 dev/test)	
		NONE	CONCAT	NONE	CONCAT
1 MAX_POOL	[CLS]	$71.266_{0.412}$ / $68.661_{0.859}$	$71.516_{0.707}$ / **$69.269_{0.880}$**	$58.040_{0.701}$ / $46.206_{0.504}$ ↑	$57.753_{0.656}$ / $46.007_{0.845}$ →
2 SELF_ATT	[CLS]	$62.426_{0.789}$ / $60.942_{0.778}$	$71.876_{0.618}$ / $69.118_{0.852}$	$49.996_{0.703}$ / $40.415_{0.709}$ ↑	$57.844_{0.550}$ / $46.113_{1.129}$ ↑
3 NONE	[CLS]	N/A	$70.976_{0.727}$ / $67.609_{0.562}$	N/A	$56.008_{0.837}$ / $45.322_{1.009}$
4 MAX_POOL	SELF_ATT	$71.363_{0.606}$ / $68.935_{1.254}$	$71.291_{0.651}$ / $68.687_{0.864}$	$58.387_{0.510}$ / $45.636_{0.478}$ →	$58.152_{1.028}$ / $46.423_{0.666}$ ↑
5 SELF_ATT	SELF_ATT	$70.979_{0.502}$ / $69.109_{0.833}$	$72.180_{0.853}$ / $68.729_{1.239}$	$57.312_{0.468}$ / $45.582_{0.902}$ →	$57.454_{0.877}$ / $45.992_{0.653}$ ↑
6 NONE	SELF_ATT	N/A	$71.051_{0.673}$ / $68.505_{0.474}$	N/A	$56.134_{0.988}$ / $45.373_{0.749}$ ↑
7 MAX_POOL	MAX_POOL	$71.383_{0.992}$ / $68.778_{0.495}$	$71.784_{0.727}$ / $69.032_{0.747}$	$57.817_{0.576}$ / $45.784_{0.646}$ ↑	$58.131_{0.515}$ / $46.400_{0.688}$ ↑
8 SELF_ATT	MAX_POOL	$71.058_{0.871}$ / $68.564_{0.849}$	$71.008_{0.579}$ / $68.976_{0.612}$	$56.856_{0.124}$ / $45.230_{0.753}$ ↑	$57.758_{0.806}$ / **$46.748_{0.822}$** ↑
9 NONE	MAX_POOL	N/A	$71.644_{0.701}$ / $68.452_{0.435}$	N/A	$56.143_{0.832}$ / $45.503_{0.750}$
[18]: BERT NER + char embed (SciBERT [26])			—-?? / $65.6_{1.0}$		—-?? / $43.8_{1.0}$
[11]: SciIE (BiLSTM + Glove; +RE/COREF)		$68.1_{??}$ / $64.2_{??}$			—-?? / $46.0_{??}$
[27]: DYGIE++ (BERT; + RE/COREF)			—-?? / 67.5		N/A
[12]: SpERT (SciBERT; +RE)			—-?? / 70.33		N/A

Note: the setting of SPAN_SUMM=MAX_POOL, CONTEX=[CLS] and SPAN_END=NONE replicates an NER-only version of SpERT

Table 4. Performances of combinations of span and context representations and the impact of END_COMB.

#	SPAN_END	SPAN_SUM	CONTEXT	SciERC: END_COMB (micro F1 dev/test) NONE	SciERC: END_COMB (micro F1 dev/test) DIFF_SUM		ScienceIE2017: END_COMB (micro F1 dev/test) NONE	ScienceIE2017: END_COMB (micro F1 dev/test) DIF_SUM	
1	CONCAT	NONE	NONE	$70.757_{0.853}$ / $68.458_{0.779}$	$70.816_{0.519}$ / $68.202_{0.646}$	→	$55.890_{0.508}$ / $45.833_{0.681}$	$55.870_{0.352}$ / $45.318_{0.353}$	→
2	CONCAT	NONE	[CLS]	$70.976_{0.727}$ / $67.609_{0.562}$	$71.331_{0.635}$ / $68.094_{0.577}$	←	$56.008_{0.837}$ / $45.322_{1.009}$	$56.626_{0.503}$ / $46.624_{0.160}$	←
3	CONCAT	NONE	SELF_ATT	$71.051_{0.673}$ / $68.505_{0.474}$	$71.179_{0.388}$ / $68.480_{0.933}$	←	$56.134_{0.988}$ / $45.373_{0.749}$	$56.714_{0.576}$ / $45.852_{0.276}$	←
4	CONCAT	NONE	MAX_POOL	$71.644_{0.701}$ / $68.452_{0.435}$	$71.422_{0.482}$ / $69.038_{0.465}$	←	$56.143_{0.832}$ / $45.503_{0.750}$	$56.465_{0.367}$ / $45.976_{0.622}$	←
5	NONE	MAX_POOL	NONE	$71.295_{1.209}$ / $68.954_{0.568}$	$71.720_{0.522}$ / $69.085_{0.971}$	←	$57.713_{1.209}$ / $45.118_{0.568}$	$57.556_{0.501}$ / 45.984	←
6	NONE	MAX_POOL	[CLS]	$71.266_{0.412}$ / $68.661_{0.859}$ *	$71.846_{0.865}$ / $68.952_{0.355}$	←	$58.040_{0.701}$ / $46.206_{0.504}$	$57.889_{0.656}$ / $46.305_{0.845}$	←
7	NONE	MAX_POOL	SELF_ATT	$71.363_{0.606}$ / $68.935_{1.254}$	$71.408_{0.679}$ / $69.002_{0.714}$	←	$58.387_{0.510}$ / $45.636_{0.478}$	$58.149_{0.923}$ / $46.740_{0.191}$	←
8	NONE	MAX_POOL	MAX_POOL	$71.383_{0.592}$ / $68.778_{0.495}$	$71.456_{0.669}$ / $69.533_{0.945}$	←	$57.817_{0.576}$ / $45.784_{0.646}$	$57.786_{0.865}$ / $46.183_{0.522}$	←
9	CONCAT	MAX_POOL	NONE	$71.381_{0.627}$ / $69.099_{1.269}$	$72.192_{0.767}$ / $69.413_{0.351}$	←	$57.667_{0.501}$ / $46.194_{0.902}$	$58.042_{0.620}$ / $45.978_{0.816}$	←
10	CONCAT	MAX_POOL	[CLS]	$71.516_{0.707}$ / $69.269_{0.880}$	$71.992_{0.739}$ / $69.266_{0.833}$	←	$57.753_{0.656}$ / $46.007_{0.845}$	$57.879_{1.187}$ / $46.934_{1.737}$	←
11	CONCAT	MAX_POOL	SELF_ATT	$71.291_{0.651}$ / $68.687_{0.864}$	$71.873_{0.749}$ / $68.648_{0.700}$	←	$58.152_{1.028}$ / $46.423_{0.666}$	$58.315_{0.378}$ / $46.641_{0.686}$	←
12	CONCAT	MAX_POOL	MAX_POOL	$71.784_{0.727}$ / $69.032_{0.747}$	$71.768_{0.418}$ / $68.581_{1.119}$	←	$58.131_{0.515}$ / $46.400_{0.688}$	$57.870_{0.529}$ / $45.945_{0.535}$	→
13	NONE	SELF_ATT	NONE	$62.177_{0.615}$ / $60.613_{0.561}$	$71.475_{0.831}$ / $68.875_{1.090}$	←	$49.810_{0.508}$ / $39.625_{0.681}$	$58.401_{0.501}$ / $46.358_{0.488}$	←
14	NONE	SELF_ATT	[CLS]	$62.426_{0.789}$ / $60.942_{0.778}$	$71.813_{0.369}$ / $69.202_{0.528}$	←	$49.996_{0.703}$ / $40.415_{0.709}$	$57.846_{0.616}$ / $46.177_{1.032}$	←
15	NONE	SELF_ATT	SELF_ATT	$70.979_{0.502}$ / $69.109_{0.833}$	$71.946_{0.819}$ / $69.385_{0.681}$	←	$57.312_{0.468}$ / $45.582_{0.902}$	$58.117_{0.605}$ / $46.639_{0.681}$	←
16	NONE	SELF_ATT	MAX_POOL	$71.058_{0.871}$ / $68.564_{0.849}$	$71.470_{0.754}$ / $69.086_{0.396}$	←	$56.856_{0.124}$ / $45.230_{0.753}$	$58.358_{0.576}$ / $\mathbf{47.134}_{0.916}$	←
17	CONCAT	SELF_ATT	NONE	$71.212_{0.668}$ / $68.522_{0.328}$	$71.209_{0.490}$ / $68.873_{0.811}$	←	$58.432_{0.386}$ / $46.585_{0.353}$	$58.119_{0.841}$ / $46.602_{0.923}$	←
18	CONCAT	SELF_ATT	[CLS]	$71.876_{0.618}$ / $69.118_{0.852}$	$71.621_{0.659}$ / $\mathbf{69.780}_{0.645}$	←	$57.844_{0.550}$ / $46.113_{1.129}$	$57.812_{0.831}$ / $46.071_{1.090}$	→
19	CONCAT	SELF_ATT	SELF_ATT	$72.180_{0.853}$ / $68.729_{1.239}$	$72.109_{1.175}$ / $69.045_{1.462}$	←	$57.454_{0.877}$ / $45.992_{0.653}$	$58.376_{0.542}$ / $46.434_{0.421}$	←
20	CONCAT	SELF_ATT	MAX_POOL	$71.008_{0.579}$ / $68.976_{0.612}$	$71.799_{0.503}$ / $68.673_{1.192}$	→	$57.758_{0.806}$ / $\mathbf{46.748}_{0.822}$	$58.202_{0.428}$ / $46.626_{0.673}$	→
[18]: BERT NER + char embed (SciBERT)				$68.1_{??}$ / $64.2_{??}$	$--_{??}$ / $65.6_{1.0}$			$--_{??}$ / $43.8_{1.0}$	
[11]: SciIE (BiLSTM + Glove; +RE/COREF)								$--_{??}$ / $46.0_{??}$	
[27]: DYGIE++ (BERT; + RE/COREF)					$--_{??}$ / 67.5			N/A	
[12]: SpERT (SciBERT; +RE)					$--_{??}$ / 70.33			N/A	

* This is the NER-only version of SpERT.

3   Conclusions

This paper investigates the performances of span modeling options on two decent Science NER datasets. Simple classical methods, e.g., concatenation of span end points and max pooling based span summary, perform surprisingly competitively. On the contrary, self-attentive span summary, though being very popular, is significantly poorer. Span representation combination introduces further improvements. In most cases, additional NER power is added when certain context encodings are combined with span encodings. Context encodings do complement when span endpoints are not used. However, no conclusion can be made as to which context encoding is consistently better.

Appendix (Experimental Setup)

Probing experiments are done on two recent challenging scientific information extraction datasets popular among the NLP community. The first is SciERC [11] – 2687 sentences from 500 abstracts of AI papers annotated with entity, relation and coreference information with a 1861/275/551 train/dev/test split. Only the 8089 entity annotations are used. The six entity types are Problem, Method, Material, Metric, OtherScientificTerm and Generic (term). The second is the dataset published with SemEval 2017 Shared Task 10 [28]–3432 sentences from 500 abstracts of computer science, materials sciences, and physics papers with a 2293/371/768 train/dev/test split, named as ScienceIE2017. The raw data was preprocessed by tokenizing using Stanford's Stanza[1] and removing entity annotations which start in the middle of a meaningful word. Both datasets are transformed into the JSON format used by SpERT [12].

The codes are written in PyTorch using HuggingFace's Transformers library[2] by modifying SpERT [12], i.e., by adding the span and context representations and turning off the relation extraction component. Because SciBERT is used, the dimensionalities of $\mathbf{h}$, $\mathbf{c}^l$ and $\mathbf{c}^r$ are all fixed to 768. The dimensionality of $\mathbf{s}$ depends on choices of span and context encoding. The length of $\mathbf{w}$ is typically set to 25 (choice of this paper, not tuned) or 30. To make results comparable, most hyperparameter choices follow the SpERT paper, except that 40 epochs are run for model selection and a larger batch size $B = 16$ is chosen to speed up training. The attention hidden size, i.e., the size of the FFN output in Eq. (1) is set to half of SciBERT hidden size; it is not tuned. As in [9], micro F1 is averaged over five runs, with standard deviation underscripted to save space.

References

1. Augenstein, I., Søgaard, A.: Multi-task learning of keyphrase boundary classification. In: Proceedings of the 55th Annual Meeting of the Association for Computational Linguistics, vol. 2, pp. 341–346. Association for Computational Linguistics, Stroudsburg (2017)
2. Ouchi, H., Shido, H., Matsumoto, Y.: A span selection model for semantic role labeling. In: Proceedings of the 2018 Conference on Empirical Methods in Natural Language Processing, pp. 1630–1642. Association for Computational Linguistics, Stroudsburg (2018)

---

[1] https://stanfordnlp.github.io/stanza/.
[2] https://huggingface.co/transformers/.

3. Rajpurkar, P., Zhang, J., Lopyrev, K., Liang, P: SQuAD: 100,000+ questions for machine comprehension of text. In: Proceedings of the 2016 Conference on Empirical Methods in Natural Language Processing, pp. 2383–2392. Association for Computational Linguistics, Stroudsburg (2016)

4. Rajpurkar, P., Robn, J., Liang, P.: Know what you don't know: unanswerable questions for SQuAD. In: Proceedings of the 56th Annual Meeting of the Association for Computational Linguistics (Volume 2: Short Papers), pp. 784–789. Association for Computational Linguistics, Stroudsburg (2018)

5. Swayamdipta, S., Thomson, S., Lee, K., Zettlemoyer, L., Dyer, C., Smith N.A.: Syntactic scaffolds for semantic structures. In: Proceedings of the 2018 Conference on Empirical Methods in Natural Language Processing, pp. 3772–3782. Association for Computational Linguistics, Stroudsburg (2018)

6. Lee, K., He, L., Lewis, M., Zettlemoyer, L.: End-to-End neural Coreference resolution. In: Proceedings of the 2017 Conference on Empirical Methods in Natural Language Processing, pp. 188–197. Association for Computational Linguistics, Stroudsburg(2017).

7. Guo, J., Che, W., Liu, T., Xu, J.: A unified architecture for semantic role labeling and relation classification. In: Proceedings of COLING 2016, the 26th International Conference on Computational Linguistics: Technical Papers, pp. 1264–1274. Association for Computational Linguistics, Stroudsburg (2016)

8. Zhao, H.., Huang, L., Zhang, R., Lu, Q., Xue, H.: SpanMlt: a span-based multi-task learning framework for pair-wise aspect and opinion terms extraction. In: Proceedings of the 58th Annual Meeting of the Association for Computational Linguistics, pp. 3239–3248. Association for Computational Linguistics, Stroudsburg (2020)

9. Jiang, Z., Xu, W., Araki, J., Neubig, G.: Generalizing natural language analysis through Span-relation representations. In: Proceedings of the 58th Annual Meeting of the Association for Computational Linguistics, pp. 2120–2133. Association for Computational Linguistics, Stroudsburg (2020).

10. Sohrab, M.G., Miwa, M.: Deep exhaustive model for nested named entity recognition. In: Proceedings of the 2018 Conference on Empirical Methods in Natural Language Processing, pp. 2843–2849. Association for Computational Linguistics, Stroudsburg (2018).

11. Luan, Y., He, L., Ostendorf, M., Hajishirzi, H.: Multi-task identification of entities, relations, and coreference for scientific knowledge graph construction. In: Proceedings of the 2018 Conference on Empirical Methods in Natural Language Processing, pp. 3219–3232. Association for Computational Linguistics, Stroudsburg (2018)

12. Eberts, M., Ulges, A.: Span-based joint entity and relation extraction with transformer pre-training. In: 24th European Conference on Artificial Intelligence-ECAI 2020, European Association for Artificial Intelligence (2020).

13. Xia, C., et al.: Multi-grained named entity recognition. In: Proceedings of the 57th Annual Meeting of the Association for Computational Linguistics, pp. 1430–1440. Association for Computational Linguistics, Stroudsburg (2019)

14. Tan, C., Qiu, W., Chen, M., Wang, R., Huang, F.: Boundary enhanced neural span classification for nested named entity recognition. In: Proceedings of the AAAI Conference on Artificial Intelligence, vol. 34(05), pp. 9016–9023. Association for the Advancement of Artificial Intelligence, Palo Alto (2020)

15. Devlin, J., Chang, M.-W., Lee, K., Toutanova, K.: BERT: pre-training of deep bidirectional transformers for language understanding. In: Proceedings of the 2019 Conference of the North American Chapter of the Association for Computational Linguistics: Human Language Technologies, Volume 1 (Long and Short Papers), pp. 4171–4186. Association for Computational Linguistics, Stroudsburg (2019)

16. Toshniwal, S., Shi, H., Shi, B., Gao, L., Livescu, K., Gimpel, K.: A cross-task analysis of text span representations. In: Proceedings of the 5th Workshop on Representation Learning for NLP, pp. 166–176. Association for Computational Linguistics, Stroudsburg (2020)

17. Taillé, B., Guigue, V., Gallinari, P.: Contextualized embeddings in named-entity recognition: an empirical study on generalization. In: Jose, J.M., et al. (eds.) ECIR 2020. LNCS, vol. 12036, pp. 383–391. Springer, Cham (2020). https://doi.org/10.1007/978-3-030-45442-5_48

18. Brack, A., D'Souza, J., Hoppe, A., Auer, S., Ewerth, R.: Domain-independent extraction of scientific concepts from research articles. In: Jose, J.M., et al. (eds.) ECIR 2020. LNCS, vol. 12035, pp. 251–266. Springer, Cham (2020). https://doi.org/10.1007/978-3-030-45439-5_17

19. Hu, Z., Yin, H., Xu, G., Zhai, Y., Pan, D., Liang, Y.: An empirical study on joint entities-relations extraction of Chinese text based on BERT. In: Proceedings of the 2020 12th International Conference on Machine Learning and Computing, pp. 473–478. ACM, New York (2020)

20. Seo, M., Lee, J., Kwiatkowski, T., Parikh, A., Farhadi, A., Hajishirzi, H.: Real-time open-domain question answering with dense-sparse phrase index. In: Proceedings of the 57th Annual Meeting of the Association for Computational Linguistics, pp. 4430–4441. Association for Computational Linguistics, Stroudsburg (2019)

21. Lin, Z., Feng, M., Xu, M., Xiang, B., Zhou, B., Bengio, Y.: A structured self-attentive sentence embedding. In: Proceedings of the 5th International Conference on Learning Representations. https://openreview.net/references/pdf?id=SyLIO1tte.

22. Ouchi, H., Shindo, H., Matsumoto, Y.: A span selection model for semantic role labeling. In: Proceedings of the 2018 Conference on Empirical Methods in Natural Language Processing, pp. 1630–1642. Association for Computational Linguistics, Stroudsburg (2018).

23. Zhan, J., Zhao, H.: Span model for open information extraction on accurate corpus. In: Proceedings of the AAAI Conference on Artificial Intelligence, vol. 34(05), pp. 9523–9530. https://doi.org/10.1609/aaai.v34i05.6497.

24. Collobert, R., Weston, J., Bottou, L., Karlen, M., Kavukcuoglu, K., Kuksa, P.: Natural language processing almost from scratch. J. Mach. Learn. Res. **12**, 2493–2537 (2011)

25. Hashimoto, K., Xiong, C., Tsuruoka, Y., Socher, R.: A joint many-task model: growing a neural network for multiple NLP tasks. In: Proceedings of the 2017 Conference on Empirical Methods in Natural Language Processing, pp. 1923–1933. Association for Computational Linguistics, Stroudsburg (2017)

26. Beltagy, I., Lo, K., Cohan, A.: SciBERT: a pretrained language model for scientific text. In: Proceedings of the 2019 Conference on Empirical Methods in Natural Language Processing and the 9th International Joint Conference on Natural Language Processing (EMNLP-IJCNLP), pp. 3615–3620. Association for Computational Linguistics, Stroudsburg (2019)

27. Wadden, D., Wennberg, U., Luan, Y., Hajishirzi, H.: Entity, relation, and event extraction with contextualized span representations. In: Proceedings of the 2019 Conference on Empirical Methods in Natural Language Processing and the 9th International Joint Conference on Natural Language Processing (EMNLP-IJCNLP), pp. 5784–5789. Association for Computational Linguistics, Stroudsburg (2019)

28. Augenstein, I., Das, M., Riedal, S., Vikraman, L., McCallum, A.: SemEval 2017 task 10: scienceIE-extracting keyphrases and relations from scientific publications. In: Proceedings of the 11th International Workshop on Semantic Evaluation (SemEval-2017), pp. 546–555. Association for Computational Linguistics, Stroudsburg (2017).

Terminology/Keyphrase Extraction for Creation of Book Indexes in Polish

Małgorzata Marciniak[ID], Agnieszka Mykowiecka[ID], and Piotr Rychlik[(✉)][ID]

Institute of Computer Science Polish Academy of Sciences, Jana Kazimierza 5, Warsaw, Poland
{mm,agn,rychlik}@ipipan.waw.pl

Abstract. The paper addresses the problem of automatic identification of phrases to be included in back-of-book indexes. We analyzed books in Polish and English published with subject indexes compiled by their authors. We checked what kinds of phrases are placed in those indexes and how often they actually occur in the corresponding books. In the experiments, we use existing terminology and keyphrase extraction tools. For Polish, the first tool is better than the second one, but for English texts, the results are inconclusive.

Keywords: Back-of-book index · Extraction tools · Polish

1 Introduction

Scientific and technical books in their traditional printed form need indexes. They help readers to find a description of a term, identify groups of related terms, and recognize synonyms. The importance of book indexes is well supported by practice – most publishing houses have their own guidelines for preparing indexes, there are courses for teaching how to prepare the most informative ones, and there are books describing these issues, e.g., [14,23,26]. Issues strictly related to the index phrase extraction for English are discussed, among others, in [7,28], and [9]. The problem was considered also for other languages, e.g., Chinese [3,11], or Thai [4].

As preparing an index is a laborious task, there are quite a few tools which facilitate this job, but only for selected natural languages. For English, several systems are listed on the page of the American Society for Indexing. But, we are not aware of such tools for Polish and we were only able to find a few publications on this subject concerning Polish texts, e.g., [19,27]. However, there are applications for the related tasks, i.e.: for extracting terminology phrases [13] and for multilingual keywords extraction [2]. In both tasks, candidates (n-grams/phrases) are selected from texts and, the most representative sequences for the analyzed data are chosen from among these candidates to create a list of keyphrases and terminological vocabulary. The goal of the work presented in this paper was to analyze if these tools are adequate for identification of index entries. Although we are mainly interested in using these tools for Polish books, we also check their performance for a few books in English.

© Springer Nature Switzerland AG 2021
G. Berget et al. (Eds.): TPDL 2021, LNCS 12866, pp. 49–54, 2021.
https://doi.org/10.1007/978-3-030-86324-1_5

2 Processing of Polish Books

For the experiments, we selected eight copyright books from linguistics (MJ [22], AP [20], EH [6], MO [17]) and economics (EE [10], ZR [18], KI [24], ZW [29]). All the books were available in pdf format. For each one, we prepared three separate files: the table of contents, the main content, and the index. To allow us to recognize different inflectional forms of the index entries, we analyzed the text files using Korpusomat [8]. The books length varies from 50,000 to 100,000 tokens.

Table 1. POS of words in the indexes: *subst*antives, *ger*unds, *adj*ectives, *ppas* – passive adj. participle, *adja* – ad-adjectival adjective, *adv*erbs, *prep*ositions, *conj*unctions, *preat* – l-participle, *pact* – active adj. participle, *xxx* – uninterpreted words, *rest* types of POS.

POS	subst	ger	adj	ppas	adja	adv	prep	conj	preat	pact	xxx	rest
#	2748	110	932	66	12	22	113	45	13	19	34	53
%	65.9	2.6	22.4	1.6	0.3	0.5	2.7	1.1	0.3	0.5	0.8	1,3

The statistics of the index phrase length shows that the vast majority of phrases are up to 4 words long, up to 10% of them are longer than 4 words. The majority of phrases have two words, the statistics of the POS is given in Table 1. Most phrases consist of nouns (*subst*antives) and *adj*ectives, which can appear before or after a modified noun, as Polish is a free word order language, e.g., *struktury$_{subst}$ mentalne$_{adj}$* 'mental structures' and *etyczne$_{adj}$ kwestie$_{subst}$* 'ethical issues'. The index entries can consist only of nouns, e.g., *teoria$_{subst.nom}$ wymiany$_{subst.gen}$ darów$_{subst.gen}$* 'gift exchange theory'. Both types of phrases make up at least 75% of indexes. There are also quite a few *ger*unds and *ppas* as they play the role of nouns and adjectives in phrases, respectively. Indexes contain also some more complex constructions. Depending on the book, up to 14% of index phrases contain prepositions. These phrases are usually longer than 3 words, e.g., *[automat$_{subst}$ skończony$_{adj}$] [z$_{prep}$ wyjściem$_{subst}$]* 'finite-state machine with the output'. Conjunctions only appear in few entries in the linguistics books (which is less than 1.5%), but in the economics books they constitute up to 7.3% index phrases. Conjunctions usually combine very simple phrases, i.e., *wariancja [międzygrupowa i$_{conj}$ wewnątrzgrupowa]* 'intergroup and intragroup variance'. A relatively small number of phrases contains adverbs, e.g., *tłumaczenie$_{subst}$ wspomagane$_{ppas}$ maszynowo$_{adv}$* 'machine-assisted translation'. It should also be mentioned that in almost all the analyzed Polish indexes, there are terms in English, acronyms and some named entities.

We identified about 0.65–0.82 of all index entries within the text, but only half of them appear in the text in the same form as in the index. The indexes from the linguistic books were covered in a greater degree than those from the economics books (more than 10% difference). On average, index phrases occur

Table 2. Index entries found for STD and EXT lists

Book		MJ	AP	EE	ZR	EH	MO	KI	ZW
Index size		217	429	309	200	369	53	51	178
STD	terms	17428	10471	15999	17241	15135	8188	10552	16039
	found	179	271	158	168	251	38	47	135
EXT	terms	23372	13488	21803	24887	19237	10609	15635	23724
	found	181	283	177	171	255	38	48	149

Table 3. Precision and recall for Polish books for the top part of the TermoPL lists and for YAKE! keywords. The number of tested terms is adequate to the length of the book, without dividing groups terms with the same TermoPL score; # – number of index entries in the selected top part of the terms list.

Book	Index size	TermoPL								YAKE!			
		STD				EXT							
		terms	#	P	R	terms	#	P	R	terms	#	P	R
MJ	224	479	62	0.13	0.28	436	57	0.13	0.25	479	7	0.01	0.03
AP	429	491	69	0.14	0.16	466	67	0.14	0.16	491	31	0.06	0.07
EH	369	571	97	0.16	0.36	530	87	0.16	0.32	571	21	0.04	0.06
MO	54	107	6	0.05	0.11	93	4	0.04	0.07	107	3	0.03	0.06
EE	309	468	53	0.11	0.17	526	62	0.12	0.20	468	1	0.00	0.00
ZR	238	419	54	0.13	0.23	435	52	0.12	0.22	419	24	0.06	0.10
KI	51	176	23	0.14	0.46	174	19	0.11	0.38	176	15	0.09	0.29
ZW	181	194	31	0.16	0.17	192	35	0.18	0.19	194	8	0.04	0.04

quite frequently within the text, but quite a few of them (16 to 30%) occur only once.

We use a publicly available tool, TermoPL [13], for extracting domain-specific terminology from texts. For each book, we extracted two lists of terms. The first one (STD) consists of phrases recognized by the standard grammar of TermoPL, which accepts adjective-noun phrases, possibly modified by other adjective-noun phrases in the genitive case. The second list (EXT) is the extension of the STD list augmented by simple prepositional phrases, adverbial phrases and conjunctions connecting two adjectives or two nouns. These lists were compared with indexes, the results are shown in Table 2. As we can see, extending the STD list with extra terms does not increase the number of found index entries.

Testing if using TermoPL could be an adequate solution to the problem of index phrase extraction, we assumed that on average there could be about one and half index entries per an average page. We took the top of the TermoPL output of this size and compared it with the index entries. The precision and recall in all cases were quite similar and rather low – about 0.2. Low recall is mainly caused by the absence or low frequency of terms within the text. The reasons of low precision is mainly caused by the presence of the phrases from general language and too general domain phrases.

We compared the performance of TermoPL with YAKE! [2], a language independent keyword extraction tool that uses an unsupervised method based on numerous local text features and statistics, such as term frequencies, co-occurrence, position in a text or even a text case. The authors of YAKE! compared their method with several other tools using an unsupervised approach to the task and proved that YAKE! significantly outperforms them [2]. The results depicted in Table 3 show that for Polish data, YAKE! keywords are not good candidates for index entries. Only with the KI book the results seem slightly better than others, but in this case, the total number of index entries is very small.

3   Experiments on English Indexes

To compare the results obtained for Polish with similar experiments for English, we collected five, recently published, open access books with indexes. We selected three economics books: PE [5], PPE [21], OB [1], and two linguistic: GT [16], and MM [12]. We check how many index entries can be found within the text of the books. The results are similar to those obtained for Polish, i.e., 60%–90%. Then, we used TermoPL with a grammar of English nominal phrases to extract index candidates. The results are given in Table 4. For the linguistics books, the results are similar to the Polish books – a relatively small number of index terms (about 10%) are in the top part of the terminology list. But for the economics books, the results are better – even a quarter of the index entries can be found with similar precision. We also extracted English key phrases with the help of YAKE! (the last three columns of Table 4). The results for the linguistics books are better for YAKE! than TermoPL. For the economics books, the results of TermoPL are better.

Table 4. Precision and recall for English books counted for the different top segments of the TermoPL (the list length defined as in Table 3) and YAKE! (1000 elements) lists.

Book	Index size	TermoPL											YAKE! top 1000		
		Approx. size				Top 1000				Entire list					
		terms	#	P	R	terms	#	P	R	#-total	R		#	P	R
GT	790	2475	115	0.04	0.15	1237	95	0.07	0.12	10402	0.44		95	0.10	0.13
MM	92	245	9	0.04	0.10	1312	22	0.02	0.24	5892	0.74		36	0.04	0.39
OB	759	1214	137	0.11	0.18	1008	123	0.12	0.16	36257	0.68		76	0.08	0.10
PE	836	2306	308	0.13	0.37	1010	215	**0.21**	**0.26**	41794	0.67		132	0.13	0.14
PPE	863	1569	241	0.15	0.28	1049	184	0.18	0.21	27708	0.67		147	0.15	0.19

4   Conclusion and Further Work

For the top part of the TermoPL list of extracted Polish phrases, the average F-measure for 8 books is 0.16, which is similar to the results reported in [9] for English. The comparison of the results obtained for TermoPL and YAKE! confirms the conclusion of the paper [25], that linguistically motivated methods gives better results. The results obtained by TermoPL for English are slightly worse than for Polish. The results for YAKE! are better for English texts than for Polish ones, probably due to a much smaller number of phrase variants. Results for the linguistics books in English are better for YAKE!, while for the economics book are better for TermoPL.

The analysis of the TermoPL results shows that it is useful to add information about named entities and acronyms related to them as we saw quite a few such entries in the book indexes. We also plan to check if it is possible to increase the efficiency of the automatic index creation methods by applying machine learning algorithms, in particular neural networks. We plan to use and enhance methods for general terms identification proposed in [15] among other things.

References

1. Black, J.S., et al.: Organizational Behavior. OpenStax, Houston (2019)
2. Campos, R., Mangaravite, V., Pasquali, A., Jorge, A., Nunes, C., Jatowt, A.: Yake! keyword extraction from single documents using multiple local features. Inf. Sci. **509**, 257–289 (2020)
3. Chang, J.S., et al.: A corpus-based statistical approach to automatic book indexing. In: Proceedings of the Third Conference on Applied Natural Language Processing, pp. 147–151. Trento, Italy (1992)
4. Chumwatana, T., Wong, K., Xie, H.: An automatic indexing technique for Thai texts using frequent max substring. In: Proceedings of the 8th International Symposium on Natural Language Processing, pp. 67–72 (2009)
5. Greenlaw, S.A., David, S.: Principles of Economics 2e. OpenStax, Houston (2018)
6. Hajnicz, E.: Automatyczne tworzenie semantycznego słownika walencyjnego. Problemy Współczesnej Nauki. Teoria i Zastosowania: Inżynieria Lingwistyczna, Akademicka Oficyna Wydawnicza EXIT, Warszawa (2011)
7. Hulth, A.: Improved automatic keyword extraction given more linguistic knowledge. In: Proceedings of the 2003 Conference on Empirical Methods in Natural Language Processing, pp. 216–223 (2003)
8. Kieraś, W., Kobyliński, Ł., Ogrodniczuk, M.: Korpusomat – a tool for creating searchable morphosyntactically tagged corpora. Comput. Methods Sci. Technol. **24**(1), 21–27 (2018). https://doi.org/10.12921/cmst.2018.0000005
9. Koutropoulou, T., Gallopoulos, E.: TMG-BoBI: generating back-of-the-book indexes with the text-to-matrix-generator. In: 2019 10th International Conference on Information, Intelligence, Systems and Applications (IISA), pp. 1–8 (2019)
10. Krawczyk, M.: Ekonomia eksperymentalna. Wolters Kluwer Polska Sp. z o.o., Warszawa (2012)
11. Lv, S., Li, N., Tian, Y.: Improving index term extraction for Chinese books with professional score. In: 2016 4th International Conference on Electrical & Electronics Engineering and Computer Science (ICEEECS 2016). Atlantis Press (2016/12)

12. Marciniak, M.: Domain corpora as a source of information, Monograph Series, vol. 4. Institute of Computer Science, Polish Academy of Sciences, Warsaw (2015)
13. Marciniak, M., Mykowiecka, A., Rychlik, P.: TermoPL – a flexible tool for terminology extraction. In: Proceedings of LREC, pp. 2278–2284. ELRA, Portorož, Slovenia (2016)
14. Mulvany, N.C.: Indexing Books. The University of Chicago Press, Chicago (2005)
15. Mykowiecka, A., Marciniak, M., Rychlik, P.: Recognition of irrelevant phrases in automatically extracted lists of domain terms. Terminology. Int. J. Theo. Appl. Issues Spec. Commun. **24**, 66–90 (2018)
16. Müller, S.: Grammatical Theory. Language Science Press, Berlin (2018)
17. Ogrodniczuk, M.: Automatyczne wykrywanie nominalnych zależności referencyjnych w polskich tekstach współczesnych. Wydawnictwa Uniwersytetu Warszawskiego, Warszawa (2019)
18. Olesiński, Z.: Zarządzanie relacjami międzyorganizacyjnymi. Wydawnictwo C.H. Beck, Warszawa (2010)
19. Pacek, J.: Indeksowanie w XXI wieku. Ewolucja i współczesne funkcje pojęcia. Zagadnienia Informacji Naukowej (2), 32–49 (2006)
20. Przepiórkowski, A.: Powierzchniowe przetwarzanie języka polskiego. Akademicka Oficyna Wydawnicza EXIT, Warszawa (2008)
21. Saros, D.E.: Principles of Political Economy, 3e: A Pluralistic Approach to Economic Theory. bepress, Valparaiso (2020)
22. Stelmaszczyk, P. (ed.): Metodologie językoznawstwa. Podstawy teoretyczne. Wydawnictwo Uniwersytetu Łódzkiego, Łódź (2006)
23. The University of Chicago Press Editorial Staff: Indexes: A Chapter from The Chicago Manual of Style, Seventeenth Edition. University of Chicago Press (2017)
24. Ujwary-Gil, A.: Kapitał intelektualny a wartość rynkowa przedsiębiorstwa. Wydawnictwo C.H. Beck, Warszawa (2009)
25. Wacholder, N., Liu, L.: Assessing term effectiveness in the interactive information access process. Inf. Process. Manag. **44**, 1022–1031 (2008)
26. Wellisch, H.: Indexing from A to Z. H.W Wilson, Bronx (1991)
27. Wolański, A.: Edycja tekstów. Praktyczny poradnik. Państwowe Wydawnictwo Naukowe (2016)
28. Wu, Z., Li, Z., Mitra, P., Giles, C.L.: Can back-of-the-book indexes be automatically created? In: He, Q., Iyengar, A., Nejdl, W., Pei, J., Rastogi, R. (eds.) 22nd ACM International Conference on Information and Knowledge Management, CIKM 2013, San Francisco, CA, USA, October 27–November 1 2013, pp. 1745–1750. ACM (2013)
29. Łada, M., Kozarkiewicz, A.: Zarządzanie wartością projektów. Wydawnictwo C.H. Beck, Warszawa (2010)

Token-Level Multilingual Epidemic Dataset for Event Extraction

Stephen Mutuvi[1,2](✉)(iD), Emanuela Boros[2](iD), Antoine Doucet[2](iD),
Gaël Lejeune[3](iD), Adam Jatowt[4](iD), and Moses Odeo[1](iD)

[1] Multimedia University, Nairobi, Kenya
[2] University of La Rochelle, La Rochelle, France
[3] Sorbonne University, Paris, France
[4] University of Innsbruck, Innsbruck, Austria

Abstract. In this paper, we present a dataset and a baseline evaluation for multilingual epidemic event extraction. We experiment with a multilingual news dataset which we annotate at the token level, a common tagging scheme utilized in event extraction systems. We approach the task of extracting epidemic events by first detecting the relevant documents from a large collection of news reports. Then, event extraction (disease names and locations) is performed on the detected relevant documents. Preliminary experiments with the entire dataset and with ground-truth relevant documents showed promising results, while also establishing a stronger baseline for epidemiological event extraction.

Keywords: Epidemiological surveillance · Multilingualism · Sequence labeling

1 Introduction

While disease surveillance has in the past been a critical component in epidemiology, conventional surveillance methods are limited in terms of both promptness and coverage, while at the same time requiring labor-intensive human input. Recently, approaches that complement the traditional surveillance methods with data-driven approaches which rely on internet-based data sources such as online news articles have been advanced [1,3]. With the progress in natural language processing (NLP), processing and analyzing news data for epidemic surveillance has become feasible. Although this research is promising, the scarcity of available annotated multilingual corpora for data-driven epidemic surveillance is a major hindrance.

Online news data contains critical information about emerging health threats such as what happened, where it happened, when, and to whom it happened [11].

This work has been supported by the European Union's Horizon 2020 research and innovation program under grants 770299 (NewsEye) and 825153 (Embeddia). It has also been supported by the French Embassy in Kenya and the French Foreign Ministry.

© Springer Nature Switzerland AG 2021
G. Berget et al. (Eds.): TPDL 2021, LNCS 12866, pp. 55–59, 2021.
https://doi.org/10.1007/978-3-030-86324-1_6

When processed into a structured and more meaningful form, the information can foster early detection of disease outbreaks, a critical aspect of epidemic surveillance. News reports on epidemics often originate from different parts of the world and events are likely to be reported in other languages than English. Hence, efficient multilingual approaches are necessary for effective epidemic surveillance [2].

Several works have tackled the detection of events related to epidemic diseases. For example, the Data Analysis for Information Extraction in any Language (DAnIEL) was proposed as a multilingual dataset and a news surveillance system that leverages repetition and saliency (salient zones in the structure of a news article), properties that are common in news writing [9]. Models based on neural network architectures which take advantage of the word embeddings representations have been used in monitoring social media content for health events [8]. Other methods were based on long short-term memory networks (LSTMs) [12] that approached the epidemic detection task from the perspective of classification of documents (in this case, tweets) to extract influenza-related information.

In this study, we formulate the problem of extracting the disease names and locations in the text as a sequence labeling task. We use the DAnIEL multilingual dataset (Chinese, English, French, Greek, Polish, and Russian) comprising news articles from the medical domain with diverse morphological structures. We establish a baseline performance using a specialized baseline system and experiment with the most recent neural sequence labeling architectures.

2   Dataset

Due to the lack of dedicated datasets for epidemic event extraction from multilingual news articles, we adapt a freely available epidemiological dataset[1], called DAnIEL [9]. The dataset consists of news articles in six different languages, namely French, Polish, English, Chinese, Greek, and Russian. In this dataset, an epidemiological event is represented by a disease name and the location of the reported event.

However, the DAnIEL dataset is annotated at document level, which differentiates it from typical datasets (token or word level annotations) utilized in research for the event extraction task (i.e., ACE 2005[2], TAC KBP 2014–2015[3]). A document is either reporting an event of interest (a disease-place pair appears in a relevant document) or not (an irrelevant document).

An example of a relevant document is contained in the following sentence: *Ten tuberculosis patients in India described as having an untreatable form of the lung disease may be quarantined to thwart possible spread, a health official said [...].*

---

[1] The dataset is available at https://daniel.greyc.fr/public/index.php?a=corpus.

[2] https://catalog.ldc.upenn.edu/LDC2006T06.

[3] https://catalog.ldc.upenn.edu/LDC2020T13.

In this case, the document is annotated with *Tuberculosis* as the disease name, and *India* as the location.

We begin by performing sentence segmentation, thus obtaining the individual sentences from the text corpus. The data is then annotated using the Doccano annotation tool[4], a collaborative annotation tool that provides annotation features for various tasks, among them sequence labelling task. The annotation guidelines required the annotators to identify and mark the spans for the key entities from the text. The occurrence of an epidemic event is characterized by mentions of disease name and the location of the disease outbreak, labeled DIS and LOC, respectively. Three native speakers annotators were recruited for each language.

The annotations were then transformed into IOB (Inside, Outside, Beginning) tagging scheme. For example, each token of a disease name, based on the spans, is assigned the tags B-DIS, I-DIS, and O, marking the beginning (B-), intermediate (I-), and out-of-span markers (O). We then compute the Interannotator agreement (IAA) using the Kappa coefficient introduced by Cohen [4]. The average IAA for all languages was of 0.66.

Table 1. Number of relevant tokens and sentences per dataset split per language.

Split	Sentences	Tokens	French	English	Polish	Chinese	Greek	Russian
Training	6,638	201,043	156,221	13,404	11,741	4,853	7,028	7,796
Validation	861	26,022	19,427	2,321	1,453	346	819	1,656
Test	862	26,134	21,634	1,221	1,498	434	687	660

Table 1 presents the statistics for this dataset from which we can observe the particularities and challenges of this dataset. DAnIEL dataset is not only multilingual, but it is also imbalanced considering the low-resourced languages (Chinese, Greek, and Russian).

3   Experiments and Results

We first consider the specialized event extraction system, DAnIEL [9], which we consider as a strong baseline. Then, we experiment with deep learning models based on a bidirectional LSTM (BiLSTM) [7,10] that use character and word representations[5]. Additionally, due to the multilingual characteristic of the dataset, we use the multilingual BERT pre-trained language models [6] for token sequential classification and fine-tune them on our dataset. We will refer to these models as BERT-multilingual-cased[6] and BERT-multilingual-uncased[7]. We also

---

[4] https://github.com/doccano/doccano.
[5] The hyperparameters for both models are detailed in the papers [7,10].
[6] https://huggingface.co/bert-base-multilingual-cased.
[7] https://huggingface.co/bert-base-multilingual-uncased.

experiment with the XLM-RoBERTa-base model [5] that has shown significant performance gains for a wide range of cross-lingual transfer tasks. We consider this model appropriate for our task and dataset due to the multilingual nature of the data[8].

As shown in Table 2, BERT-multilingual-uncased recorded the highest F1, recall and precision scores with 80.99%, 79.77% and 82.25% respectively, on the dataset comprising both relevant and irrelevant examples. We observe in Table 2 that all the models significantly outperform our DAnIEL baseline.

Table 2. Evaluation results for the detection of disease names and locations on all languages and all data instances (relevant and irrelevant documents).

Models	P	R	F1
All data instances (relevant and irrelevant)			
BiLSTM+LSTM	79.68	70.07	74.57
BiLSTM+CNN	73.38	71	72.17
BERT-multilingual-cased	80.66	79.72	80.19
BERT-multilingual-uncased	**82.25**	**79.77**	**80.99**
XLM-RoBERTa-base	82.41	76.81	79.52
Only relevant documents			
BiLSTM+LSTM	**91.32**	85.38	88.25
BiLSTM+CNN	87.29	84.45	85.85
BERT-multilingual-cased	85.40	**90.95**	88.08
BERT-multilingual-uncased	87.16	89.79	88.46
XLM-RoBERTa-base	88.53	89.56	**89.04**

When evaluating the ground-truth relevant examples only, the task is obviously easier, particularly in terms of precision. Overall, XLM-RoBERTa-base attained the best F1-measure score of 89.04%. The model with the best recall was BERT-multilingual-cased (90.95%), while the BiLSTM+LSTM model had the highest precision.

4   Conclusions

In this paper, we present a token-level dataset and a strong baseline evaluation for multilingual epidemic event extraction. The results of the preliminary experiments suggest that the approaches based on pre-trained language models performed better than other deep learning models, thus, they can be utilized as strong baselines for epidemic event extraction. As future work, a further investigation of these preliminary results could reveal the underlying reasons of the

[8] XLM-RoBERTa-base was trained on 2.5TB of CommonCrawl data in 100 languages.

different performance values, and thus, further work will focus on a more fine-grained analysis of the methods. Moreover, we also propose to further examine the classification of relevant and irrelevant documents, in order to ascertain the level of error propagation from the document classification.

References

1. Aiello, A.E., Renson, A., Zivich, P.N.: Social media-and internet-based disease surveillance for public health. Annu. Rev. Public Health **41**, 101–118 (2020)
2. Brixtel, R., Lejeune, G., Doucet, A., Lucas, N.: Any language early detection of epidemic diseases from web news streams. In: 2013 IEEE International Conference on Healthcare Informatics, pp. 159–168. IEEE (2013)
3. Choi, J., Cho, Y., Shim, E., Woo, H.: Web-based infectious disease surveillance systems and public health perspectives: a systematic review. BMC Public Health **16**(1), 1–10 (2016). https://doi.org/10.1186/s12889-016-3893-0
4. Cohen, J.: A coefficient of agreement for nominal scales. Educ. Psychol. Measur. **20**(1), 37–46 (1960)
5. Conneau, A., et al.: Unsupervised cross-lingual representation learning at scale. In: Proceedings of the 58th Annual Meeting of the Association for Computational Linguistics, ACL 2020, Online, 5–10 July 2020, pp. 8440–8451. Association for Computational Linguistics (2020). https://www.aclweb.org/anthology/2020.acl-main.747/
6. Devlin, J., Chang, M.W., Lee, K., Toutanova, K.: BERT: pre-training of deep bidirectional transformers for language understanding. In: Proceedings of the 2019 Conference of the North American Chapter of the Association for Computational Linguistics: Human Language Technologies, Volume 1 (Long and Short Papers), pp. 4171–4186. Association for Computational Linguistics, Minneapolis (2019). https://doi.org/10.18653/v1/N19-1423
7. Lample, G., Ballesteros, M., Subramanian, S., Kawakami, K., Dyer, C.: Neural architectures for named entity recognition. In: Conference of the North American Chapter of the Association for Computational Linguistics: Human Language Technologies (2016)
8. Lampos, V., Zou, B., Cox, I.J.: Enhancing feature selection using word embeddings: The case of flu surveillance. In: Proceedings of the 26th International Conference on World Wide Web, pp. 695–704 (2017)
9. Lejeune, G., Brixtel, R., Doucet, A., Lucas, N.: Multilingual event extraction for epidemic detection. Artif. Intell. Med. **65**, 131–143 (2015). https://doi.org/10.1016/j.artmed.2015.06.005
10. Ma, X., Hovy, E.: End-to-end sequence labeling via bi-directional LSTM-CNNs-CRF. In: Proceedings of the 54th Annual Meeting of the Association for Computational Linguistics (Volume 1: Long Papers), pp. 1064–1074. Association for Computational Linguistics, Berlin (2016). https://doi.org/10.18653/v1/P16-1101. https://www.aclweb.org/anthology/P16-1101
11. Ng, V., Rees, E.E., Niu, J., Zaghool, A., Ghiasbeglou, H., Verster, A.: Application of natural language processing algorithms for extracting information from news articles in event-based surveillance. Can. Commun. Dis. Rep. **46**(6), 186–191 (2020)
12. Wang, C.K., Singh, O., Tang, Z.L., Dai, H.J.: Using a recurrent neural network model for classification of tweets conveyed influenza-related information. In: Proceedings of the International Workshop on Digital Disease Detection using Social Media 2017 (DDDSM-2017), pp. 33–38 (2017)

A Semantic Search Engine for Historical Handwritten Document Images

Vuong M. Ngo[1]([✉]) [iD], Gary Munnelly[1] [iD], Fabrizio Orlandi[1] [iD], Peter Crooks[2] [iD], Declan O'Sullivan[1] [iD], and Owen Conlan[1] [iD]

[1] ADAPT Centre, SCSS, Trinity College Dublin, Dublin, Ireland
{vuong.ngo,gary.munnelly,fabrizio.orlandi}@adaptcentre.ie,
{declan.osullivan,Owen.Conlan}@tcd.ie
[2] Department of History, Trinity College Dublin, Dublin, Ireland
pcrooks@tcd.ie

Abstract. A very large number of historical manuscript collections are available in image formats and require extensive manual processing in order to search through them. So, we propose and build a search engine for automatically storing, indexing and efficiently searching the manuscript images. Firstly, a handwritten text recognition technique is used to convert the images into textual representations. In the next steps, we apply the named entity recognition and historical knowledge graph to build a semantic search model, which can understand the user's intent in the query and the contextual meaning of concepts in documents, to return correctly the transcriptions and their corresponding images for users.

Keywords: Handwriting transcription · Named entity · Knowledge graph

1 Introduction

Every year, the great collections of historical handwritten manuscripts in museums, libraries and other organisations are digitised as electronic images. The digitisation makes the manuscripts available to a wider audience, and preserves the cultural heritage. The automatic recognition of textual corpora and named entities generated from medieval and early-modern manuscript sources with high accuracy is a challenge [2,20,22]. Manuscript images are often processed through keyword spotting or word recognition to be accessed and searched, such as [4,8,14,17] and [18]. There are some papers build a search system for handwritten images, such as [1,5,15,16,21] and [23]. However, their systems only offer keyword search.

Unlike keyword search, semantic search improves search precision and recall by understanding the user's intent and the contextual meaning of concepts in documents and queries [3,12,19,24]. This paper proposes a semantic search engine for full-text retrieval of historical handwritten document images based

© The Author(s) 2021
G. Berget et al. (Eds.): TPDL 2021, LNCS 12866, pp. 60–65, 2021.
https://doi.org/10.1007/978-3-030-86234-1_7

on named entity (NE), keyword (KW) and knowledge graph (KG). This would help not only in processing, storing and indexing automatically, but also would allow users to access quickly and retrieve efficiently manuscripts.

2   System Architecture

The Public Record Office of Ireland (PROI) was destroyed on 30 June 1922, resulting in the loss of 700 years of Irish history. The Beyond 2022 Project (https://beyond2022.ie) is combining historical research, archival discovery, and technical innovation to create a virtual reconstruction of the PROI. There are over 300 volumes of surviving and collected handwritten copies of lots documents, with some 100,000 pages containing 25 million words of text.

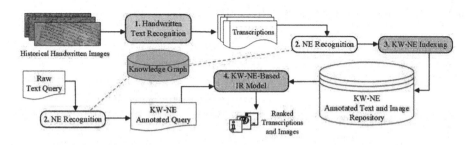

Fig. 1. The system architecture

Our system architecture of the search engine is illustrated in Fig. 1 which has four separate processing modules being `Handwritten Text Recognition`, `NE Recognition`, `KW-NE Indexing` and `KW-NE-Based IR Model`. Firstly, the historical handwritten document images are digitised to transcriptions through the `Handwritten Text Recognition` module. Then, the transcriptions are annotated by NEs through the `NE Recognition` module. This module needs to connect to the `Knowledge Graph` to extract the classes and identifiers of NEs. Next, KWs and NEs of the annotated transcriptions and the respective original images are presented and indexed by the `KW-NE indexing` module and stored in `KW-NE Annotated Text and Image Repository`. The raw text query is also annotated NEs through the `NE Recognition` module to become a KW-NE annotated query. Finally, the `KW-NE-Based IR Model` module compares the annotated query and the annotated documents to return the ranked transcriptions and images.

3   Image Representation and Knowledge Graph

Transkribus [13] is used for training and deploying Handwritten Text Recognition (HTR) models to derive text transcription from image scans. Given the rate at which transcriptions can be generated, NE Recognition (NER) and Entity

Linking (EL) are required to automated annotate all instances of entities occurring in the transcription text. We used SpaCy [11] for NER and had highly results on 18th century English text. To provide flexibility, an NLP pipeline has been implemented as a thin layer over a number of standard NLP tools. The output of the pipeline is a NLP Interchange Format [10] in which a NER tool has annotated classes of entities and, where possible, an EL tool has connected the recognized entities to KG.

The KG collects structured data from various historical sources. Part of the data is manually curated by historians through spreadsheets. Other data sources (e.g. geographical data from OSi [6]) are imported automatically as RDF for direct insertion into KG. The schema (or ontology) used to structure KG, is mainly based on the popular CIDOC-CRM ontology [7]. A short excerpt of KG is depicted in Fig. 2. It shows a few main entities and relationships related to a person (of type `CIDOC-CRM:E21_Person`) named "William Sutton", who was member of a few relevant offices in Ireland.

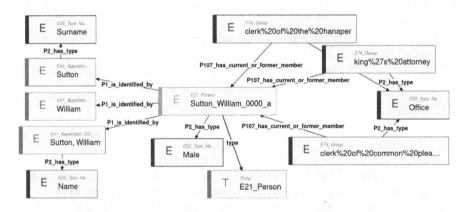

Fig. 2. A portion of our historical KG about "William Sutton".

4   Information Retrieval Model and Demo

A search engine needs to not only return the best documents, but also be fast. We implemented the index and search functions based on Elasticsearch to have a real-time search engine [9]. The Okapi BM25 model was proposed to find and rank the relevant handwritten manuscripts for queries. In the model, documents and queries are presented by sets of concepts being NEs or KWs. Figure 3 presents an image of a handwritten medieval historical manuscript, its transcription and its concept set d, applied in the model. In the transcription, there are three kinds of words determined by our NER tool: (1) stop-words being *the, to, of, we* and *you*; (2) NEs being *sheriff, Meath, clerk* and *William Sutton*; and (3) KWs being *king, &c, greeting, direct, pay, shilling* and *silver*. The stop-words are not added into the concept set d.

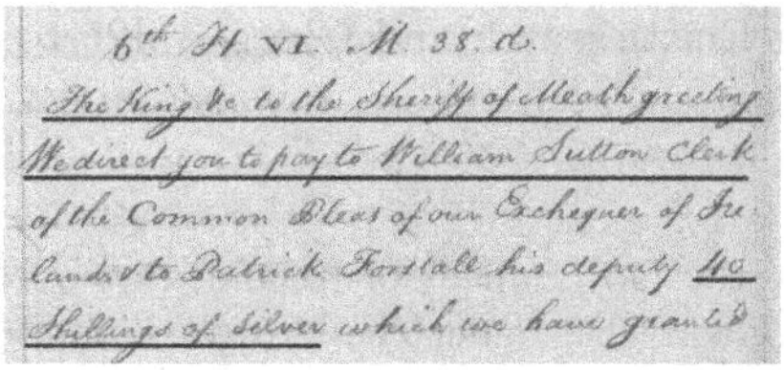

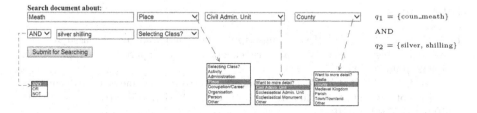

"... The King &c to the Sheriff of Meath greeting We direct you to pay to William   Sutton clerk ... 40 Shillings of silver ..."

$d = \{..., \text{king}, \&c, \text{occu\_sheriff}, \text{coun\_meath}, \text{greeting}, \text{direct}, \text{pay}, \text{william\_sutton/person}, \text{occu\_clerk}, 40, \text{shilling}, \text{silver}, ...\}$

Fig. 3. An example about NE and KW annotation of a medieval historical manuscript

Fig. 4. User interface of our deployed search engine

Figure 4 presents the interface of our search engine[1], and the concept sets of q_1 and q_2. In that, $coun\_meath$ is the identifier of an entity named *Meath* and classed *Country*, which is determined by our NER algorithm. While, *silver* and *shilling* are keywords. To exploit the features of NEs for semantic search, a NE needs to be presented by its most specific meaning in the concept set d. It means that, with a NE in the transcription,

- If our NER can determine its identifier, the NE will be presented by its identifier in d. For example, $occu\_sheriff$, $coun\_meath$ and $occu\_clerk$ are identifiers of entities named *sheriff*, *Meath* and *clerk*, and added into d.
- If our NER only determines its most specific class, the NE will be presented by a combined information including its name and class. For example, the entity named *William Sutton* does not exist in our historical KG, so its identifier cannot be extracted. However, the NER determines its most specific class being *Person*. So $william\_sutton/person$ is added into d.

5 Conclusion

We proposed a novel semantic full-text search system for images of historical handwritten manuscripts. Unlike the existing approach only using KW extracted from images, we exploited NE, KW and KG of increase search performance. In that, NER and HTR tools were built to recognise transcriptions and NEs from the manuscript images. Besides, to increase the precision of our NER tool, the historical KG was designed and proposed. Then, we implemented the index and

---

[1] https://by2022.adaptcentre.ie/conf_demo.

search functions for transcriptions based on Elasticsearch and Okapi BM25 to search images in real-time. Finally, the semantic search engine was also implemented and deployed.

Acknowledgment. Beyond 2022 is funded by the Government of Ireland, through the Department of Culture, Heritage and the Gaeltacht, under the Project Ireland 2040 framework. The project is also partially supported by the ADAPT Centre for Digital Content Technology under the SFI Research Centres Programme (Grant 13/RC/2106_P2).

References

1. Aghbari, Z., Brook, S.: HAH manuscripts: a holistic paradigm for classifying and retrieving historical Arabic handwritten documents. Expert Syst. Appl. **36**(8), 10942–10951 (2009)
2. Ahmed, R., Al-Khatib, W., Mahmoud, S.: A survey on handwritten documents word spotting. Int. J. Multimed. Inf. Retr. **6**(1), 31–47 (2017). https://doi.org/10.1007/s13735-016-0110-y
3. Cao, T., Ngo, V.: Semantic search by latent ontological features. Int. J. New Gener. Comput. **30**(1), 53–71 (2012). https://doi.org/10.1007/s00354-012-0104-0
4. Cheikhrouhou, A., Kessentini, Y., Kanoun, S.: Multi-task learning for simultaneous script identification and keyword spotting in document images. Pattern Recogn. **113**, 107832 (2021)
5. Colutto, S., Kahle, P., Guenter, H., Muehlberger, G.: Transkribus. A platform for automated text recognition and searching of historical documents. In: Proceedings of the 15th International Conference on eScience (eScience), pp. 463–466 (2019)
6. Debruyne, C., et al.: Ireland?s authoritative geospatial linked data. In: d'Amato, C., et al. (eds.) ISWC 2017. LNCS, vol. 10588, pp. 66–74. Springer, Cham (2017). https://doi.org/10.1007/978-3-319-68204-4_6
7. Doerr, M.: The CIDOC conceptual reference module: an ontological approach to semantic interoperability of metadata. AI Mag. **24**(3), 75–92 (2003)
8. Frinken, V., Palakodety, S.: Handwritten keyword spotting in historical documents. In: Handwritten Historical Document Analysis, Recognition, and Retrieval—State of the Art and Future Trends, Series in MP&AI, vol. 89, pp. 81–99. World Scientific Publishing (2021)
9. Gheorghe, R., Hinman, M., Russo, R.: Elasticsearch in Action, 1st edn. Manning Publications Co., Shelter Island (2015)
10. Hellmann, S., Lehmann, J., Auer, S., Brümmer, M.: Integrating NLP using linked data. In: Alani, H., et al. (eds.) ISWC 2013. LNCS, vol. 8219, pp. 98–113. Springer, Heidelberg (2013). https://doi.org/10.1007/978-3-642-41338-4_7
11. Honnibal, M., Montani, I., Van Landeghem, S., Boyd, A.: SpaCy: industrial-strength natural language processing in Python (2020). https://doi.org/10.5281/zenodo.1212303
12. Jiang, Y.: Semantically-enhanced information retrieval using multiple knowledge sources. Clust. Comput. **23**(4), 2925–2944 (2020). https://doi.org/10.1007/s10586-020-03057-7
13. Kahle, P., Colutto, S., Hackl, G., Mühlberger, G.: Transkribus - a service platform for transcription, recognition and retrieval of historical documents. In: 2017 14th IAPR International Conference on Document Analysis and Recognition (ICDAR), vol. 04, pp. 19–24 (2017). https://doi.org/10.1109/ICDAR.2017.307

14. Kang, L., Riba, P., Villegas, M., Fornés, A., Rusiñol, M.: Candidate fusion: integrating language modelling into a sequence-to-sequence handwritten word recognition architecture. Pattern Recogn. **112**, 107790 (2021)
15. Lang, E., Puigcerver, J., Toselli, A.H., Vidal, E.: Probabilistic indexing and search for information extraction on handwritten German parish records. In: Proceedings of 16th International Conference on Frontiers in Handwriting Recognition (ICFHR), pp. 44–49 (2018)
16. Leydier, Y., Lebourgeois, F., Emptoz, H.: Text search for medieval manuscript images. Pattern Recogn. **40**(12), 3552–3567 (2007)
17. Li, Z., Wu, Q., Xiao, Y., Jin, M., Lu, H.: Deep matching network for handwritten Chinese character recognition. Pattern Recogn. **107**, 107471 (2020)
18. Martínek, J., Lenc, L., Král, P.: Building an efficient OCR system for historical documents with little training data. Neural Comput. Appl. **32**(23), 17209–17227 (2020). https://doi.org/10.1007/s00521-020-04910-x
19. Ngo, V., Cao, T.: Discovering latent concepts and exploiting ontological features for semantic text search. In: Proceedings of the 5th International Joint Conference on Natural Language Processing (IJCNLP-2011), pp. 571–579. ACL (2011)
20. Nozza, D., Manchanda, P., Fersini, E., Palmonari, M., Messina, E.: LearningToAdapt with word embeddings: domain adaptation of named entity recognition systems. Inf. Process. Manag. **58**(3), 102537 (2021)
21. Stauffer, M., Fischer, A., Riesen, K.: Filters for graph-based keyword spotting in historical handwritten documents. Pattern Recogn. Lett. **134**, 125–134 (2020)
22. Toledo, J., Carbonell, M., Fornés, A., Lladós, J.: Information extraction from historical handwritten document images with a context-aware neural model. Pattern Recogn. **86**, 27–36 (2019)
23. Vidal, E., et al.: The carabela project and manuscript collection: large-scale probabilistic indexing and content-based classification. In: The 17th International Conference on Frontiers in Handwriting Recognition (ICFHR), pp. 85–90 (2020)
24. Wang, J., et al.: A pseudo-relevance feedback framework combining relevance matching and semantic matching for information retrieval. Inf. Process. Manag. **57**(6), 102342 (2020)

Temporal Analysis of Worldwide War

Devansh Bajpai and Rishi Ranjan Singh$^{(\boxtimes)}$

Department of Electrical Engineering and Computer Science,
Indian Institute of Technology, Bhilai, Chhattisgarh, India
{devanshb,rishi}@iitbhilai.ac.in

Abstract. In this paper, we study the wars fought in history and draw conclusions by analysing a curated temporal multi-graph. We explore the participation of countries in wars and the nature of relationships between various countries during different timelines. This study also attempts to shed light on different countries' exposure to terrorist encounters.

Keywords: Temporal network analysis · War networks · Data visualization

1 Introduction

Wars are one of the most important factors in deciding the state of the world. Several literature study about cause [5,9,11], damage [2,10] and outcomes [8,12] associated with interstate and civil wars. In the network of military alliances, wars and international trade, the relation between the international trade and wars happening among the countries have been studied [3,6]. In [7], authors have done a neural network based analysis of militarized disputes. Network theoretic analysis for international relations is done in [3]. A similar work to this paper [4], analysed temporal network of international relations based on the wars fought between 1816 and 2007. In this paper, we carry out a temporal analysis of the wars that have been fought in the history and report the inter-country relationships during different timelines. We focus only on the wars fought after 1500 CE due to availability of data and with the assumption that wars fought before 1500 CE might have only minor effects on the present inter-country relationships. We use temporal multi-graph to analyze the wars fought during 1500–2020 timeline.

2 Data Collection

One of the main reasons for limited related research is the limited availability of data-sets. A data-set maintained by Sarkees and Wayman[13] covers the wars from 1816–2007 timeline. It only covers a small portion of time-line that we plan to cover. Therefore, we create a data-set for more wider timeline which we collect based on the data available on Wikipedia pages [1]. These set of pages list war history of 165 different countries. Each country has a page listing wars and conflicts that the country has participated in. The temporal multi-graph was built based on the data available on these pages. *Requests* and *Beautiful Soup* libraries available with Python3 are used for scraping the web pages.

© Springer Nature Switzerland AG 2021
G. Berget et al. (Eds.): TPDL 2021, LNCS 12866, pp. 66–70, 2021.
https://doi.org/10.1007/978-3-030-86324-1_8

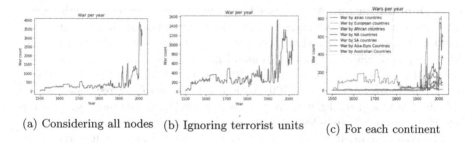

(a) Considering all nodes   (b) Ignoring terrorist units   (c) For each continent

Fig. 1. Year-wise number of wars (Color figure online)

3   Network Description

Nodes in the network represent the fighting entity which could be a nation (e.g. India), an empire which existed in past (e.g. Ottoman empire), terrorist organisations (e.g. ISIS), inter-governmental country alliances (e.g. NATO). Edges of the network represent the wars fought between nodes. Network is in the form of a temporal multi-graph with a total of 3000 nodes and 27721 edges. The average degree of the graph, considering edges over the whole timeline, is 18.5. The maximum degree is 1321 and the minimum degree is 1. Here, the degree of a node represents the number of wars that country/empire/terrorist organization was a part of.

4   Results and Discussion

We have considered wars that have happened between 1500 CE and 2020 CE. It is a period of 520 years. Analysis of the whole timeline at once doesn't give us good results as an ally in the fifteenth century might be enemy in the twenty first century. It is also difficult to do analysis on each year separately as there are a total of 520 years. To decide the segments, we created a plot Fig. 1a between years and number of wars fought in a specific year. After analyzing the plot in Fig. 1a and b, we concluded to divide the timeline from 1500 CE to 2020 CE into three parts and study all of them separately as well. The first one is labelled as Early wars [1500–1800], part in the graph which has almost same number of wars. The wars are mostly dominated by European countries. The second is labeled as During and pre-world wars [1801–1945] the part that covers the incidents of World wars. Both the world wars fall in this timeline. The last one is labelled as Post world wars [1946–2020], the part which is closest to the present state of different countries. We drew, another plot, given in Fig. 1b, similar to Fig. 1a, but without the terrorist encounters. In the new plot total wars fought reduced heavily, which shows impact of war against terrorism in modern world. We also plot the number of wars fought by countries from different regions/continents in Fig. 1c. Only the nodes having degree more than 40 are only considered for making this plot.

Most Dominating and Arch-Rival Countries: The nodes having high degrees in the constructed network correspond to the countries or empires fighting most number of wars in that timeline. The powerful countries generally become condescending and fight more wars. Ottoman Empire, Russia, and United States are the top degree nodes in [1500–1800], [1801–1945], [1946–2020] timelines respectively. For the overall timeline [1500–2020], Russia is the top degree node followed by United Kingdom and France. We can observe that for all the timelines, countries having top degrees were indeed the most dominating countries.

The nodes having highest number of edges between them in our graph corresponds to the pair of countries fighting most number of wars against each other during a timeline. List of pair of nodes with highest number of edges between them gives us the list of countries with strong rivalries between them. United Kingdom-France, United Kingdom-Germany, and United States-Russia are the top arch-rivals in [1500–1800], [1801–1945], [1946–2020] timelines respectively. For the overall timeline [1500–2020], United Kingdom-France are the arch rival countries.

Inter-Country Relationship: We studied the inter-country relations between different countries by analyzing the number of wars they fought against each other and number of wars they fought along the same side. Analysis of some inter-country relationship pairs are plotted in Fig. 2. In these figures, we plotted two lines of blue and orange color for each pair of nodes. The blue line is at 1 when two nodes fought a war along the same side in that year, where as the orange line touches 1 when two nodes fought against each other in that year. For example, in Fig. 2b, show the relationship between United Kingdom and France. Orange line has value 1 for almost all the time between 1500 CE and 1820 CE due to the Anglo-French war. Blue line has value 1 for some time between 1550CE to 1650 CE due to the long war in which France and UK both fought against Spain from 1568 CE to 1648 CE. In 1830 France accepted Britain as ally as orange line doesn't touch y = 1 value for long duration after that. Blue line touches y = 1 constantly after 1970 as both developed nations were helping other countries in fighting civil wars and in mitigating terrorism.

(a) UK and France   (b) USA and Russia   (c) UK and USA

Fig. 2. Relations between two countries

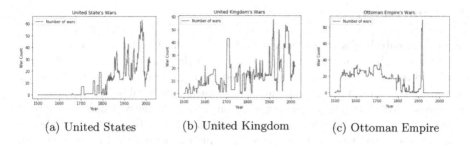

(a) United States   (b) United Kingdom   (c) Ottoman Empire

Fig. 3. Number of wars participated by countries/Empires over timeline

Analysis of Countries' History: Some of the major events in the history of a country can be predicted by analysing its degree in the temporal network. This sections sheds light on the year-wise number of war-fronts in which some countries and empires were involved in while ignoring wars involving terrorist organizations for clear understanding of inter-country wars. The plot for few countries are given in Fig. 3. We can note that in the case of Ottoman Empire, the curve takes significant value after 1520 CE, as Ottoman Empire came in the total power. Empire starts loosing power after 1710 CE but the curve has a huge spike in 1914 CE during the first world war. The Empire was defeated in 1918.

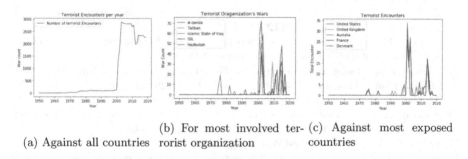

(a) Against all countries   (b) For most involved terrorist organization   (c) Against most exposed countries

Fig. 4. Year-wise number of wars involving terrorist organizations

Wars involving Terrorist Organisations. In this section, we analyse the wars involving terrorist organization. These wars consider both: the attacks by terrorist organization on a country and attack by nations on the hubs of terrorist organizations. All the plots in this section is for timeline 1950 CE to 2020 CE because before 1950 CE, there is very limited number of such wars. Figure 4a shows year-wise number of wars involving terrorist organization. Figure 4b shows the distribution of number of wars fought by top 5 terrorist organisations which have been involved in most wars. Figure 4c shows the distribution of terrorist engagements by top 5 countries which have been involved in most wars against terrorism.

5 Conclusion

Temporal analysis of wars fought after 1500 CE is done by curating data available on Wikipedia. The analysis results comply with the historical events. The powerful and dominating nations are identified during different timelines. Rivalries and allies based on wars explain the inter-country relationships during different timelines. Most active terrorist organizations and most active countries against terrorism were also identified using this analysis. The data did not include the damage associated with wars, considering which is a possible future direction. The full version of this paper is available at https://arxiv.org/abs/2107.01098.

References

1. https://en.m.wikipedia.org/wiki/category:lists_of_wars_by_country (2020)
2. Glick, R., Taylor, A.M.: Collateral damage: trade disruption and the economic impact of war. Rev. Econ. Stat. **92**(1), 102–127 (2010)
3. Hafner-Burton, E.M., Kahler, M., Montgomery, A.H.: Network analysis for international relations. Int. Organ. **63**(3), 559–592 (2009)
4. Roman, H.R., Gaffney, C.P., Varela, L.F.: Temporal analysis of international relations networks (2018). http://snap.stanford.edu/class/cs224w-2018/reports/CS224W-2018-99.pdf
5. Houweling, H., Siccama, J.G.: Power transitions as a cause of war. J. Conflict Resolut. **32**(1), 87–102 (1988)
6. Jackson, M.O., Nei, S.: Networks of military alliances, wars, and international trade. Proc. Natl. Acad. Sci. **112**(50), 15277–15284 (2015)
7. Lagazio, M., Russett, B.: A neural network analysis of militarized disputes, 1885–1992: temporal stability and causal complexity (2004)
8. Mason, T.D., Joseph P Weingarten, J., Fett, P.J.: Win, lose, or draw: predicting the outcome of civil wars. Polit. Res. Q. **52**(2), 239–268 (1999)
9. McMahan, J.: Just cause for war. Ethics Int. Affairs **19**(3), 1–21 (2005)
10. Murthy, R.S., Lakshminarayana, R.: Mental health consequences of war: a brief review of research findings. World Psychiatry **5**(1), 25 (2006)
11. Organski, A., Kugler, J.: The War Ledger, June 1981
12. de Karl, R., Rouen, J., Sobek, D.: The dynamics of civil war duration and outcome. J. Peace Res. **41**(3), 303–320 (2004)
13. Sarkees, M.R., Wayman, F.: Resort to war: 1816–2007 (2010). https://correlatesofwar.org/data-sets/COW-war

Data Repositories and Archives

Where Did the Web Archive Go?

Mohamed Aturban[1]([✉])[iD], Michael L. Nelson[2][iD], and Michele C. Weigle[2][iD]

[1] Columbia College, Columbia, MO 65216, USA
maturban@ccis.edu
[2] Old Dominion University, Norfolk, VA 23529, USA
{mln,mweigle}@cs.odu.edu

Abstract. To perform a longitudinal investigation of web archives and detecting variations and changes replaying individual archived pages, or mementos, we created a sample of 16,627 mementos from 17 public web archives. Over the course of our 14-month study (November, 2017–January, 2019), we found that four web archives changed their base URIs and did not leave a machine-readable method of locating their new base URIs, necessitating manual rediscovery. Of the 1,981 mementos in our sample from these four web archives, 537 were impacted: 517 mementos were rediscovered but with changes in their time of archiving (or *Memento-Datetime*), HTTP status code, or the string comprising their original URI (or *URI-R*), and 20 of the mementos could not be found at all.

Keywords: Web archives · Memento · Archive-It.

1 Introduction

Web archives are established with the objective of providing permanent access to archived web pages, or *mementos*. Mementos should be accessible in web archives even after the corresponding live web page is no longer available. The Uniform Resource Identifier (URI) [12] of the archived web page should not change over time, otherwise this defeats the purpose of using archived URIs. When web archives change their infrastructure, resulting in new base URIs for mementos, there should be machine-readable breadcrumbs left so that the older mementos still work.

We wanted to study the fixity of captured web pages, so we gathered a diverse set of mementos from 17 web archives distributed over 1996–2017. Our longitudinal experiment involved replaying the same mementos over the course of 14 months [7–10]. During our study, we noticed that we were no longer able to access any mementos from four web archives (Library and Archives Canada, the National Library of Ireland, the Public Record Office of Northern Ireland, and Perma.cc) at certain points, and there was no machine-readable redirection to the new URIs. This paper outlines our discovery of the disappearance of these mementos and our efforts to find their new locations.

© Springer Nature Switzerland AG 2021
G. Berget et al. (Eds.): TPDL 2021, LNCS 12866, pp. 73–84, 2021.
https://doi.org/10.1007/978-3-030-86324-1_9

2 Background

Memento [19] is an HTTP protocol extension that allows for content-negotiation of web resources in the time dimension. The Memento protocol is supported by most public web archives, including those included in this study. In the Memento framework, the identifier of an original resource from the live Web is a *URI-R*, and the identifier of an archived version of that resource at a particular point in time is a *URI-M*, or *memento*.

When a request is made to a Memento-compatible web archive for a URI-M that the archive holds, the archive will include Memento headers in the HTTP response. In particular, the Memento-Datetime HTTP Response header (e.g., `Memento-Datetime: Sun, 08 Jan 2017 09:15:41 GMT`) is sent by the archive to indicate the datetime at which the resource was captured.

A request for a URI-M indicates both the URI-R and the Memento-Datetime requested. If an archive does not have a memento for the requested URI-R at that particular Memento-Datetime, the archive may return an HTTP `30x Redirect` status with a `Location` response header indicating the temporally closest URI-M that the archive does have available.

Many, though not all, Memento-compatible web archives construct URI-Ms that contain both the URI-R and the Memento-Datetime. For example, for the URI-M http://www.collectionscanada.gc.ca/webarchives/20060208075019/http://www.cdc.gov/, the URI-R is http://www.cdc.gov/ and the Memento-Datetime is represented by the 14-digit date string 20060208075019, which is Wed, 08 Feb 2006 07:50:19 GMT.

Web archives can differ in how they handle URI-Ms that returned an HTTP `404 Not Found` or `503 Service Unavailable` status code during capture. Some archives will return an HTTP `200 OK` status code and include the archived error page in the HTTP response body. Other archives, such as the Internet Archive and Archive-It, will respond with the original status code; they return an archived `404 Not Found` for URI-Ms that returned a `404 Not Found` upon capture.

When a new archive receives an archived collection from the original archive, it may apply some post-crawling techniques to the received files (e.g., WARC files) including deduplication, spam filtering, and indexing. This may result in mementos in the new archive that have different values of the Memento-Datetime compared to their corresponding values in the original archive.

3 Methodology

Our original study accessed 16,627 mementos from 17 public web archives 39 times over a period of 14 months (Nov 2017–Jan 2019); the details of data selection are described elsewhere [10]. For each URI-R chosen, we used the LANL Memento Aggregator [13] in Nov 2017 to discover URI-Ms in different web archives. The data set is available in GitHub [18]. Our goal was to study the fixity of mementos. We would expect that replaying the same memento over time should result in the same representation, but that is not always the case. During the time period of this study, we found instances where none of the mementos from particular archives were available. This led us to the investigations we report in this paper.

We used the Squidwarc headless crawler [11] to load each URI-M (including executing JavaScript to ensure loading all embedded resources) and download the contents into a WARC file [16]. Saving the data in WARC files allowed us to record all HTTP response headers and content for all of the resources that made up the *composite memento* [1].

In our analysis, we refer to the archive from which mementos have moved as the *original archive* and the archive to which the mementos have moved as the *new archive*. We are strict in our approach to determine if a memento in the new archive is the same as a corresponding memento in the original archive: we compare the Memento-Datetimes, the URI-Rs, and the final HTTP status codes, and if any of these values do not match, we declare that it is a *missing memento*.

4   Findings

Table 1 shows the original and new archives, if the Memento-Datetimes matched, if the HTTP status codes matched, and if the URI-Rs matched, along with the number of mementos in each category. The number of mementos we consider

Table 1. Web archive changes based on how mementos changed. The number of missing mementos is shown in **bold**.

Original archive → New archive	Same Memento-Datetimes?	Same status codes?	Same URI-Rs?	URI-Ms
collectionscanada.gc.ca → bac-lac.gc.ca	Yes	Yes	Yes	302
	NO	Yes	Yes	**28**
	NO	Yes	NO	**18**
	NO	NO	Yes	**1**
	NO	NO	NO	**2**
europarchive.org/NLI → internetmemory.org/NLI	Yes	Yes	Yes	979
internetmemory.org/NLI → archive-it.org	Yes	Yes	Yes	787
	Yes	NO	Yes	**1**
	Yes	NO	NO	**2**
	NO	Yes	Yes	**184**
	NO	Yes	NO	**5**
proni.gov.uk → archive-it.org	Yes	Yes	Yes	355
	Yes	NO	Yes	**2**
	NO	Yes	Yes	**106**
	NO	Yes	NO	**6**
perma-archives.org → perma.cc	NO	Yes	Yes	**164**
	NO	NO	NO	**18**

as missing are in **bold**. We studied a total of 1,981 mementos from these four archives (we only count the NLI mementos once), classified 537 as missing (i.e., different Memento-Datetimes, status codes, or URI-Rs), and were unable to rediscover any version of 20 mementos in their corresponding new archives (these have NO in all columns in the table).

4.1   Library and Archives Canada

In our study, we had 351 mementos from collectionscanada.gc.ca, maintained by Library and Archives Canada (LAC). In July 2018 we discovered that all 351 URI-Ms from this archive were redirecting to http://www.bac-lac.gc.ca/eng/discover/archives-web-government/Pages/web-archives.aspx, the main webpage of the Government of Canada Web Archive. By viewing that live webpage, we discovered that the contents of this web archive had moved to webarchive.bac-lac.gc.ca. Additional details of our findings regarding LAC can be found in our blog post [4].

(a) In collectionscanada.gc.ca

(b) In webarchive.bac-lac.gc.ca

Fig. 1. An example of a memento moved from collectionscanada.gc.ca to webarchive.bac-lac.gc.ca.

Because LAC still controls the domain of the original archive (collectionscanada.gc.ca), it would be possible for requests to the original archive to redirect to the corresponding URI-Ms in the new archive using Apache mod_rewrite rules, for example. This would maintain link integrity via "follow-your-nose" [15] from the old URI-M to the new URI-M. But since we found that every memento request to the original archive redirected to the home page of the new archive, we had to manually intervene to detect the corresponding URI-Ms of the mementos in the new archive. This was done by replacing www.collectionscanada.gc.ca/webarchives with webarchive.bac-lac.gc.ca:8080/wayback in the URI-Ms of the

original archive. For instance, http://www.collectionscanada.gc.ca/webarchives/
20051228174058/http://nationalatlas.gov/ is now available at http://webarc
hive.bac-lac.gc.ca:8080/wayback/20051228174058/http://nationalatlas.gov/

Many of the mementos from LAC have been archived by the Internet
Archive, meaning that the URI-Ms are archived, not just the URI-Rs. For
instance, http://web.archive.org/web/20160720232234/http://www.collections
canada.gc.ca/webarchives/20071125005256/http://www.phac-aspc.gc.ca/publi
cat/ccdr-rmtc/95vol21/index.html is a URI-M captured in the Internet Archive
in July 2016 of a URI-M captured by LAC in Nov 2007. Because of this, we
were able to estimate when LAC made the change from www.collectionscanada.
gc.ca to webarchive.bac-lac.gc.ca. It appears that LAC began using the new
archive around Dec 2011, with http://web.archive.org/web/20111211144417/
http://www.collectionscanada.gc.ca/ linking to http://web.archive.org/web/
20111207015200/http://www.bac-lac.gc.ca/eng/Pages/default.aspx. Starting in
Feb 2017, the Internet Archive was capturing mementos from both webarchive.
bac-lac.gc.ca:8080/wayback/ and collectionscanada.gc.ca/webarchives/, indicating that LAC had two separate archives operational concurrently, but only URI-
Ms from collectionscanada.gc.ca were being returned to the Memento LANL
Aggregator.

We classified 49 out of 351 mementos from www.collectionscanada.gc.ca as
missing because they cannot be retrieved exactly from the new archive as they
were in the old archive. Instead, the new archive responds with other mementos that have different Memento-Datetimes. For example, when we requested
the URI-M http://www.collectionscanada.gc.ca/webarchives/20060208075019/
http://www.cdc.gov/ from the original archive on Feb 27, 2018, we received the
HTTP status 200 OK and a Memento-Datetime of Wed, 08 Feb 2006 07:50:19
GMT. Then, we requested the corresponding URI-M, http://webarchive.bac-
lac.gc.ca:8080/wayback/20060208075019/http://www.cdc.gov/, from the new
archive. This request is redirected to another URI-M, http://webarchive.bac-lac.
gc.ca:8080/wayback/20061026060247/http://www.cdc.gov/, which has a different Memento-Datetime (Thu, 26 Oct 2006 06:02:47 GMT), resulting in a delta
of about 260 days. In addition, the content of the memento in the new archive
is different from the content of the memento from the original archive.

Additionally, as of this writing, it appears that all URI-Ms in the new
archive are redirecting to https://www.bac-lac.gc.ca/eng/discover/archives-
web-government/Pages/web-archives.aspx which states that "the Government
of Canada Web Archive is currently not available". This message has been displayed on the webpage since April 2020[1].

4.2 National Library of Ireland

In May 2018, we discovered that 979 mementos from the National Library of
Ireland (NLI) collection that were originally hosted by The European Archive

---

[1] Although this is outside of our 14-month study, this effectively means that all 351
LAC mementos are currently missing.

at europarchive.org were moved to internetmemory.org, hosted by the Internet Memory Foundation. This appears to have just been a domain name change, as The European Archive announced its name change to the Internet Memory Foundation in 2011 (Fig. 2b), but had been still returning URI-Ms with the domain europarchive.org to the LANL Memento Aggregator. Although there was a human-readable notice that the domain name would be changing, there was no machine-readable notice provided. In addition to using `mod_rewrite` to provide automatic redirects, another option would be to use the Sunset HTTP response header [20] on requests for URI-Ms from the original archive. In September 2018, we found that the collection of mementos had been moved to Archive-It (archive-it.org) in collection https://archive-it.org/collections/10702. Figure 2 shows a single memento represented in the three different archives. Additional details of our findings regarding NLI can be found in our blog post [5].

(a) In europarchive.org

(b) European Archive announcing their name change to IMF

(c) In internetmemory.org

(d) In archive-it.org

Fig. 2. An example of a memento moved from europarchive.org to internetmemory.org, and then to archive-it.org

There were no changes in the 979 mementos (other than their URIs) when they moved from europarchive.org to internetmemory.org, thus our assumption that this was only a domain name change. In addition, as shown in Fig. 2, the archive banner appears to be the same. As with LAC, the European Archive did not use URL rewriting to automatically redirect requests for URI-Ms with the collection.europarchive.org domain to collections.internetmemory.org; we had to manually make the changes in our dataset. In addition after the changeover, the main webpage for europarchive.org itself was no longer maintained, and by August 2018 it had been taken over by an apparent spam site. Currently, the main website for internetmemory.org does not respond, and it has not been archived by the Internet Archive's Wayback Machine since January 2019. The movement of mementos from these archives will affect link integrity across web resources that contain links to mementos from europarchive.org and internetmemory.org.

We found that upon moving to Archive-It, 192 of the original 979 mementos were missing and cannot be retrieved from the new archive. For these missing mementos, the new archive responds with other mementos that have different values for the Memento-Datetime, the URI-R, or the HTTP status code. One example shows a memento that cannot be found in the new archive with the same Memento-Datetime as it was in the original archive. When requesting the URI-M http://collections.internetmemory.org/nli/20121221162201/http://bbc.co.uk/n ews/ from the original archive on September 3, 2018, the archive responded with 200 OK, and the Memento-Datetime was Friday, 21 December 2012 16:22:01 GMT. Then, we requested the corresponding URI-M, http://wayback.archive-it.org/10702/20121221162201/http://bbc.co.uk/news/, from the new archive. The request redirected to another URI-M, http://wayback.archive-it.org/10702/20121221163248/http://www.bbc.co.uk/news/. Although the representations of both mementos are identical (except for the archival banners), we consider the memento from the original archive as missing because both mementos have different values for Memento-Datetime (i.e., Friday, 21 December 2012 16:32:48 GMT in the new archive) for a delta of about 10 min. Even though the 10-minute delta might not be semantically significant, we do not consider it to be the same since the values of the Memento-Datetime are not identical.

Another change we found was in the way the archives handle archived HTTP 4xx/5xx status codes. The replay tool in the original archive was configured so that it returns the status code 200 OK for archived 4xx/5xx. As described in Sect. 2, Archive-It properly returns the status code 503 Service Unavailable for an archived 503 response.

Finally, we found that some HTTP status codes of URI-Ms in the new archive might not be identical to the HTTP status code of the corresponding URI-Ms in the original archive. For example, the HTTP request of the URI-M http://collections.internetmemory.org/nli/20121223031837/http://www2008.org/ to the original archive resulted in 200 OK. The request to the corresponding URI-M http://wayback.archive-it.org/10702/20121223031837/http://www2008.org/ from Archive-It results in 404 Not Found.

We note that the move to Archive-It included a change of web archiving platform, which can affect the replay of mementos. Therefore, when the original WARC files were moved to the new platform, differences in indexing, replay, URI canonicalization, and handling of HTTP redirections may explain some of the differences in the values of Memento-Datetime, URI-R, and HTTP status code in the new archive.

4.3   Public Record Office of Northern Ireland (PRONI)

The Public Record Office of Northern Ireland (PRONI) Web Archive was also hosted by the European Archive/IMF, but using a custom domain, webarchive.proni.gov.uk. In October 2018, mementos in the PRONI archive were moved to Archive-It (archive-it.org) in the collection at https://archive-it.org/collections/11112. After the move, we found that 114 of the original 469 mementos in our study were missing. Additional details of our findings regarding PRONI can be found in our blog post [6].

As with LAC and NLI, requests for URI-Ms in PRONI do not automatically redirect to mementos at Archive-It. In fact, every request to a URI-M in the PRONI archive now returns a 404 Not Found status code. However, users of the archive can indirectly find the corresponding URI-Ms because https://webarchive.proni.gov.uk provides a list of the URI-Rs for which mementos have been created. Let us consider finding the corresponding memento in Archive-It for the PRONI memento http://webarchive.proni.gov.uk/20150318223351/http://www.afbini.gov.uk/, which has a URI-R of http://www.afbini.gov.uk/ and a Memento-Datetime of Wed 18 Mar 2015 22:33:51 GMT. From the index at webarchive.proni.gov.uk, we can click on the URI-R www.afbini.gov.uk, which will redirect to an Archive-It HTML page that contains all available mementos for the selected URI-R. Then, we choose 2015-03-18, the same Memento-Datetime as in the original archive. In addition, once the Archive-It collection ID (11112) is known, URI-Ms from PRONI can be transformed to corresponding Archive-It URI-Ms. For example, the memento http://webarchive.proni.gov.uk/20100218151844/http://www.berr.gov.uk/ is now available at http://wayback.archive-it.org/11112/20100218151844/http://www.berr.gov.uk/.

Even though the PRONI collection was hosted by the European Archive, its URI-Ms did not change when europarchive.org became internetmemory.org. It appears that PRONI served mementos under proni.gov.uk while using the hosting services provided by the European Archive/IMF. Thus, the regular users of the PRONI archive did not notice any change in URI-Ms. We do not believe custom domains are available with Archive-It, so PRONI was unable to continue to host their mementos in their own URI namespace.

Unlike the European Archive and IMF, PRONI still owns the domain name of the original archive, webarchive.proni.gov.uk. Therefore, to maintain link integrity via "follow-your-nose", PRONI could issue redirects (even though it currently does not) to the corresponding URI-Ms in Archive-It.

For the 114 missing mementos, the new archive responds with other mementos that have different values for the Memento-Datetime, the URI-

R, or the HTTP status code. For example, when requesting the URI-M http://webarchive.proni.gov.uk/20160901021637/https://www.flickr.com/ from the original archive on December 1, 2017, the archive responded with 200 OK, and a Memento-Datetime of Thu, 01 September 2016 02:16:37 GMT. When we requested the corresponding URI-M http://wayback.archive-it.org/ 11112/20160901021637/https://www.flickr.com/ from the new archive, the request was redirected to another URI-M, http://wayback.archive-it.org/11112/ 20170401014520/https://www.flickr.com/. The representations of both mementos are identical (except for the archival banners). However, these mementos have different Memento-Datetime values (i.e., Friday, 21 April 2017 01:45:20 GMT in the new archive) for a delta of about 211 days.

We found that 63 of the 114 missing mementos have Memento-Datetime values with a delta of less than 11 s. For example, the request to the memento http://webarchive.proni.gov.uk/20170102004044/http://www.fws.gov/   from the original archive on Nov 18, 2017 returned a 302 redirect to http:// webarchive.proni.gov.uk/20170102004044/https://fws.gov/. The request to the corresponding memento http://wayback.archive-it.org/11112/20170102004044/ http://www.fws.gov/ from the new archive redirects to the memento http:// wayback.archive-it.org/11112/20170102004051/https://www.fws.gov/. There is a 10-s difference between the values of the Memento-Datetimes, which might not be semantically significant, but we do not consider the mementos identical because of the difference in the Memento-Datetime values.

Since PRONI used the same replay engine as NLI (when both were hosted by the European Archive/IMF), it returned the status code 200 OK for archived 4xx/5xx responses. Archive-It properly returns the status code 403 for an archived 403 response.

Mementos may disappear when moving from the original archive to the new archive. For example, the request to the URI-M http://webarchive.proni.gov.uk/ 20140408185512/http://www.www126.com/ from the original archive resulted in 200 OK. The request to the corresponding URI-M http://wayback.archive-it. org/11112/20140408185512/http://www.www126.com/ from Archive-It results in 404 Not Found. Before transferring collections to the new archive, it is possible that the original archive reviews collections and removes URI-Rs/URI-Ms that are considered off-topic [2,3,17] or spam (e.g., the URI-R www.www126. com is about auto insurance).

4.4   Perma.cc

The Perma.cc archive [21] is maintained by the Harvard Law School Library and has the goal of providing permanent URIs for archived webpages for use in academic publications. When a user archives a webpage in Perma.cc, the user is provided a unique "Perma Link" as the URI-M (e.g., https://perma.cc/T8U2-994F. This is different than the URI-Ms from many other archives that include the 14-digit Memento-Datetime and URI-R in the URI-M.

Prior to 2020, mementos were accessible via long-form URI-Ms, for instance http://perma-archives.org/warc/20170731024959/https://www.tmall.com/. These long-form URI-Ms were what had been returned to the LANL Memento Aggregator and are the form we used in our longitudinal study.

On Feb 5, 2020, Perma.cc deployed new support for Memento, which involved changing the endpoints for Memento services and the URI-Ms provided [14]. Some of the changes included removing access to the URI-Ms of the form http://perma-archives.org/warc/... that we had been using and only returning mementos with the Perma Link URI-Ms, such as https://perma.cc/T8U2-994F. Another change removed embedded resources from Memento access and began only providing access to top-level pages that were public, user-initiated captures. Requests for mementos of non-top level pages would return 404 Not Found.

Our original study included 182 long-form URI-Ms from Perma.cc. After the change, we were able to find only 164 corresponding short-form URI-Ms, resulting in 18 mementos that could not be found at all. It is possible that these missing mementos were not top-level URI-Ms or that they were private Perma Links, both of which are no longer replayable. However, in all 164 cases, the corresponding mementos had different Memento-Datetime values, with delta ranging from one second to three years. Figure 3 shows each URI-M and the difference between the original Memento-Datetime and the new Memento-Datetime.

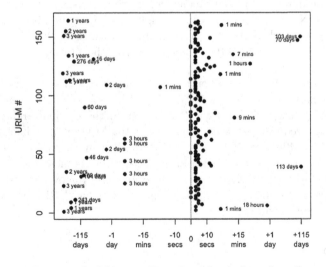

Fig. 3. Difference between the Memento-Datetimes for the long-form Perma.cc URI-Ms and the corresponding short-form URI-Ms.

5 Conclusion

The main goal of web archives is to provide permanent access to web resources using consistent URIs. Links to such archived resources are used in academic publications so that the information cited remains available even if the resource on the live Web changes or disappears. Our study provides a cautionary tale for archives that have to change domains or web archiving platforms. In a study of 16,627 mementos over 17 public web archives, we found that four archives changed their domains without providing a machine-readable notification, affecting 1,981 mementos from our study. Of these, we were not able to find 537 identical mementos in the new archives, 20 of which had disappeared completely. The data set is available in GitHub [18].

References

1. Ainsworth, S.G., Nelson, M.L., Van de Sompel, H.: A framework for evaluation of composite memento temporal coherence. Tech. Rep. arXiv:1402.0928, arXiv (2014)
2. AlNoamany, Y., Weigle, M.C., Nelson, M.L.: Detecting off-topic pages in web archives. In: Proceedings of Theory and Practice of Digital Libraries (TPDL), pp. 225–237 (2015). https://doi.org/10.1007/978-3-319-24592-8_17
3. AlNoamany, Y., Weigle, M.C., Nelson, M.L.: Detecting off-topic pages within TimeMaps in Web archives. Int. J. Digit. Libr. **17**(3), 203–221 (2016). https://doi.org/10.1007/s00799-016-0183-5
4. Aturban, M.: Where did the archive go? Part 1: library and archives Canada (2019). https://ws-dl.blogspot.com/2019/08/2019-08-30-where-did-archive-go-part1.html
5. Aturban, M.: Where did the archive go? Part 2: National Library of Ireland (2019). https://ws-dl.blogspot.com/2019/09/2019-09-10-where-did-archive-go-part-2.html . https://ws-dl.blogspot.com/2019/09/2019-09-10-where-did-archive-go-part-2.html
6. Aturban, M.: Where did the archive go? Part 3: Public Record Office of Northern Ireland. https://ws-dl.blogspot.com/2019/09/2019-09-25-where-did-archive-go-part-3.html (2019)
7. Aturban, M.: A Framework for verifying the fixity of archived web resources. Ph.D. thesis, Old Dominion University (2020). https://doi.org/10.25777/PC8D-Y213
8. Aturban, M., Alam, S., Nelson, M.L., Weigle, M.C.: Archive assisted archival fixity verification framework. In: Proceedings of the 19th ACM/IEEE Joint Conference on Digital Libraries (JCDL), pp. 162–171 (2019). https://doi.org/10.1109/JCDL.2019.00032
9. Aturban, M., Nelson, M.L., Weigle, M.C.: It is hard to compute fixity on archived web pages. In: Proceedings of the Workshop on Web Archiving and Digital Libraries (WADL) held in conjunction with the 18th ACM/IEEE Joint Conference on Digital Libraries (JCDL) (2018), https://vtechworks.lib.vt.edu/bitstream/handle/10919/97988/WADL2018.pdf
10. Aturban, M., Nelson, M.L., Weigle, M.C., Klein, M., Van de Sompel, H.: Collecting 16K archived web pages from 17 public web archives. Tech. Rep. arXiv:1905.03836, arXiv, May 2019

11. Berlin, J.: Squidwarc - A high fidelity archival crawler that uses Chrome or Chrome Headless, July 2017. https://github.com/N0taN3rd/Squidwarc
12. Berners-Lee, T., Fielding, R., Massinter, L.: Uniform Resource Identifier (URI): Generic Syntax, Internet RFC-3986, January 2005. https://datatracker.ietf.org/doc/html/rfc3986
13. Bornand, N.J., Balakireva, L., Van de Sompel, H.: Routing memento requests using binary classifiers. In: Proceedings of the 16th ACM/IEEE Joint Conference on Digital Libraries (JCDL), pp. 63–72 (2016). https://doi.org/10.1145/2910896.2910899
14. Cremona, R.: New memento support at perma.cc, February 2020. https://groups.google.com/g/memento-dev/c/XHB4IezBiqA/m/BpB4u8DjBQAJ
15. Fielding, R.T.: REST APIs must be hypertext-driven (2008). https://roy.gbiv.com/untangled/2008/rest-apis-must-be-hypertext-driven
16. International Organization for Standardization (ISO): WARC file format. ISO 28500:2017 (2017). https://www.iso.org/standard/68004.html
17. Jones, S.M., Weigle, M.C., Nelson, M.L.: The off-topic memento toolkit. In: Proceedings of iPRES (2018). https://doi.org/10.17605/OSF.IO/UBW87
18. Mohamed Aturban: Mementos-Fixity (2019). https://github.com/oduwsdl/mementos-fixity/blob/master/final_urims.txt
19. Van de Sompel, H., Nelson, M.L., Sanderson, R.: HTTP framework for time-based access to resource states - Memento, Internet RFC 7089 (2013). http://tools.ietf.org/html/rfc7089
20. Wilde, E.: The Sunset HTTP Header Field, Internet RFC 8594 (2019). https://tools.ietf.org/html/rfc8594
21. Zittrain, J., Albert, K., Lessig, L.: Perma: scoping and addressing the problem of link and reference rot in legal citations. Legal Inf. Manag **14**(02), 88–99 (2014). https://doi.org/10.1017/S1472669614000255

What's Data Got to Do with It? An Agenda for a New Generation of Digital Libraries

George Buchanan[1]([⊠]), Dana McKay[2], and David Bainbridge[3]

[1] University of Melbourne, Swanston Street, Melbourne, VIC 3010, Australia
George.buchanan@unimelb.edu.au
[2] RMIT University, La Trobe Street, Melbourne, VIC 3000, Australia
[3] University of Waikato, Private Bag 3105, Hamilton 3240, New Zealand
david.bainbridge@waikato.ac.nz

Abstract. Digital libraries have matured rapidly in recent years: practical large-scale libraries are now ubiquitous, and many fundamental problems are resolved. This paper addresses the future of one area of DL theory and practice, identifying common requirements and needs that are found in contemporary DLs. This shows that a new wave of research and engineering problems need to be solved, and that corresponding theories and principles need to be developed. We draw on both the current literature and four ongoing data DL projects to demonstrate the next generation of data DL systems, and where new DL theory is needed.

Keywords: Data digital libraries · Digital repositories · Digital infrastructure

1 Introduction

Digital libraries are now so ubiquitous as to appear to be mature and unremarkable pieces of technology [1]. Similarly, digital repositories [2] are commonplace and their use is routine [3]. The two technologies are very similar, with libraries emphasising access, and repositories storage. Both are primarily focussed on conventional text documents, with occasional excursions into supporting music, audio, and multimedia—there are several exemplar collections of the latter to be found at the Internet Archive, for instance. Data digital libraries for storing and accessing large datasets—from scientific data to mass-scale social media—are now emerging. This new type of library provides a need for revolutionary sea-change: existing approaches are entirely inadequate to deliver effective tools for data digital library users, librarians and administrators.

There have been widespread claims that data sharing will accelerate progress in the sciences, social sciences, the humanities, and government, however this acceleration requires facilities to store, access, and manage data—data digital libraries [4, 5]. This white paper outlines some of the key pain-points in data digital libraries that require urgent research attention to realise the vision of data sharing. We start, in Sect. 2, by introducing four key specifics to data digital libraries that are driving the need for change: dynamic content, access control, presenting datasets, and maintenance/administration. Next we place these driving forces in context through a review of the literature, before

© Springer Nature Switzerland AG 2021
G. Berget et al. (Eds.): TPDL 2021, LNCS 12866, pp. 85–96, 2021.
https://doi.org/10.1007/978-3-030-86324-1_10

presenting four use-cases: the first focuses on social media; the second on enriched research repositories; the third on worksets; and the last on in-situ data analysis. We round out the paper with a discussion that reflects on the factors that have led us to the current situation, and an agenda for future work in data digital libraries.

2 Data Digital Libraries: Data not Documents

Data digital libraries provide access to collections of data, rather than of documents. While what counts as 'data' is contested, storing new forms of content—e.g. sensor data, databases of scientific measurements, social media streams and astronomical observations—create new challenges for digital libraries (DLs). For the purposes of this paper we take data to mean all information that is not in long-form linear text, with an emphasis on databases of all forms.

Fundamental assumptions of DL architecture, such as text-based retrieval, long continuous text strands and low frequency updates to individual items, are turned on their heads, and new DLs need to account for:

- Retrieval based on metadata and non-textual data forms
- Data in many formats, often within a single item
- Frequently updating or dynamic items

This leads to major changes in how users might plausibly expect to find items in a library, the ways in which items in the library can be read, the rate of change of individual items, and the needs of administrators and users alike to identify and engage with the library's content. While systems exist that claim to match these needs (e.g. DataDryad, Invenio) these have not received systematic analysis in the literature, and in fact have very similar architectures, and suffer very similar problems, to mainstream DL systems.

2.1 Dynamic Content

Even state-of-the-art DLs perform poorly when handling content that changes regularly. This stems from several sources, including: poor (often no) support for multiple document versions, or version control; expensive re-indexation time costs when content changes; little or no support for administrative oversight and management; and a high dependence on manual intervention for providing descriptive metadata.

However, digital data is dynamic in ways that far exceed current DL systems: first, existing data changes frequently as it is updated; second, version control and support can be fundamental user needs; and third, data may be being extended continually as new information arrives from monitoring stations or social media streams, for example.

It is not clear what problems may emerge for users or administrators from this change, but there are significant technical challenges to ensure data is properly indexed, and users can retrieve not only the current, but previous versions of a document. The ability to choose versions will itself create usability problems in the interface, ensuring that users can retrieve the version that they expect with ease.

2.2 Access Controls

While early conventional DLs struggled to provide access control, state-of-the-art systems provide some support for embargoing documents, or allowing access to users based on what type of user they are (e.g. staff or student at a university). However, data digital libraries create a much more challenging set of constraints. Users may require individual accreditation to gain access to an item, and items may come with more complex constraints on who has potential access, for what purposes, for how long and in what volume. Research data, for example, may be limited only to the original team, or those from their wider research group, or only for very specific purposes, though available to others with permission.

Providing unfettered access to the raw data may itself be inappropriate due to the terms of access, and as a result the library may only be able to allow users access via a mediated process. In practice, this will mean embedding analytical tools in the library, and allowing access to summative reports and analyses, rather than the raw data itself.

Most archival and library policies have been shaped around a few key principles of access. In general, access to physical archives may be restricted to those with a strong need for, rather than merely curiosity in, the available materials. However, once someone is given access to an archive, they can access almost all of the material. Some acquisitions will be embargoed for a period of time before being available to archive users, and some material may need to be withheld to ensure its conservation. New research on policy making for repository and library services, and how to support the created policies in operating services, needs to be urgently undertaken.

Datasets in data digital libraries and repositories can hold data that addresses or relates to issues that are of concern due to human privacy, political debates around the data, or as a result of societal emergencies such as pandemics or natural disasters. As a result, there is a significant threat of a loss of authority due to failure to disclose data appropriately, and conversely disclosing data inappropriately. Technology alone cannot address these concerns. A rethinking of library and information science and practice is required to both enable the successful administration of data access, and to develop appropriate technologies to enact access policies effectively.

2.3 Presenting Datasets

In traditional digital libraries, most documents are a mixture of text and images, often presented in HTML or PDF format. In cases where video or audio is a major component of the collection this is presented through standard multimedia players in a web browser. However, complex data is not simply accessed in the same manner; further, while PDF, MP4 and other media have standard formats, this is not true of data. As a result, unless users are simply allowed to download entire datasets, presentation tools are required. These may be generic, or specific to particular formats. DL systems that are designed to support a wider range of data formats, such as Greenstone, could be extended appropriately [6, 7]. However, many production DL systems and digital repository systems are not designed to be extensible in this way. As a result, existing DL and DR systems cannot meet the needs of Data Digital Libraries and Repositories.

2.4 Maintenance and Administration

Conventional libraries and repositories have relatively fixed needs for administering and maintaining collections. To date, digital libraries and repositories have provided only limited facilities for collection administration, preservation, and gaining an overview of the collection for administrative purposes. This can be indirectly seen in the fact administrative interfaces only began to be systematically developed and evaluated after 15 years of DL research [8]. However, the need to administrate diverse data formats and types, dynamic collection content, with flexible access controls, plus other factors, adds significant complexity to the administrative work of DLs and DRs. This raises both policy-making and technical questions.

3 Literature Review

The question of what is a digital library has been the subject of long debate. Tefko Saracevic [9] noted several differing and contested definitions twenty years ago. While the agenda mapped out here in this paper will no doubt fuel this debate further, remembering the previous contributions to the dialogue is important, to avoid repetition, but also to inform the ongoing discussion in this paper. In this section we draw upon literature from the areas of digital rights access, continuous data, and content analysis. Digital libraries have still not been precisely defined, but the digital library research community has been active in many circumstances where large digital collections of searchable material have been required, including the digital humanities [10, 11], institutional repositories [12] and—key to this paper—data digital libraries [13, 14].

3.1 Mandatory Digital Data Access

A number of major changes in the information policy landscape have altered the context in which organisations set their accession and holding policies. For example, the U.K.'s Engineering and Physical Sciences Research Council (EPSRC) adopted a framework in 2011 that obliged institutions to make research data publicly available after the original researchers have benefitted from a "limited time of privileged access...to work on and publish their results"[1]. The EPSRC are far from unusual, and many research funders in the UK, Europe and globally have taken the same approach. As a result, institutions increasingly need to store and make discoverable their research data, as well as the papers that their researchers have produced. Ideally, papers should be linked to the research data that they are built on [15, 16]. This brings the digital library closer to the age of digital scholarship anticipated by Christine Borgman [17], where publication and dissemination of original data become closely coupled.

Searching across collections of data overlaps with fundamental challenges in information retrieval: run-time merging collections is computationally expensive, and negatively impacts search results; searching in tabulated datasets has not yet established conceptual foundations; and searching of short texts is hard to optimise [18].

---

[1] https://epsrc.ukri.org/about/standards/researchdata/.

Furthermore, an individual project or paper may itself build on multiple datasets in different digital and conceptual formats. In a given institution, more significant differences will occur between research domains, even where all data is kept in one store. This readily produces a fragmented set of data silos, all of which makes reproducing science, reusing data, and providing transparent and accountable research more difficult. Clear connections ideally need to be made between long-form text research papers and complex digital data that is likely best stored in a different database that optimises for content other than text.

3.2 Continuous Data

For the first DLs, document indexes were built for the entire collection. When it was re-indexed, a new index was built from scratch [6]. This was known to be sub-optimal for continuously changing collections [18]. However, most DLs were archival, and the need to support continuous, daily or hourly, changes was not seen, at the time, as a critical requirement [19]. Furthermore, the most likely changes to an existing document was replacement with a new version, or deletion. Between periodic re-indexations, documents were static. However, this is no longer an accurate depiction of the material that libraries, archives, and researchers work with. Live feeds from field observations [20] are just one example of data that is inherently fluid. In such cases, while some of the metadata may be changing slowly, or not at all (e.g. title), both the content and some metadata (e.g. the last capture time) can be changing rapidly. This stretches even the known efficient solutions for document re-indexation, such as Brown [19].

Social media is one particularly thorny issue, as the content of each 'document' is often short, the rate of change in an observed collection may be very high. Older approaches to changing indexes still anticipated a much less frequent rate of change, larger documents, and larger volumes of data for each additional re-indexation run. Furthermore, stream data is highly contextual, and treating a single data point or social media post in isolation is potentially meaningless. Entries are not simply discrete documents, but an interconnected graph of items.

Time-frames of data are often needed in these contexts [21], yet DL tools for supporting date-range browsing and searching are known to be limited [22]. Furthermore, recency is often desirable, but the trade-off between recency and relevance is complex, and poorly understood both technically and in terms of user needs and preferences [23]. Practical libraries cannot simply take general-case tradeoffs that may not fit well with their users or data: new skills of librarianship and DL administration are needed.

3.3 Supporting Data and Collection Analysis

Analysis can be performed and presented in many different ways, e.g. visualisation or automatic summarisation. While there was extensive early work on visualising digital libraries, there was only weak evidence for the efficacy of those visualisations [24]. There has been continuing interest in automatic extraction of textual patterns such as keyphrases [25, 26]. However, major gaps remain in the toolset. Worksets of user-selected documents need to be supported by DL systems (none of the major systems do), and then be analysed by user-chosen analytical tools: ideally within the DL infrastructure so this cannot be used to bypass access and copyright controls. While existing DL systems provide limited gateways for textual analysis and visualisation, we now require structured gateways to analysis of arbitrary worksets of documents and data.

3.4 Controlling Access

DLs have long needed to control access to content for copyright and licensing reasons. However, there are increasingly other constraints. For example, research data can be embargoed, with staged release to different communities, and retain restrictions in the long term. Furthermore, cultural sensitivities of communities can be equally important. Images of the deceased are unacceptable to Australian Aboriginal communities [27], and New Zealand Māori strongly associate access to cultural material with membership of particular groups [28, 29]. While rights-based access controls are common, they are typically binary and use a few user types that apply across whole collections [6, 30]. Finally, researchers may want or need to restrict access to ensure data is being used in a way consistent with the principles under which it is gathered [31]. In data DLs, access varies between individual users, and between documents, or even parts of a dataset. This complexity is far beyond the range of previous work.

3.5 Summary

This section has shown that many of our key requirements have already been noted in the literature (e.g. administrative interfaces and access control). The need for future development was recognised at the time, but then seemed to be required only by a few DLs. We now examine use-cases to see how frequently requirements overlap.

4 Use Cases

Digital library software design has built on known requirements for library systems [7, 25, 32]. In this section, we reflect on a number of ongoing data digital library projects that demonstrate the shortcomings of existing DL systems and DL system design. We draw on example projects involving the Universities of Melbourne and Waikato, to demonstrate the overlap of needs between superficially dissimilar areas. Each use case describes the purpose of the system, and briefly highlights some functional requirements. We then list key requirements currently unsupported by established DL systems.

4.1 Digital Libraries of Social Media

The University of Melbourne is undertaking a strategic initiative on social media digital libraries, with support from the Australian Research Data Commons (ARDC). Across the University, research teams are collecting different social media streams, with the agreement of the specific platforms involved (e.g. Twitter, Facebook, Reddit). Each stream involves the ingest of social media posts on a regular and frequent basis, with hourly captures being run of the most recent data. The library users are mostly social media researchers who want to search for and analyse social media content.

The emerging integrated DL will provide a central point-of-service for all these groups, providing built-in analysis of the social media data, as well as conventional search facilities. As the project advances, it will form a national infrastructure.

The DL indexes hashtags (e.g. "#covid"), user ids (e.g. "@TheBBC") and text, plus URLs of any links in the post. This allows users to identify multiple posts related to the same external image, or hashtags. Users regularly wish to partition posts into time-frame buckets, and track changes over time–e.g. how often a hashtag is used per week over several months. Social network analysis is often used on the social network structures that underpin discussions. However, the different platform licence terms mean that this must be done within the DL, rather than exported or transmitted to a third party. While posts can be identified using their unique identifier, and related identifiers supplied to a third party, they then will also have to gain permission to process and abstract data separately. Analysis must occur within the platform, to ensure compliance with the terms of use. Traceability of content use is critical, to comply with terms of use.

Social media content posts are short-form text, but a post may respond to a previous one, and be responded to by further posts. This leads to a collection of trees, and a user may want to return individual posts, posts and responses only, the entire message tree, or some other fragment. There is a strong demand for the latest social media content, and hence reindexations for search should be done as frequently as possible.

- Large collection (several terabytes) of short-form social media.
- Tree structures of social media posts and responses.
- Hourly re-indexation.
- Social network analysis support.
- Support for selective access controls.
- Provision of summary data, but not raw data.

4.2 Enriched Research Repositories

Research repositories have conventionally used simpler deposit digital library systems such as ePrints or DSpace. These provide for static documents, and today primarily address the need for 'green' open-access, where the publisher permits the original author's institution to provide a pre-print of a journal article or conference paper. However, increasingly there are requirements to enrich institutional repositories by also providing access to the original datasets used in research, or at least some summary data to facilitate meta-analysis, checking of the original work, or re-analysis for a different purpose. The University of Melbourne is constructing a future series of repositories, including support for both published and unpublished research papers, diagrammatic content from ongoing and previous research using FigShare, plus a range of databases of research data across the University's many disciplines.

While in theory FigShare could provide many of Melbourne's requirements, evaluations have shown that users struggle to find material, and many datasets can be indexed, but not stored in, FigShare. The university aims to link datasets and the original papers they provided source material for, and between diagrams in FigShare and the datasets from which they were abstracted, whether kept in FigShare or separately. The original papers already have established repositories with superior search and browsing facilities. Support for consistent management of datasets, diagrams and paper, supported by validation and automated checks for missing material is a necessity, in order to minimise operational costs and realise greater benefits. FigShare has received a limited degree of analysis from DL researchers, and our experience in practice is that it is in many ways much more primitive than DL systems such as Fedora and Greenstone.

As seen in the previous subsection, datasets may have restrictions placed on access, due to ethical considerations, licencing of data sources, or in some cases legal constraints. There are also cases where the raw data may be stored in the library, but only summative data provided to external users on demand. This mirrors the needs of the social media libraries, where privacy, legal or licencing considerations constrain the information that can be provided to a user. A classic context for this is medical data, where raw data runs particular risks of, and consequences from, de-anonymisation.

This provides new problems, such as the following:

- Interconnected (sub-)collections of long-form text and raw digital data
- Support for selective access controls
- Analysis across larger collections of related datasets (e.g. visualisation)
- Provision of summary data, not raw data

4.3 Digital Humanities Worksets

While enriched repositories and social media DLs stretch different elements of DL infrastructure, there are also novel use cases in what are at first sight conventional digital libraries. DLs of historic publications see low rates of change, and have no separate datasets to complement the text. However, digital humanists of various forms of expertise often need to create worksets for their research, deploy analysis over selected documents, and do so automatically or semi-automatically, and at scale. This is an avenue of work being pursued by work at the HathiTrust Research Center, where Waikato University is a partner, which gives scholars access to their 17+million volume (6+billion page) DL collection [33]. Using the tools they are developing a scholar can produce a workset that can be shared with others, and—notably—be directly imported into the Data Capsule environment they have devised for non-consumptive research [34].

While the sole scholar was once the epitome of humanities work, a more contemporary picture is one where they work on large-scale scholarly projects as part of a research team working together on shared artefacts. However, the integration of that approach, and its broadening to other forms of digital collaboration, to open gateways to multiple tools in established DL systems is almost unknown.

4.4 In-Situ Data Analysis

The previous use-case touches on the benefits of being able to undertake data analysis once items of interest within the DL have been established. In the HathiTrust this is currently done using tools that are external to the DL. Going beyond this, the integration of tools into the digital library is not simply a matter of convenience, but one of better research management, and means the tools are available to the full set of users.

In the (Unofficial) Eurovision Linked Open Data DL project[2], at the University. Of Waikato, we have developed an experimental version of the Greenstone3 architecture that maps, at ingest-time, document and browsing-related metadata to linked data, which is stored in the DL alongside the more traditional activities of full-text indexing, and database storage of metadata. Configuring the DL this way means it is possible for a user of the DL to perform in-situ data analysis, which can in turn be visualized if desired. For example, in addition to viewing the list of winners over the years—information that is relatively easy to locate in static form elsewhere on the web—the user is able to adjust the data analysis undertaken by the DL to list the Top 3 performances, control the date-range of the information display, and have (where alignment with Linked Open Data in MusicBrainz is possible) the DL include musical content analysis features such as displaying the time-signature and musical key the song was in.

Targeting voting data in the DL, Sankey plots that tally how countries have voted over a given time-period can be generated, as can Treemaps that help bring out where differences occur between a country's Jury votes and Televote, cast by viewers in their country watching the contest. While there is some support in the user interface for non-expects to develop these forms of analysis, here is much room for improvement, and consequently where attention is currently focussed.

5 Discussion

Expectations and requirements of digital libraries have grown since the genesis of the field over 25 years ago. While in the last few years, DL system innovation has appeared to be static, the call for extended functionality has been growing. However, the question that rebuts these calls is whether any new requirements are enduring and common to many use cases. As we have seen in our four example cases, in fact there are considerable overlaps for data digital libraries. Many requirements appear in two or more of the four cases, e.g. the need for workset support. This is one requirement that has been suggested before [33], but it is pertinent across our scenarios, and yet not seen in general purpose DL architectures such as Greenstone, DSpace, etc.

However, to understand how to construct DLs with these new facilities is not merely implementation. We need to return to the whole range of stakeholders.

A key stakeholder group is **librarians**, who must contribute the metadata schemas needed to help manage and provide access to data. There are no current general standards equivalent to Dublin Core for research data [35], though some field-specific ones have emerged out of necessity [36, 37].

Researchers need to participate in generating requirements for worksets; there has been some work already (e.g. [38]), however it has generally been about rather than with researchers. They key contribution needed from research communities though is the development of credit and attribution mechanisms, to incentivize the publication of datasets, making an often time-consuming and complex activity worthwhile. [12, 39].

If librarians and researchers represent the users of data DLs, we need to consider the technical problems too. While search is a well-understood problem in the context of long-form text, as we noted above, indexation is often only done periodically, and short-form

---

[2] https://so-we-must-think.space/eurovision-let-it-sparql.

text search has multiple known problems [18, 23]. Research now needs to prioritise table retrieval, and the searching and filtering of large-scale collections of datasets, among other challenges. Subjectively, we do not yet know how readily users find data worth using, but the initial data suggests much more remains to do [40]. **Developers** of DLs now have a new suite of requirements to organise, and new solutions to design, implement and test. While the existing DL software landscape has been stable for many years, it is clear new initiatives are needed to provide unmet needs.

Our examples here are only that. Other fields have similar needs: e.g. digital human-ities collections require hyperlinking and annotation, and digital artwork support is embryonic. While some of these needs will be domain specific, image analysis for example will likely be as relevant to the arts as they are to geographers and physical scientists.

The development of Greenstone in its three versions resulted in extensive support for a flexible digital library system for the early 21st century. It remains, alongside oth-ers such as Fedora, the backbone of many practical DLs. However, the needs of users have expanded. While individual features presented here could be added ad-hoc to such software architectures, there is a fundamental difference between making an implemen-tation that functions, and a systematic theoretical and practical approach that can readily implement specific libraries for particular uses. Just as Greenstone contributed plugin architectures for document processing, and communication support to connect separate libraries, we now need gateways for analytical tools and workset construction. Similarly, even with Greenstone3's use of Solr to provide incremental indexing, its current imple-mentation lacks agility and needs to be supplemented by indexation that better supports fluid rather than fixed streams of data, and search that discovers datasets large and small, and interconnected social media content as well as PDF documents.

6   Conclusions

Digital libraries have advanced significantly in the last thirty years. While the needs of gradually growing collections of seldom-changing text documents are generally well-addressed, many other forms of digital libraries remain challenging. Libraries are now expanding to support research and other original data, collect dynamic streams of content, address complex access issues, and the preservation of complex content. The gap between those needs and our current technologies is at least as large as that of the early years of DL research. The DL research community needs clarity about what the research agenda now is, and this paper provides a starting point for that future discussion. The current status of DL research should more be viewed as the end of the beginning, than as the beginning of the end.

References

1. Bainbridge, D.: Digital libraries: mission accomplished? SRELS J. Inf. Manag. **56**, 159–170 (2019)
2. Lynch, C.A.: Institutional repositories: essential infrastructure for scholarship in the digital age. Libr. Acad. **3**, 327–336 (2003)

3. Smith, I.: Open Access Infrastructure. UNESCO Publishing
4. Costello, M.J.: Motivating online publication of data. Bioscience **59**, 418–427 (2009)
5. Arzberger, P., et al.: Promoting access to public research data for scientific, economic, and social development. Data Sci. J. **3**, 135–152 (2004)
6. Witten, I.H., Bainbridge, D., Nichols, D.M.: How to Build a Digital Library. Morgan Kaufmann Publishers Inc. (2009)
7. Suleman, H., Edward, A.: Designing protocols in support of digital library componentization. In: Agosti, M., Thanos, C. (eds.) ECDL 2002. LNCS, vol. 2458, pp. 568–582. Springer, Heidelberg (2002). https://doi.org/10.1007/3-540-45747-X_43
8. Witten, I.H., Bainbridge, D.: Creating digital library collections with Greenstone. Library Hi Tech **23**, 541–560 (2005)
9. Saracevic, T., Covi, L.: Challenges for digital library evaluation. In: Proceedings of the Annual Meeting of the American Society for Information Science, vol. 37, pp. 341–350. Citeseer (2000)
10. Fenlon, K., Senseney, M., Green, H., Bhattacharyya, S., Willis, C., Downie, J.S.: Scholar-built collections: a study of user requirements for research in large-scale digital libraries. Proc. Am. Soc. Inf. Sci. Technol. **51**, 1–10 (2014)
11. Buchanan, G., Cunningham, S.J., Blandford, A., Rimmer, J., Warwick, C.: Information seeking by humanities scholars. In: Rauber, A., Stavros Christodoulakis, A., Tjoa, M. (eds.) ECDL 2005. LNCS, vol. 3652, pp. 218–229. Springer, Heidelberg (2005). https://doi.org/10.1007/11551362_20
12. Herrmannova, D., Pontika, N., Knoth, P.: Do authors deposit on time? Tracking open access policy compliance. In: 2019 ACM/IEEE Joint Conference on Digital Libraries (JCDL), pp. 206–216. IEEE (2019)
13. Borgman, C., Wallis, J.C., Enyedy, N.: Building digital libraries for scientific data: an exploratory study of data practices in habitat ecology. In: Gonzalo, J., Costantino Thanos, M., Verdejo, F., Carrasco, R.C. (eds.) ECDL 2006. LNCS, vol. 4172, pp. 170–183. Springer, Heidelberg (2006). https://doi.org/10.1007/11863878_15
14. Agosto, D.E., Hughes-Hassell, S.: People, places, and questions: an investigation of the everyday life information-seeking behaviors of urban young adults. Libr. Inf. Sci. Res. **27**, 141–163 (2005)
15. Schopfel, J., Chaudiron, S., Jacquemin, B., Prost, H., Severo, M., Thiault, F.: Open access to research data in electronic theses and dissertations: an overview. Libr. Hi Tech (2014)
16. Pakstis, J., Calkins, H., Dobrzynski, C., Lamm, S., McNamara, L.: Advancing reproducibility through shared data: bridging archival and library practice. In: 2019 ACM/IEEE Joint Conference on Digital Libraries (JCDL), pp. 49–52. IEEE (2019)
17. Borgman, C.L.: Scholarship in the Digital Age: Information, Infrastructure, and the Internet. MIT press, Cambridge (2010)
18. Baeza-Yates, R., Ribeiro-Neto, B.: Modern Information Retrieval: The Concepts and Technology Behind Search, 2nd edn. Addison-Wesley, Pearson (2011)
19. Brown, E.W., Callan, J.P., Croft, W.B.: Fast incremental indexing for full-text information retrieval. In: Very Large Databases (VLDB), vol. 94, pp. 192–202. Morgan Kaufmann (1994)
20. Borgman, C.L., Wallis, J.C., Enyedy, N.: Little science confronts the data deluge: habitat ecology, embedded sensor networks, and digital libraries. Int. J. Digit. Libr. **7**, 17–30 (2007)
21. Preotiuc-Pietro, D., Samangooei, S., Cohn, T., Gibbins, N., Niranjan, M.: Trendminer: An architecture for real time analysis of social media text. In: Proceedings of the International AAAI Conference on Web and Social Media, vol. 6 (2012)
22. McKay, D., Shukla, P., Hunt, R., Cunningham, S.J.: Enhanced browsing in digital libraries: three new approaches to browsing in Greenstone. Int. J. Digit. Libr. **4**, 283–297 (2004)
23. Hearst, M.A.: Search User Interfaces. Cambridge University Press, Cambridge (2009)

24. Börner, K., Chen, C.: Visual interfaces to digital libraries: motivation, utilization, and socio-technical challenges. In: Börner, K., Chen, C. (eds.) Visual Interfaces to Digital Libraries. LNCS, vol. 2539, pp. 1–9. Springer, Heidelberg (2002). https://doi.org/10.1007/3-540-362 22-3_1

25. Paynter, G.W., Witten, I.H., Cunningham, S.J., Buchanan, G.: Scalable browsing for large collections: a case study. In: Proceedings of the fifth ACM conference on Digital libraries, pp. 215–223. ACM, San Antonio (2000)

26. Witten, I.H., Paynter, G.W., Frank, E., Gutwin, C., Nevill-Manning, C.G.: Kea: Practical automated keyphrase extraction. In: Design and Usability of Digital Libraries: Case Studies in the Asia Pacific, pp. 129–152. IGI Global (2005)

27. Michaels, E.: A primer of restrictions on picture-taking in traditional areas of aboriginal Australia. Vis. Anthropol. **4**, 259–275 (1991)

28. Brown, D., Nicholas, G.: Protecting indigenous cultural property in the age of digital democracy: institutional and communal responses to Canadian first nations and Māori heritage concerns. J. Mater. Cult. **17**, 307–324 (2012)

29. Walter, M., Suina, M.: Indigenous data, indigenous methodologies and indigenous data sovereignty. Int. J. Soc. Res. Methodol. **22**, 233–243 (2019)

30. Goh, D.H.L., Chua, A., Khoo, D.A., Khoo, E.B.H., Mak, E.B.T., Ng, M.W.M.: A checklist for evaluating open source digital library software. Online Inf. Rev. (2006)

31. McKay, D.: Oranges are not the only fruit: an institutional case study demonstrating why data digital libraries are not the whole answer to e-research. In: Chowdhury, G., Koo, C., Hunter, J. (eds.) ICADL 2010. LNCS, vol. 6102, pp. 236–249. Springer, Heidelberg (2010). https://doi.org/10.1007/978-3-642-13654-2_29

32. Witten, I.H., Bainbridge, D., Paynter, G., Boddie, S.: Importing documents and metadata into digital libraries: requirements analysis and an extensible architecture. In: Agosti, M., Thanos, C. (eds.) ECDL 2002. LNCS, vol. 2458, pp. 390–405. Springer, Heidelberg (2002). https://doi.org/10.1007/3-540-45747-X_29

33. Weigl, D.M., Page, K.R., Organisciak, P., Downie, J.S.: Information-seeking in large-scale digital libraries: strategies for scholarly workset creation. In: ACM/IEEE Joint Conference on Digital Libraries (JCDL), pp. 253–256. ACM (2017)

34. Murdock, J., Jett, J., Cole, T., Ma, Y., Downie, J.S., Plale, B.: Towards Publishing Secure Capsule-Based Analysis. In: 2017 ACM/IEEE Joint Conference on Digital Libraries (JCDL), 17 261–264 (2017)

35. Ball, A., Chen, S., Greenberg, J., Perez, C., Jeffery, K., Koskela, R.: Building a disciplinary metadata standards directory. (2014)

36. Farnel, S., Shiri, A.: Metadata for research data: current practices and trends. In: International Conference on Dublin Core and Metadata Applications, pp. 74–82 (2014)

37. Alves, C., Castro, J.A., Ribeiro, C., Honrado, J.P., Lomba, Â.: Research data management in the field of ecology: an overview. In: International Conference on Dublin Core and Metadata Applications, pp. 87–94 (2018)

38. Karasti, H., Baker, K.S., Halkola, E.: Enriching the notion of data curation in e-science: data managing and information infrastructuring in the long term ecological research (LTER) network. Comput. Support. Coop. Work (CSCW) **15**, 321–358 (2006)

39. Narayan, B., Luca, E.: Issues and challenges in researchers adoption of open access and institutional repositories: a contextual study of a university repository. Inf. Res. Int. Electron. J. (2017)

40. Martinez-Uribe, L., Macdonald, S.: User engagement in research data curation. In: Agosti, M., Borbinha, J., Kapidakis, S., Papatheodorou, C., Tsakonas, G. (eds.) ECDL 2009. LNCS, vol. 5714, pp. 309–314. Springer, Heidelberg (2009). https://doi.org/10.1007/978-3-642-04346-8_30

Semantic Tagging via Entity-Level Analytics: Assessment of Concise Content Tagging

Amit Kumar[(✉)] and Marc Spaniol[(✉)]

Department of Computer Science Campus Côte de Nacre,
Université de Caen Normandie, 14032 Caen Cedex, France
{amit.kumar,marc.spaniol}@unicaen.fr

Abstract. Digital curation requires substantial human expertise in order to achieve and maintain document collections of high quality. This necessitates usually expert knowledge of a librarian or curator in order to interpret the content and categorize it accordingly. This process is at the same time expensive and time-consuming. With the advent of knowledge bases and the plenitude of information contained within them new opportunities emerge at the horizon. In particular, entity-level analytics allows to semantically enrich contents via linked open data (LOD). To this end, we assess in this paper the approach of concise content annotation as a means of supporting the process of digital curation. In particular, we compare various entity-level annotation methods and highlight the importance of concise semantic tagging based on qualitative as well as quantitative evaluations.

Keywords: Digital curation · Linked open data · Entity-level analytics

1 Introduction

Concise content annotations are an indispensable prerequisite for efficient and effective digital curation. In particular, it is crucial to capture the essence of a document by extracting its semantic. To this end, experts such as librarians or curators index contents by keywords and (potentially) connect them with an underlying taxonomy (or ontology) in order to facility structured search and retrieval. However, this process is time-consuming and labor-intensive. At the same time, digital preservation and digitization leads to a sheer abundant amount of data to be curated. In an era of artificial intelligence (AI) the question therefore arises: how to support digital curation and assist curators in concisely annotating the data? One the hand side, we observe a need for an a flexible as possible tagging-like content annotation [18] while, on the other hand side, a way of linking these annotations with an underlying taxonomy (or ontology) is desired in order to support "guided" retrieval. With the availability of automatically generated knowledge bases knowledge (KBs) such as DBpedia [2] or

© Springer Nature Switzerland AG 2021
G. Berget et al. (Eds.): TPDL 2021, LNCS 12866, pp. 97–105, 2021.
https://doi.org/10.1007/978-3-030-86324-1_11

YAGO [24] software for named entity disambiguation such as Open Calais [23] or AIDA [12] has emerged. Thus, it becomes now possible to "distill" the semantic of a document by identifying the named entities contained and analyzing them. As a result, a document might be "summarized" by its named entities and the type(s) they belong to. For instance, a document containing entities of type ATHLETE and PLAYER might be associated with SPORTS, while another document holding entities of type POLITICIAN and LAWYER might be linked with POLITICS. However, YAGO contains around half a million of types. Thus, digital curation requires the right balance between too fine-grained and too abstract annotations by focusing onto the most concise types. We therefore employ our PURE framework [13] in order to identify the most concise types out of the abundance of information captured in KBs about (prominent) entities such as *Kamala Harris* or the *International Monetary Fund*. To this end, we address in this paper the assessment of concise content tagging based on entity-level analytics.

2   Related Work

Semantic content annotation has been widely investigated in the digital libraries (DL), information retrieval (IR) and natural language processing (NLP) communities. An overview over approaches that are aligned along four key sub-tasks, i.e., Named Entity Recognition, Relation Extraction, Entity Linking, and Ontology Development can be found in [15]. However, these approaches are not suitable for a coherent semantic annotation of an entire document. In [1], the authors propose an annotation method for research papers presented in JCDL and ECDL based on the Digital Library Evaluation Ontology. However, neither a demonstrator nor an API has been released. GoNTogle [3,8] generates semantic annotation of the document. It utilizes kNN text clustering and is strictly fixed to the ACM ontology classes. WebAnno [4] is a generic web-based annotation tool for distributed teams. As such, it supports semantic annotation tasks, but not document tagging. ANNIE [5] is an information extraction system build on top of the GATE [6] framework. Supported are, e.g., tokenization, named entity recognition, part-of-speech tagging and semantic tagging of annotated entities. However, there is no type-specific semantic content tagging that might assist in digital curation. Support for document annotation through semantic tagging is not supported. Open Calais provides services for named entity recognition, instance recognition and facts for certain predefined properties with a focus on News contents [23]. It is ontology-based and returns extraction results in RDF, however the coverage with links to other Linked Open Data sets is very limited. AIDA [12,26] provides an online interface for named entity recognition and disambiguation. Similar to ANNIE, AIDA does not provide contextual support for digital curation. STICS [10], however, supports semantic retrieval via named entities, but does not provide typed annotations. TagTheWeb [21] and CALVADOS [9] aim at generating semantic fingerprints of Web documents for analysis and comparison purposes, only. The first based on Wikipedia category graph, the latter based on YAGO. The generation of RDF collections and containers is proposed in [7].

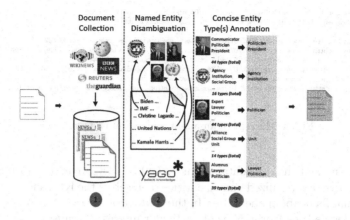

Fig. 1. Steps in entity-driven semantic tagging

However, this is an application specific solution and a minimal extension to the R2RML language, only. Semantator [25] is a Protégé [22] plug-in that attempts to convert biomedical text to linked data. In particular, it provides facilities for creating and removing ontology instances, managing instance relationships, and annotating relationships. In [19], RDF-enabled cataloguing tool for a university library is presented. It aims at generating bibliographic records so that Metadata Object Description Schema (MODS) [16] and Metadata Authority Description Schema (MADS) [17] contents can be published and interlinked. NAISC [20] is an interlinking approach for the library domain. In particular, it supports the creation of interlinks between entities, such as people, places, or works, stored in a library dataset to related entities held in another institution.

The aforementioned approaches offer only to a very limited extent support for digital curation (if at all). Apart from that, these approaches are usually application specific solutions and, thus, limited to a dedicated domain. In contrast, our assessment of concise semantic tagging is purely semantic and solely based on the information related to named entities contained in a document. Hence, additional contextualization becomes possible due to seamless linkage with data in the LOD cloud.

3   Conceptual Approach

In the following, we introduce the conceptual approach of entity-driven semantic tagging. Figure 1 presents the consecutive steps employed in entity-driven semantic tagging. The process begins with a document upload (cf. ① in Fig. 1) to a collection or a digital archive. The two main steps relevant for digital curation follow then subsequently by automatically exploiting the document's inherent semantic from the named entities contained. To this end, we employ the named entity disambiguation tool AIDA [12] (cf. ② in Fig. 1). Thus, we are able to

```
<My_Document_123> <http://www.w3.org/2000/01/rdf-schema#member> <company>.
<My_Document_123> <http://www.w3.org/2000/01/rdf-schema#member> <minister>.
...
<company> <http://www.w3.org/2002/07/owl#sameas> yago3:<wordnet_company_108058098>.
<company> <http://www.w3.org/2002/07/owl#sameas> <http://dbpedia.org/class/yago/Company108058098>.
<minister> <http://www.w3.org/2002/07/owl#sameas> yago3:<wordnet_minister_110320863>.
<minister> <http://www.w3.org/2002/07/owl#sameas> <http://dbpedia.org/class/yago/Minister110320863>.
<journalist> <http://www.w3.org/2002/07/owl#sameas> yago3:<wordnet_journalist_110224578>.
<journalist> <http://www.w3.org/2002/07/owl#sameas> <http://dbpedia.org/class/yago/Journalist110224578>.
...
```

Fig. 2. Excerpt of an annotated example document

extract the named entities contained in YAGO [11,24]. Apart from the information about the canonicalized named entities themselves the KB contains a wealth of additional facts about them, too. In the context of digital curation, the underlying ontology's type hierarchy is of particular interest, because it gives insights for a more fine-grained content annotation. Considering the example highlighted in Fig. 1, we observe, for instance, for US vice-president *Kamala Harris* a total of 39 types derived from the transitive closure or a total of 16 types for the *International Monetary Fund* stored in YAGO. These types "stem" from only 10 directly associated types for *Kamala Harris* and 3 directly associated types for the *International Monetary Fund*. Considering the "inflation" of types obtained when computing the transitive closure, it becomes evident that a concise type annotation is required. To this end, the most relevant types should be selected from the extensive type set contained in the transitive closure. For this purpose, we employ as a third - and optional - step the PURE (Pattern Utilization for Representative Entity type classification) framework [13] (cf. ③ in Fig. 1), which builds upon more than 300 types structured by the 5 top-level types from the YAGO ontology. By doing so, we derive the most representative types of each named entity and a concisely annotated pseudo document as indicated by the dotted overlay of types in step ③ of Fig. 1. A resulting example document is shown in Fig. 2. It consists of RDF triples (subject-predicate-object). 'rdf-schema#member' and 'owl#sameas' are used as the predicates in the annotated document. The object part of the triple represents the generated concise annotations where predicate is 'rdf-schema#member'. These annotations are based on the AnnoTag system [14]. In order to ensure best possible interpretability of the types a reference to their instances in YAGO and (exploiting the `sameAs` link also directly to) DBpedia is provided so that they can be understood in the context of the underlying ontology. A fully annotated document is available provided via the Website[1]. Ultimately, the resulting automatically annotated document (like the example mentioned before) can then be refined or revised by a human annotator.

---

[1] Annotation of an example document https://spaniol.users.greyc.fr/research/Anno Tag/Example_Annotation.txt.

4   Semantic Content Tagging Assessment

4.1   Assessment Dataset and Measures

The performance of semantic content tagging was assessed by conducting a qualitative and quantitative analysis on the goodness of the automatically generated semantic tags and report results on Precision and Mean Reciprocal Rank (MRR). To this end, we compared three variations of entity-driven semantic tagging:

- *Transitive Entity Types*: all types obtained from computing the transitive closure of a named entity
- *Direct Entity Types*: the types that are directly linked with a named entity
- *Concise Entity Types*: the concise types derived for a named entity by employing PURE [13]

Experiments were performed by utilizing a large data set[2] consisting of 3,824 articles for annotation. Out of the aforementioned documents, we drew a random sample of 50 documents. The 50 documents in the evaluation data set contained on average slightly more than 500 words and 25 entities, each. Based on the entities from this evaluation data set, there were in total 811 types identified for annotation with the *Transitive Entity Types* method, 430 for the *Direct Entity Types* method and 114 for the *Concise Entity Types* method of AnnoTag. In order to provide a more detailed overview about the corresponding types related to our experimental data set, a detailed list is provided on our Website[3]. The actual assessment was manually performed based on an individual evaluation and a three-level grading scheme (2: "highly concise annotation(s)", 1: "concise annotation(s)", 0: "unsuitable annotation(s)"). Evaluation data are publicly available here[4]. Based on these evaluations, we computed the following measures:

$$
\begin{aligned}
&1)\ \text{``Hard'' Precision:} && 2 \rightsquigarrow \text{relevant, 1 or 0} \rightsquigarrow \text{irrelevant} \\
&2)\ \text{``Soft'' Precision:} && 2 \text{ or } 1 \rightsquigarrow \text{relevant, 0} \rightsquigarrow \text{irrelevant} \\
&3)\ \text{``Emulated'' MRR:} && 2 \rightsquigarrow 1^{st} \text{ rank, score} = 1 \\
& && 1 \rightsquigarrow 2^{nd} \text{ rank, score} = 0.5 \\
& && 0 \rightsquigarrow \text{no rank, score} = 0
\end{aligned}
$$

4.2   Qualitative Assessment

The evaluation results of our qualitative assessment are summarized in Table 1. It can be observed that those methods that limit the perimeter of annotations (i.e. *Direct Entity Types* and *Concise Entity Types*) achieve the highest scores in both, Precision and emulated MRR. In particular, *Concise Entity Types* achieves

---

[2] Harvard Dataverse News Articles https://doi.org/10.7910/DVN/GMFCTR.

[3] List of possible annotation types in DBpedia and YAGO https://spaniol.users.greyc. fr/research/AnnoTag/Annotation_Types.zip.

[4] Semantic Tagging Assessment https://spaniol.users.greyc.fr/research/AnnoTag/ Evaluation_Data.zip.

Table 1. Qualitative assessment over 50 randomly sampled documents

Entity-level analytics method	Measure		
	"Hard" Precision	"Soft" Precision	"Emulated" MRR
Transitive entity types	0	0.28	0.14
Direct entity types	0.4	0.78	0.59
Concise entity types	0.72	0.92	0.82

92% in "Soft" Precision. Considering the fact, that the automatically generated semantic tags are supposed to be used as an assistance in a (semi-)automatic digital curation process involving a human curator, the remaining annotation errors might be easily corrected while saving valuable human time and labor due to the high quality of the automatically generated annotations.

4.3 Quantitative Assessment

In a second evaluation we now study the quantitative dimension of entity-level semantic content tagging. Not surprisingly, the number of created tags differs significantly for the various methods (cf. Table 2 for details). Exploiting the information by computing the transitive closure as in *Transitive Entity Types* leads to an "explosion" of tags. Inline with the observations from the qualitative assessment in Sect. 4.2 it becomes clear that this methods somewhat overshoots the target. This is due to the fact, that at the upper part of the ontology very generic types (such as ORGANISM, LIVING_THING or ABSTRACTION) are located. As these types are not sufficiently specific, they lead to an overall decay in Precision and MRR. In contrast, the order of tags assigned by *Direct Entity Types* and *Concise Entity Types* are about 3 to 10 times less and, thus, leading to a more concise result with higher Precision and emulated MRR scores. In particular, the method of *Concise Entity Types* extraction by PURE [13] shows that a few (concise) types are best suited in order to capture a content's semantic. At the same time, an Average of 9.28 and a Median of 8 implies that the amount of tags to be verified and/or corrected by a human curator is manageable.

Table 2. Quantitative assessment over 50 randomly sampled documents

Entity-level analytics method	Annotated type counts		
	Total	Average	Median
Transitive entity types	5,161	103.22	99.5
Direct entity types	1,760	35.2	32
Concise entity types	464	9.28	8

5   Conclusion and Outlook

In this paper we presented an assessment of semantic tagging via entity-level analytics. From our evaluation it can be observed that entity-level analytics is capable of achieving a high annotation quality based on a considerable small, but concise, amount of tags. To this end we believe, that a method utilizing tagging such as *Concise Entity Types* might become a valuable asset in digital curation.

In future work, we aim at deploying the approach of *Concise Entity Types* and making the system available to the scientific community. To this end, we have just released a Web-based demonstrator [14] and provide an API subsequently. In addition, we plan to study the performance of entity-level analytics when applying it to a specific application domain, e.g., by concept matching.

References

1. Afiontzi, E., Kazadeis, G., Papachristopoulos, L., Sfakakis, M., Tsakonas, G., Papatheodorou, C.: Charting the digital library evaluation domain with a semantically enhanced mining methodology. In: Downie, J.S., McDonald, R.H., Cole, T.W., Sanderson, R., Shipman, F. (eds.) 13th ACM/IEEE-CS Joint Conference on Digital Libraries, JCDL 2013, Indianapolis, IN, USA, 22–26 July 2013, pp. 125–134. ACM (2013). https://doi.org/10.1145/2467696.2467713
2. Auer, S., Bizer, C., Kobilarov, G., Lehmann, J., Cyganiak, R., Ives, Z.: DBpedia: a nucleus for a web of open data. In: Aberer, K., et al. (eds.) ASWC/ISWC - 2007. LNCS, vol. 4825, pp. 722–735. Springer, Heidelberg (2007). https://doi.org/10.1007/978-3-540-76298-0_52
3. Bikakis, N., Giannopoulos, G., Dalamagas, T., Sellis, T.: Integrating keywords and semantics on document annotation and search. In: Meersman, R., Dillon, T., Herrero, P. (eds.) OTM 2010. LNCS, vol. 6427, pp. 921–938. Springer, Heidelberg (2010). https://doi.org/10.1007/978-3-642-16949-6_19
4. Eckart de Castilho, R., et al.: A web-based tool for the integrated annotation of semantic and syntactic structures. In: Proceedings of the Workshop on Language Technology Resources and Tools for Digital Humanities (LT4DH), pp. 76–84. The COLING 2016 Organizing Committee, Osaka, Japan, December 2016. https://www.aclweb.org/anthology/W16-4011
5. Cunningham, H., Maynard, D., Bontcheva, K., Tablan, V.: GATE: a framework and graphical development environment for robust NLP tools and applications. In: Proceedings of the 40th Anniversary Meeting of the Association for Computational Linguistics (ACL 2002) (2002)
6. Cunningham, H., et al.: Text Processing with GATE (Version 6) (2011). http://tinyurl.com/gatebook
7. Debruyne, C., McKenna, L., O'Sullivan, D.: Extending R2RML with support for RDF collections and containers to generate MADS-RDF datasets. In: Kamps, J., Tsakonas, G., Manolopoulos, Y., Iliadis, L., Karydis, I. (eds.) TPDL 2017. LNCS, vol. 10450, pp. 531–536. Springer, Cham (2017). https://doi.org/10.1007/978-3-319-67008-9_42
8. Giannopoulos, G., Bikakis, N., Dalamagas, T., Sellis, T.: GoNTogle: a tool for semantic annotation and search. In: Aroyo, L., et al. (eds.) ESWC 2010. LNCS, vol. 6089, pp. 376–380. Springer, Heidelberg (2010). https://doi.org/10.1007/978-3-642-13489-0_27

9. Govind, Kumar, A., Alec, C., Spaniol, M.: CALVADOS: a tool for the semantic analysis and digestion of web contents. In: Hitzler, P., et al. (eds.) ESWC 2019. LNCS, vol. 11762, pp. 84–89. Springer, Cham (2019). https://doi.org/10.1007/978-3-030-32327-1_17

10. Hoffart, J., Milchevski, D., Weikum, G.: STICS: searching with strings, things, and cats, pp. 1247–1248, July 2014. https://doi.org/10.1145/2600428.2611177

11. Hoffart, J., Suchanek, F.M., Berberich, K., Weikum, G.: YAGO2: a spatially and temporally enhanced knowledge base from Wikipedia. Artif. Intell. **194**, 28–61 (2013)

12. Hoffart, J., et al.: Robust disambiguation of named entities in text. In: Proceedings of the 2011 Conference on Empirical Methods in Natural Language Processing (EMNLP 2011), Edinburgh, UK, 27–31 July 2011, pp. 782–792. ACL (2011)

13. Kumar, A., Govind, Alec, C., Spaniol, M.: Blogger or president? Exploitation of patterns in entity type graphs for representative entity type classification. In: Proceedings of the 12th International ACM Web Science Conference (WebSci 2020), pp. 59–68 (2020)

14. Kumar, A., Spaniol, M.: AnnoTag: concise content annotation via LOD tags derived from entity-level analytics. In: Proceedings of the 25th International Conference on Theory and Practice of Digital Libraries (TPDL 2021) (2021, to appear), 6 p

15. Liao, X., Zhao, Z.: Unsupervised approaches for textual semantic annotation, a survey. ACM Comput. Surv. **52**(4), 66:1–66:45 (2019). https://doi.org/10.1145/3324473

16. Library of Congress: Metadata Object Description Schema (MODS) (2020). http://www.loc.gov/standards/mods/. Accessed 26 Apr 2021

17. Library of Congress: Metadata Authority Description Schema (MADS) (2021). http://www.loc.gov/standards/mads/. Accessed 26 Apr 2021

18. Macgregor, G., McCulloch, E.: Collaborative tagging as a knowledge organisation and resource discovery tool. Libr. Rev. **55**(5), 291–300 (2006)

19. McKenna, L., Bustillo, M., Keefe, T., Debruyne, C., O'Sullivan, D.: Development of an RDF-enabled cataloguing tool. In: Kamps, J., Tsakonas, G., Manolopoulos, Y., Iliadis, L., Karydis, I. (eds.) TPDL 2017. LNCS, vol. 10450, pp. 612–615. Springer, Cham (2017). https://doi.org/10.1007/978-3-319-67008-9_55

20. McKenna, L., Debruyne, C., O'Sullivan, D.: NAISC: an authoritative linked data interlinking approach for the library domain. In: Bonn, M., Wu, D., Downie, J.S., Martaus, A. (eds.) 19th ACM/IEEE Joint Conference on Digital Libraries, JCDL 2019, Champaign, IL, USA, 2–6 June 2019, pp. 11–20. IEEE (2019). https://doi.org/10.1109/JCDL.2019.00012

21. Medeiros, J.F., Pereira Nunes, B., Siqueira, S.W.M., Portes Paes Leme, L.A.: TagTheWeb: using Wikipedia categories to automatically categorize resources on the web. In: Gangemi, A., et al. (eds.) ESWC 2018. LNCS, vol. 11155, pp. 153–157. Springer, Cham (2018). https://doi.org/10.1007/978-3-319-98192-5_29

22. Musen, M.A.: The Protégé project: a look back and a look forward. AI Matters **1**(4), 4–12 (2015). https://doi.org/10.1145/2757001.2757003

23. REFINITIV: Open Calais (2021). http://www.opencalais.com. Accessed 26 Apr 2021

24. Suchanek, F.M., Kasneci, G., Weikum, G.: YAGO: a core of semantic knowledge - unifying WordNet and Wikipedia. In: 16th International World Wide Web Conference (WWW 2007), pp. 697–706. ACM (2007)

25. Tao, C., Song, D., Sharma, D.K., Chute, C.G.: Semantator: semantic annotator for converting biomedical text to linked data. J. Biomed. Inform. **46**(5), 882–893 (2013). https://doi.org/10.1016/j.jbi.2013.07.003
26. Yosef, M.A., Hoffart, J., Bordino, I., Spaniol, M., Weikum, G.: AIDA: an online tool for accurate disambiguation of named entities in text and tables. Proc. VLDB Endow. **4**, 1450–1453 (2011)

Automating the Selection of Emulated Rendering Environments for Born-Digital Data-Sets

Julian Giessl[1], Rafael Gieschke[1], Klaus Rechert[1(✉)], and Euan Cochrane[2]

[1] Albert-Ludwigs-Universität Freiburg, Freiburg im Breisgau, Germany
`klaus.rechert@rz.uni-freiburg.de`
[2] Yale University Library, New Haven, CT, USA

Abstract. Digital, and born digital, collections in libraries and archives are growing. Managing growing backlogs of unprocessed and inaccessible digital content they cannot afford to manually process and make accessible requires automation. To support users in both creating useful setups covering a relevant set of objects as well as choosing from a list of available setups for a given object, tool support is required. In this paper, we propose a method based on co-occurrence of file formats to automate the selection of ready-made software setups for a given artifact to be accessed through emulation.

Keywords: Emulation · File formats · Access automation

1 Introduction

Digital, and born digital, collections in libraries and archives are growing at a incredibly fast rate. With the growth in collections has come an accompanying growth in complexity of file types and software dependencies. Archives in particular are also often put in a position where they are acquiring collections that are 10–30+ years old at the point of acquisition. This can mean that the digital objects they are acquiring are often in practically-obsolete formats that depend on legacy software that is no longer available on the market. Unfortunately the budgets of archives and libraries have not kept pace with their acquisition rate and libraries and archives are increasingly faced with huge and growing backlogs of unprocessed and inaccessible digital content that they cannot afford to manually process and make accessible. Hence, automation is crucial.

To automate analysis of born-digital content, a wide range of tools for file format identification [2], metadata extraction, and file format validation are available as well as file format registries and frameworks combining various tools to increase coverage. For media objects (e.g., hard disk images) also a variety of tools from the domain of digital forensics have been adapted [5,6].

To provide access to a digital artifact rendering software, e.g., a viewer application is required. For text or audio-visual content, there are many viewer applications available, usually already part of the catalog or repository software and

© Springer Nature Switzerland AG 2021
G. Berget et al. (Eds.): TPDL 2021, LNCS 12866, pp. 106–111, 2021.
https://doi.org/10.1007/978-3-030-86324-1_12

already association with file format IDs. Container formats that wrap multiple sub-files into one "container file", such as media objects, can also be accessed, e.g., though an automated file-system viewer [7].

These viewers, however, are usually not suitable for interactive multi-media content or for presenting the full experience of digital artifacts. In addition, it can be equally difficult to find and select appropriate (rendering) software for the supplementary digital material often provided with scientific publications and containing multiple files in different (obsolete) file formats. Earlier approaches of managing large multi-media collection relied on manual review [1], (semi-)manual for a limited selection of media [3], or had a limited selection of software installed to choose from [8].

With growing acceptance of emulation as access strategy, the necessity and availability of installed software setups is increasing too. To support users in both creating useful setups covering a relevant set of objects as well as choosing from a list of available setups for a given object, tool support is required. In this paper we propose a method based on co-occurrence of file formats to automate the selection of ready-made software setups for a given artifact to be accessed through emulation.

2   Building and Maintaining Rendering Software Setups

The EaaSI program of work[1] is building infrastructure and tools to create and provision configured machines with different sets of software applications installed on them. EaaSI is also creating both a network of connected EaaSI installations between which configured machines can be shared and a community of organizations to support each other. This community of organizations is pre-configuring such machines/environments with installed and documented software applications. In addition, as part of the EaaSI program of work Yale University Library alone is committed to configuring and sharing at least 3000 pre-configured software applications running in configured environments. These environments all contain an operating system and at least one software application such as a word processor, CAD program, or music composition software. The environments are being thoroughly documented with information captured about, e.g., the file formats that each application can interact with (open, save, import, export, etc.).

Given the diversity of environments and software applications becoming available in networks like EaaSI and the often broad overlap in interaction capabilities of these applications, it can be challenging for users to manually identify the best environment or environments to use when interacting with digital archives. However selecting the "best" environment to use for interaction is essential. Using an

---

[1] Emulation as a Service Infrastructure (EaaSI),
https://www.softwarepreservationnetwork.org/emulation-as-a-service-infrastructu
re/.

inappropriate environment can lead to content, context, and look-and-feel changes to the digital objects being interacted with[2].

3   Selecting a Configured Interaction Environment

To solve the problem of automatically finding system environments to render digital objects, a statistical approach was chosen. The resulting model can be seen as an experiment to see if it is possible to make sensible recommendations solely based on the distribution of file formats in digital objects.

3.1   Modeling File Format Co-occurrence

The proposed model is based upon what is often referred to as *the distributional hypothesis*. This hypothesis is motivated by the works of Harris (1954) [4] in the field of linguistics and could be translated to the aforementioned problem set as: *File formats that occur in the same context, i.e., digital objects or directories, tend to have similar uses or similar scopes of application.* We argue that this hypothesis should hold because files conceptually belonging together are grouped as compound objects and within objects organized further in directories, usually with specific purposes or applications in mind.

Following the model, we calculate co-occurrence scores for pairs of file formats. These scores can be seen as the distance between the file formats, i.e., the strength of the connections between the formats. Visually this can be depicted as a graph. This graph $G(V, E)$ is defined by a set of formats represented by its nodes $v \in V$ and by a set of co-occurrences in a specific context represented by its edges $e \in E$. Such a specific context can, e.g., be occurrences in directories. The shorter the edges (i.e., the higher their weight), the higher the co-occurrence score. Formats which are packed densely should imply format clusters which represent specific scopes of applications. The rationale of the model is that if an environment can handle a format of a cluster, it should also be able to handle the other formats of the same cluster. Given such a representation of a digital object, the model chooses the environment u out of a set of environments U which can best render the format clusters of the digital object.

Given a set of formats Y contained in the digital object d, $G(Y, E)$ is the graph representing the digital object d, and $Z(u)$ is the set of formats the environment u can handle. Then let $S(Y \cap Z(u), \tilde{E} \subset E)$ be the subgraph S of G which is induced by the environment u. The model then chooses the environment $\hat{u}$ which induces the heaviest subgraph $\hat{S}$ in graph G:

$$\hat{u} = \arg\max_{u \in U} \text{weightOf}(S(Y \cap Z(u), \tilde{E} \subset E))$$

Where weightOf(G) is the sum over all the weights of the edges in the graph G. Hence, the crucial issue for the environment recommendation of the model is the construction of the graphs representing the digital objects.

---

[2] cf. https://web.archive.org/web/20130207025446/http://archives.govt.nz/resource s/information-management-research/rendering-matters-report-results-research-digi tal-object-r.

3.2 Implementation

Every graph can be represented by an adjacency matrix. Thus, the technical representation of a digital object is translated to *co-occurrence matrices*.

The model uses four types of co-occurrence matrices. The matrices L_o and L_d form a description of a digital object. The matrix L_o represents formats co-occurring within the digital object. The interpretation of the matrix L_o is a rough indication of the potential scope, purpose, or field of the digital object. Matrix L_d stores the number of directories the respective formats co-occur within the digital object. This matrix represents a more nuanced view on potential applications. The matrices G_o and G_d store co-occurrence values on object and directory level learned from objects known to the system so far.

Usually, the entries of co-occurrence matrices simply count the co-occurrences of terms in a specific context. If the model would use these kind of co-occurrence matrices, then the model would give too much weight to very common file formats like, e.g. plain text files. There are two reasons these formats should not have such an impact on the co-occurrences. Firstly, these formats are very common and therefore most of the configured software environments should be able to read or render them anyway. The other reason is that the underlying idea of this model is to implicitly create format clusters which reflect scopes of application. If formats, i.e., nodes in the co-occurrence graph, sit closely together and are highly connected, then these closely connected formats form a cluster. If a specific format is part of most of these implicit clusters, then the information gain through these formats is rather limited. Therefore, the co-occurrence matrices describing the digital objects need to be corrected to account for the occurrence of common file formats. To achieve this, each of the co-occurrence matrices is normalized: the values of a co-occurrence matrix M will first be normalized over the individual columns of the matrix $\sum_j M_{ij} = 1$, resulting in a matrix M'. Each column j represents a distribution over the formats i co-occurring with format j. Consequently, the resulting matrix M' contains two relative values M'_{ij}, M'_{ji} for the co-occurrence of two formats i, j. The geometric mean of M'_{ij} and M'_{ji} is used to create a co-occurrence score for the formats i and j, resulting in a scoring matrix S as $\mathrm{Score}(i, j) = S_{ij} = S_{ji} = \sqrt{M'_{ij} \cdot M'_{ji}}$.

Applying these corrections to the matrices L_o, L_d, G_o, G_d and combining the resulting matrices, a matrix D describing a digital object can be written as: $D = ((\alpha G_o + \beta G_d)\lfloor + \rfloor(\gamma L_o + \delta L_d)) + \omega O$, where $(G\lfloor + \rfloor L)_{ij} = G_{ij} + L_{ij}$ if $L_{ij} \neq 0$ and 0 otherwise and where $\omega \ll \alpha, \beta, \gamma, \delta$ are weighting parameters. The matrix O is a diagonal matrix which is only used so that the model can handle digital objects which contain a single file format only.

The environments are then ranked according to the overlap of matrix D with the readable formats of the environments, i.e., the weight of the sub-graphs of the graph represented by the matrix D which are induced by the readable formats of the environments.

3.3   Preliminary Evaluation

To verify that the model makes reasonable recommendations, the co-occurrence model is compared with a baseline model based on an adaption of the Okapi BM25 [9] using a data set containing 5584 digital objects (CD-ROM ISO images).

The basic assumption is that if there is a set of handcrafted software environments and a set of randomly generated (nonsensical) environments, a useful recommendation model should overall prefer the handcrafted environments. For this, three environments were constructed by hand and seven are generated randomly. The first handcrafted environment is made of a Windows 10 system with the following software: Microsoft Access, Microsoft Excel, Microsoft Word and Microsoft PowerPoint (in total containing 107 readable file formats). The second handcrafted environment is made of a Windows 7 system with the following software: Adobe Photoshop, Adobe Reader, Adobe GoLive and Windows Media Player (in total containing 108 readable file formats). The third handcrafted environment was constructed by using file formats found in a collection of scientific data sets and combining them into a software environment, i.e., the file formats found correspond to the readable file formats of the constructed environment (in total 101 file formats). The seven random environments are generated by respectively picking 107 file formats out of the file formats occurring in the test data set randomly and combining them to an environment. For each digital object in the data set, the three handcrafted and seven random environments were ranked 50 times by both the co-occurrence and the BM25 model. In each run, the random environments were regenerated.

In around 10.5% of the cases, none of the environments can read any of files of the digital objects. In the remaining cases, the co-occurrence model ranked a handcrafted environment as the highest ranked environment in 60.1% of the cases whereas the BM25 model ranked a handcrafted environment in 46.6% of the cases as the highest ranked environment. In comparison with a random recommender, i.e., an algorithm which chooses an environment randomly, a handcrafted environment should be chosen in about 30% of the cases as best match. In some cases though, a random environment might actually be a suitable choice, especially since the handcrafted environments have limited format coverage and cannot read seldom file formats. In all cases where a random environment was ranked first by the co-occurrence model, the model ranked one of the handcrafted environments as second best in 46.5% of the cases whereas the BM25 model only ranked one of the handcrafted environments as second best in 35.8% of the cases.

Since we lack a fully labeled data set and a sophisticated set of rendering environments, the results do not fully reflect the quality of the recommendations generated by the model. But since overall the handcrafted environments should be ranked better than the random environments, the results at least indicate that the proposed model is superior to a classical approach based on a TF-IDF scheme like the BM25 model.

4 Conclusion

This work proposes a model which can recommend software rendering environments for born-digital data-sets based on the co-occurrences of file formats. The model is further enhanced by looking at how common the co-occurrence of two formats is in general and calculating biases. It is most useful for defining an order among environments which are not fully covering an object's file formats but are able to render a similar number of formats. Further work is needed to test the model on a larger set of user-labeled data.

As a future extension, the model could also be used to solve the described problem from the other end: instead of recommending environments from a given set of environments, an appropriate set of potential environments for a repository of digital objects can be recommended by creating semantic clusters of file formats. These clusters can then be used to compile suitable system environments for a given repository of digital objects. This set of environments should cover a large variety of born-digital objects while minimizing the number of software environments required.

References

1. Becker, C., Kolar, G., Küng, J., Rauber, A.: Preserving interactive multimedia art: a case study in preservation planning. In: Goh, D.H.-L., Cao, T.H., Sølvberg, I.T., Rasmussen, E. (eds.) ICADL 2007. LNCS, vol. 4822, pp. 257–266. Springer, Heidelberg (2007). https://doi.org/10.1007/978-3-540-77094-7_35
2. Brown, A.: Automatic format identification using PRONOM and DROID. Digital Preservation Technical Paper 1 (2006)
3. Espenschied, D., Rechert, K., von Suchodoletz, D., Valizada, I., Russler, N.: Large-scale curation and presentation of CD-ROM art. In: Proceedings of the 10th International Conference on Digital Preservation (IPRES), Lisbon, Portugal, 3–5 September, pp. 45–52 (2013)
4. Harris, Z.S.: Distributional structure. Word 10(2–3), 146–162 (1954)
5. Kirschenbaum, M., Ovenden, R., Redwine, G., Donahue, R.: Digital forensics and born-digital content in cultural heritage collections (2010)
6. Lee, C.A., Kirschenbaum, M., Chassanoff, A., Olsen, P., Woods, K.: Bitcurator: tools and techniques for digital forensics in collecting institutions. D-Lib Mag. 18(5/6), 14–21 (2012)
7. Misra, S., Lee, C.A., Woods, K.: A web service for file-level access to disk images. Code4Lib J. 25 (2014)
8. Rechert, K., Liebetraut, T., Stobbe, O., Valizada, I., Steinke, T.: Characterization of CD-ROMs for emulation-based access. In: iPRES, p. 144 (2015)
9. Robertson, S.E., Walker, S., Jones, S., Hancock-Beaulieu, M.M., Gatford, M., et al.: Okapi at trec-3. In: Proceedings of the Third Text REtrieval Conference, pp. 109–126 (1994)

Colabo.Space - Participatory Platform for Evolving Research and Publishing Workflows

Sasha Mile Rudan[1,2]([✉])[iD], Sinisha Rudan[3], Eugenia Kelbert[4,5],
Andrija Sagic[6], Lazar Kovacevic[7], and Matthew Reynolds[8]

[1] University of Oslo, Oslo, Norway
`sasharu@ifi.uio.no`
[2] Uppsala University, Uppsala, Sweden
[3] ChaOS NGO, Belgrade, Serbia
[4] HSE, Moscow, Russia
`ekelbert@hse.ru`
[5] UEA, Norwich, UK
[6] Milutin Bojić Library, Belgrade, Serbia
[7] Inverudio, Chicago, USA
[8] University of Oxford, Oxford, UK
`matthew.reynolds@ell.ox.ac.uk`

Abstract. We explore and evaluate the Colabo.Space ecosystem as a basis for conducting literary (and, by extension, other) research. The key principle of the ecosystem is to support participatory design at each stage to enable visual, declarative and co-creative design and evolution of the ecosystem, its infrastructure, data types and contained (research) knowledge.

Accompanied with specialized platforms, it supports describing research workflows; collecting data; distant reading research; publishing and visualizing the findings.

We argue for supporting the continuous evolution of the ecosystem, the findings and publishing content, with reference to the ecosystem and its publishing process (both the content and meta-data).

We evaluate the constituting components of the Colabo.Space ecosystem within three collaborative research projects.

Keywords: Research workflow · Participatory design

1 Introduction

This paper presents a research platform for a full research workflow, focusing on literary research, including presenting and publishing findings [3,7,18,21].

This study is supported by (i) ChaOS cha-os.org, (ii) Inverudio inverudio.com, (iii) Milutin Bojić Library milutinbojic.org.rs/, (iv) Creative Multilingualism, University of Oxford, (prismaticjaneeyre.org), (v) Retracing Connections (retracingconnections.org), Uppsala University.

G. Berget et al. (Eds.): TPDL 2021, LNCS 12866, pp. 112–117, 2021.
https://doi.org/10.1007/978-3-030-86324-1_13

Addressing the challenges [6,9,12,20] of collaborative research, we augment it through an infrastructure that enables continuous participatory design practice and supports co-design and co-creation of workflows and knowledge artefacts by all stakeholders. The workflow is described through a set of flexible phases that support dialogical processes and semantic knowledge. This infrastructure enables processes designed through workflows that (i) accurately fit particular research needs, (ii) enable a fluent flow between different research phases, (iii) can easily evolve and adapt to new community needs. Conventional tools and platforms that focus on a particular phase of the research workflow often limit knowledge and findings to the tool itself and to that research phase [1,14] which introduces considerable research friction (enforced with the *"silo"* research culture [5]), especially when participants reiterate through the workflow (for example, through different hypotheses).

By supporting a holistic research workflow, we are able to publish both the final and intermediate results and metadata on the findings and the research process. This enables research augmentation and its transparency, allowing to identify potential flaws and support reproducibility/replicability, transparency, and objectivity [3]. We approach these challenges from both technological and behavioral aspects [15,16], helping researchers to change their culture toward collaborative knowledge and process management and reusability across research phases and projects [5,10,19].

2   The Research Workflow

Research workflows we address are primarily DH workflows in literary study [8], with the following characteristics: (i) workflows "solidify" - starting as conceptual ideations the stakeholders co-evolve them into an executable workflows, (ii) workflows (should) evolve significantly to support new hypotheses, (iii) data and knowledge structures are initially unknown and evolve over time, (iv) literary scholars are not necessarily tech savvy or at least not IT experts, (v) stakeholders from different disciplines with different working methodologies should be able to unify and integrate their work, (vi) research depends on previously published literary texts and corpora either in print or digitalized/digitally-born content residing in digital repositories, (vii) the final work outcome has to be published and efficiently interlinked with the original corpora, (viii) the published work is open to continuous evolution.

Participatory design (PD) [17] is a fundamental methodology that drives our design of the whole workflow and even motivates most of our infrastructure design as it "asks for" an infrastructure that the community can co-design and implement. We found that community engagement (after communicating the benefits of such a process) was the next most important aspect of our mutual work that provided them with full trust and power of shaping the workflow and infrastructure according to their needs [2].

This was the main motivation behind introducing the following components: TopiChat, ColaboFlow, KnAllEdge and DataTalks. Together, they provide

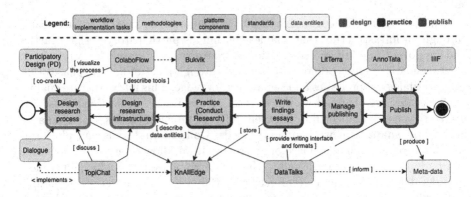

Fig. 1. Generic research workflow

dialogical and declarative support for designing, describing and executing the workflow. Therefore, the underlying *workflow implementation tasks* support the collaborative building of knowledge, ideas and hypotheses through the dialogical and brainstorming activities (Fig. 1).

The novel approach we propose through the *Colabo.Space* ecosystem[1] includes three major components (i) ColaboFlow - a declarative (and executable) language and visual interface for designing workflows in a collaborative manner, (ii) DataTalks - semantic and declarative (both human and machine interpretable) mechanism for describing knowledge artefacts and interaction interfaces, (iii) KnAllEdge - a triplestore for semantically organizing knowledge that supports knowledge ambiguity and evolution and unifies knowledge artefacts across the whole workflow. These three components support the necessary aspects of visually co-designing a declarative, transparent and low-friction infrastructure through a process receptive to all stakeholders.

The last three activities in the workflow are related to the publishing process. Our novel contribution consists in providing a continuous link between research practice, writing and publishing findings that can co-evolve and reflect the latest state across the mesh of digitized and digitally born publications cross annotated and available through the publishing infrastructures and standards.

3   Evaluations

We have (i) evaluated our platform at the formative phase [4] - we have surveyed prospective users to understand the general pains and needs of such platforms [13], (ii) worked with three communities (their representatives are co-authors of this study) to understand current DH research problems, (iii) conducted events where we *described and modelled original workflows* through ColaboFlow notation. There are two evaluation levels; (i) **platform level** - if our notation is

---

[1] https://Colabo.Space.

suitable as a *lingua franca* for describing such workflows and (ii) **application level** - if the current implementation of our platform suits particular workflows.

Evaluation 1: Prismatic Jane Eyre - This evaluation focuses on the PJE project [11]. This group of researchers works on prismatic variation in translations of "Jane Eyre" into 26 languages[2]. For example, we have traced the translations of several key words. The original workflow included selecting the key words during an in-person event. Each researcher then tracked thw key words and provided back-translations. The group leader then selected and analyzed the material across languages and results were visualized for the website.

The model of this workflow when hosted within our ecosystem looks like following: (i) with dialogue and brainstorming support, the platform supports two paths for this workflow's initial steps: virtual and face-to-virtual; in either case, the discussion is now not limited in time. (ii) Multi-annotation support ensures a streamlined path: researchers annotate the novel, nominate key words, discuss and vote in dialogue bubbles. (iii) Results are exported, visualized, augmented with the knowledge generated and published, all through the same platform. One advantage is flexibility. For example, we found that a translation was made from an intermediary text post-factum; in Colabo.Space, such discoveries do not disrupt the workflow and are automatically propagated to the published content.

Evaluation 2: Retracing Connections - The project *"Retracing connections"* deals with materials in 4 medieval languages with over 20 interdisciplinary researchersThe project requires overlapping the system co-design and practice. We thus had to introduce an innovative methodology which combines lean, agile, co-designing (Participatory Design) methodologies and Participatory Action Research practice. This enabled the concurrent process of designing, implementing and practising the ecosystem but also required a paradigm shift in DH infrastructure design itself; we had to introduce declarative system design, both (i) at the level of data structures through DataTalks and (ii) process workflows (BPMN standard) through ColaboFlow. This helped us to create core data types; *manuscript, feasts, collections, and texts* and to continue to evolve them through our critical investigation.

Evaluation 3: Milutin Bojic Collection - The digitized collection of poet Milutin Bojic consists of books, manuscript, photograph and studies about his work and the letters of Radmila Todorovic, his fiance. With the original platform (Islandora, Tesseract, Kraken HWR) there was no possibility for multi- and cross-annotations between the transcription and the related section of the scanned image. There was also no possibility to initiate dialogue about a particular transcribed word. Finally, the pipeline was not replicable as there was no possibility to preserve transcriptions and correlations within images if the images would get reprocessed. Similarly, we didn't have the possibility to show scholar essays that would address the genealogy of Bojic's work.

---

[2] https://prismaticjaneeyre.org/people/.

4 Conclusion

We presented and evaluated Colabo.Space, an ecosystem for collaborative processes and a platform for conducting continuous research and publishing. We evaluated the Colabo.Space ecosystem and accompanying components in terms of three collaborative research projects.

References

1. Amorim, R.C., Castro, J.A., Da Silva, J.R., Ribeiro, C.: A comparison of research data management platforms: architecture, flexible metadata and interoperability. Univ. Access Inf. Soc. **16**(4), 851–862 (2017)
2. Bratteteig, T., Wagner, I.: Disentangling Participation. CSCW, Springer, Cham (2014). https://doi.org/10.1007/978-3-319-06163-4
3. Chambers, C.D.: Registered reports: a new publishing initiative at cortex. Cortex **49**(3), 609–610 (2013)
4. Chen, S., Osman, N.M., Nunes, J., Peng, G.C.: Information systems evaluation methodologies. In: Proceedings of the IADIS International Workshop on Information Systems Research Trends, Approaches and Methodologies. Sheffield (2011)
5. Cromity, J., De Stricker, U.: Silo persistence: it's not the technology, it's the culture! New Rev. Inf. Network. **16**(2), 167–184 (2011)
6. Harper, G.W., Carver, L.J.: "Out-of-the-mainstream" youth as partners in collaborative research: exploring the benefits and challenges. Health Educ. Behav. **26**(2), 250–265 (1999)
7. Houghton, J.W., Oppenheim, C.: The economic implications of alternative publishing models. Prometheus **28**(1), 41–54 (2010)
8. Jänicke, S., Franzini, G., Cheema, M.F., Scheuermann, G.: Visual text analysis in digital humanities. In: Computer Graphics Forum, vol. 36, pp. 226–250. Wiley Online Library (2017)
9. LeGris, J., Weir, R., Browne, G., Gafni, A., Stewart, L., Easton, S.: Developing a model of collaborative research: the complexities and challenges of implementation. Int. J. Nurs. Stud. **37**(1), 65–79 (2000)
10. Majchrzak, A., Cooper, L.P., Neece, O.E.: Knowledge reuse for innovation. Manage. Sci. **50**(2), 174–188 (2004)
11. Reynolds, M.: Prismatic Translation. Transcript, London, England. Taylor & Francis Group (2019). https://books.google.co.uk/books?id=rqxEzQEACAAJ
12. Riger, S.: Guest editor's introduction: Working together: challenges in collaborative research on violence against women (1999)
13. Rudan, S.M., Rudan, S., Møller-Pedersen, B.: Extending BPM(N) to support face-to-virtual (F2V) process modeling. In: Proceedings of the IADIS International Workshop on Information Systems Research Trends, Approaches and Methodologies, pp. 350–361 (2021)
14. Schacht, S., Maedche, A.: A methodology for systematic project knowledge reuse. In: Razmerita, L., Phillips-Wren, G., Jain, L.C. (eds.) Innovations in Knowledge Management. ISRL, vol. 95, pp. 19–44. Springer, Heidelberg (2016). https://doi.org/10.1007/978-3-662-47827-1_2
15. Schacht, S., Morana, S., Maedche, A.: The evolution of design principles enabling knowledge reuse for projects: an action design research project. JITTA J. Inf. Technol. Theory Appl. **16**(3), 5 (2015)

16. Sein, M.K., Henfridsson, O., Purao, S., Rossi, M., Lindgren, R.: Action design research. MIS Q. **35**, 37–56 (2011)
17. Simonsen, J., Robertson, T.: Routledge International Handbook of Participatory Design. Routledge (2012)
18. Song, F., et al.: Dissemination and publication of research findings: an updated review of related biases. Health Technol. Assess **14**(8), 1–193 (2010)
19. Watson, S., Hewett, K.: A multi-theoretical model of knowledge transfer in organizations: determinants of knowledge contribution and knowledge reuse. J. Manage. Stud. **43**(2), 141–173 (2006)
20. Welsh, E., Jirotka, M., Gavaghan, D.: Post-genomic science: cross-disciplinary and large-scale collaborative research and its organizational and technological challenges for the scientific research process. Philos. Trans. Roy. Soc. A Math. Phys. Eng. Sci. **364**(1843), 1533–1549 (2006)
21. Wilson, P.M., Petticrew, M., Calnan, M.W., Nazareth, I.: Disseminating research findings: what should researchers do? A systematic scoping review of conceptual frameworks. Implementation Sci. **5**(1), 1–16 (2010)

How Can an Archive Be Characterized?

Marta Faria Araújo$^{(\boxtimes)}$ and Carla Teixeira Lopes$^{(\boxtimes)}$ (iD)

Faculty of Engineering of the University of Porto and INESC TEC, Porto, Portugal
up201704534@edu.fe.up.pt, ctl@fe.up.pt

Abstract. Archives are evolving. Analog archives are becoming increasingly digitized and linked with other cultural heritage institutions and information sources. Diverse forms of born-digital archives are appearing. This diversity asks for systematic ways to characterize existing archives managing physical or digital records. We conducted a systematic review to identify and understand how archives are characterized. From the 885 identified articles, only 15 were focused on archives' characterization and, therefore, included in the study. We found several characterization features organized in three main groups: archival materials, provided services, and internal processes.

Keywords: Archives · Cultural heritage · Web archives · Characterization

1 Introduction

The increasing amount of available information has been one of the drivers of the evolution of archives. Both national and international standards are defined for archival description [5]. On the contrary, other traditional processes, such as appraisal, selection, disposal, transfer, storage or physical space management, access control, and security, are less likely to be standardized. In these processes, each institution is developing its guidelines, methodologies, and definitions [5].

The proposal of a systematic way to characterize archives, their collections, and processes can foster works that could reveal an assortment of practices in physical and digital archives. This work is the first step towards this goal. We conducted a systematic literature review of works that analyze physical and digital archives. When we refer to archive description in this work, we mean archive characterization in a broad sense and not how records in the archive are described/indexed/enriched (e.g., which standards are used) for future access.

2 Methodology

We selected the Web of Science and Scopus databases as information sources for our systematic review because of their relevance and comprehensiveness in many scientific fields. Our final query involved conjunction of (archive OR archival OR collection OR repository), (description OR characterization OR analysis OR

© Springer Nature Switzerland AG 2021
G. Berget et al. (Eds.): TPDL 2021, LNCS 12866, pp. 118–122, 2021.
https://doi.org/10.1007/978-3-030-86324-1_14

study), and ("cultural heritage" OR historical OR Web OR ISAD OR "International Standard Archival Description" OR EAD OR "Encoded Archival Description" OR standard). The search was limited to the title, thus ensuring greater precision. We adapted this query for each database, identifying 364 articles in Scopus and 521 in Web of Science.

The screening had four major subsequent stages focusing on analyzing: title, abstract, introduction/conclusion, and full-text. All stages followed the same strategy of identifying the articles with: (1) analysis of the element under focus; (2) identification of articles to exclude; (3) identification of articles to the second author to revise. Some of the excluded articles were either related to software/data repositories or focused on the characterization of user behaviors while accessing archives, or only focused on describing metadata standards.

In the end, we selected 15 articles for assessment, 4.2% of the initial set of results, which shows that this is an understudied theme. We read the articles in two stages. First, we identified the dimensions that were the focus of analysis in the studies. In the second stage, we reread the articles to register the dimensions involved in each study.

3 Analysis of Articles

The analysis of the articles led us to identify characterization features organized in three main groups: archival materials, services, and internal processes. In each group, we arranged features according to their function, as showed in Figs. 1, 2, and 3. The double contoured boxes represent groups of features in these figures, and single contoured boxes represent features.

As represented in Fig. 1, the materials that archives hold can be depicted regarding their characteristics [1,3,4,8,10,12–14,17] and organization [3,7,13, 15,16]. Archive contents can differ in *size* (e.g., object dimensions or the size of the file); *content type* (e.g., text, audio, video, or MIME types); *last modification* date for digital records; and *age*, that conveys the temporal scope of the archive, through, for example, its oldest record. Contents can be organized by *time period*, *scope* (e.g., records from companies, personal records), *source* (e.g., a specific notary office), or *function* (e.g., current or historical documents).

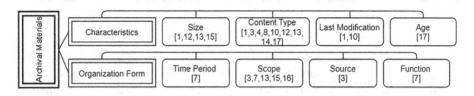

Fig. 1. Characteristics of archival materials.

The most commonly found services provided by the archives were divided into six groups, as seen in Fig. 2. The first group, *Collection* [2,3,7,8,12–15], is used whenever archives provide artificial assemblages of documents based on some common characteristic without regard to their provenance. Collections can also be associated with specific services: searching within collections and links to external collections and archives. Archives can also provide *Finding Aids* [11,14] in diverse formats (e.g., text or hypertext), searchable or not. *Reference Services* [14] are provided if the archive allows online searching of records or if it allows the user to request access to documents. Archives can also offer a *Search & Retrieval Interface* [2,6,8,13,14,17], possibly letting the user browse the existing indexes and know more about the retrieval process (e.g., if authority control was used, that is, if standardized names and index terms were used). *User Information* [14] can also be provided or received from the user. Finally, archives can also share their *Institutional Information & Policies* [1,3,6–8,12–14,17] such as annual reports, mission statement, rules of acquisition, access, copy, the development policies for new collections, and policies for growth control.

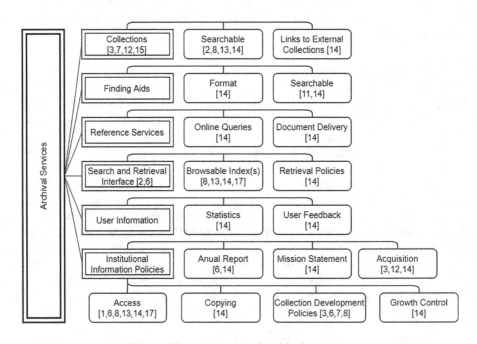

Fig. 2. Characteristics of archival services.

Figure 3 concerns the internal processes that take place within an archive. It portrays the availability of *metadata* [1,6,8,10,17] as well as the standard used [2,13], the existence of *analysis of logs* [1] and crawlers [4,6,9,10,13,17]. In archives that do so, the analysis of logs involves storing user access logs to the systems and analyze them to understand their users and necessities better. Crawlers are only used by web archives and can differ on harvesting, files used to store information, the seeds that trigger the process, rules and limits of the

algorithm, and frequency. In cases where third-party crawlers are used, the name
of the crawler can be used to detail this process.

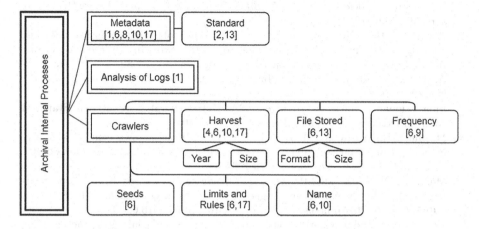

Fig. 3. Characteristics of archival internal processes.

4   Conclusion

This work is a first step towards the systematization of how archives can be
characterized. For this purpose, we conducted a systematic review and analyzed
the features identified in the articles. These features were later organized into
three main groups: materials, services, and internal processes. Most of the features apply to both analog and digital archives. Only the feature related to the
crawling process is specific to web archives.

Some features are used most often than others in the characterization of
archives. As expected, the type of content is the characteristic that is used most
often to characterize archives. Regarding services, the availability of access policies stands out as the most popular feature. On the other hand, the description
of contents through metadata is the feature most often used to characterize the
internal activities of an archive.

In conclusion, besides existing a gap in the literature regarding the characterization of archives, we found that characterization approaches are very heterogeneous. Thus, in the future, it would be interesting to create a model that would
allow this analysis and that would systematize and standardize this process,
making it easier to compare the archives.

References

1. Adams, I.F., Storer, M.W., Miller, E.L.: Analysis of workload behavior in scientific and historical long-term data repositories. ACM Trans. Storage **8**(2) (2012).
https://doi.org/10.1145/2180905.2180907

2. Bojars, U.: Case study: towards a linked digital collection of Latvian cultural heritage. In: CEUR Workshop Proceedings, vol. 1608, pp. 21–26. CEUR-WS (2016)
3. Gordon, R.S.: Suggestions for organization and description of archival holdings of local historical societies. Am. Arch. **26**(1), 19–39 (1963). https://doi.org/10.17723/aarc.26.1.h30vg72g2141m667
4. Holzmann, H., Nejdl, W., Anand, A.: The Dawn of today's popular domains: a study of the archived German Web over 18 years. In: Proceedings of the ACM/IEEE Joint Conference on Digital Libraries, pp. 73–82. Institute of Electrical and Electronics Engineers Inc., September 2016. https://doi.org/10.1145/2910896.2910901
5. International Council on Archives: ISAD(G): General International Standard Archival Description. Technical report, ICA (1999)
6. Maemura, E., Worby, N., Milligan, I., Becker, C.: If these crawls could talk: studying and documenting web archives provenance. J. Assoc. Inf. Sci. Technol. **69**(10), 1223–1233 (2018). https://doi.org/10.1002/asi.24048
7. Moreno, A.V., Ortiz, M.G.P.: Los archivos diocesanos: análisis de series documentales e importancia para la investigación histórica. Investigacion Bibliotecologica **29**(65), 73–99 (2015). https://doi.org/10.1016/j.ibbai.2016.02.015
8. Normore, L.: Studying special collections and the web: an analysis of practice. First Monday **8**(10) (2003). https://doi.org/10.5210/fm.v8i10.1085
9. Ogden, J., Halford, S., Carr, L.: Observing web archives: the case for an ethnographic study of web archiving. In: WebSci 2017 - Proceedings of the 2017 ACM Web Science Conference, pp. 299–308. Association for Computing Machinery, Inc., June 2017. https://doi.org/10.1145/3091478.3091506
10. Rauber, A., Aschenbrenner, A., Witvoet, O., Bruckner, R.M., Kaiser, M.: Uncovering information hidden in web archives: a glimpse at web analysis building on data warehouses. D-Lib Mag. **8**(12) (2002). https://doi.org/10.1045/december2002-rauber
11. Segura, S., Gallego, L., Jamin, E., Gomez, M.A., van Hooland, S., Genin, C.: Study on standard-based archival data management, exchange and publication. Technical report, ICA (2018)
12. Talbierska, J.: Researching historical library collections to discover the past and plan the future (2016). https://doi.org/10.1163/15700690-12341353
13. van Gendt, M., Isaac, A., van der Meij, L., Schlobach, S.: Semantic web techniques for multiple views on heterogeneous collections: a case study. In: Gonzalo, J., Thanos, C., Verdejo, M.F., Carrasco, R.C. (eds.) ECDL 2006. LNCS, vol. 4172, pp. 426–437. Springer, Heidelberg (2006). https://doi.org/10.1007/11863878_36
14. Wallace, D.A.: Archival repositories on the world wide web: a preliminary survey and analysis. Arch. Mus. Inform. **9**(2), 150–168 (1995). https://doi.org/10.1007/BF02770452
15. Weideman, C.: A new map for field work: impact of collections analysis on the Bentley Historical Library. Am. Arch. **54**(1), 54–60 (1991). https://doi.org/10.17723/aarc.54.1.d657136x82qlh286
16. Yin, L.: Research on development and statistical analysis of national standard archives. In: ACM International Conference Proceeding Series, pp. 239–242. Association for Computing Machinery, July 2020. https://doi.org/10.1145/3414752.3414762
17. Žabička, P., Matějka, L.: Czech Web archive analysis. New Rev. Hypermedia Multimed. **13**(1), 27–37 (2007). https://doi.org/10.1080/13614560701450383

Visualizing Copyright-Protected Video Archive Content Through Similarity Search

Kader Pustu-Iren[1]([⊠]) [iD], Eric Müller-Budack[1] [iD], Sherzod Hakimov[1] [iD],
and Ralph Ewerth[1,2] [iD]

[1] TIB – Leibniz Information Centre for Science and Technology, Hannover, Germany
{kader.pustu,eric.mueller,sherzod.hakimov,ralph.ewerth}@tib.eu
[2] L3S Research Center, Leibniz University Hannover, Hannover, Germany

Abstract. Providing access to protected media archives can be difficult due to licensing restrictions. In this paper, an alternative way to examine video content without violating terms of use is proposed. For this purpose, keyframes of the original, archived videos are replaced with images from publicly available sources using person recognition and visual similarity search for scenes and locations.

Keywords: Visualization · Person recognition · Geolocation similarity search · Place similarity search · Historical video archives

1 Introduction

The historical collection of the former German Democratic Republic (GDR) at the German Broadcasting Archive (DRA) offers a solid foundation for many research questions on East German history. Researchers who want to access videos have to submit requests and visit the archive in person. Though the archive is almost entirely digitized, showing the audiovisual content to users via a Web interface is not possible due to licensing restrictions. In contrast, there are many freely available image sources such as Flickr or Wikimedia Commons that can be used to mimic the video material. Such material could be useful to preview potentially relevant archive content to interested researchers and help them in deciding to pursue research questions in the original archive, e.g., does a historical figure occur in certain target environments and scenes?

In this paper, we suggest an novel approach to visualize copyright-protected archives without showing the original content. The visualization approach presents alternative visual content from open access repositories that is similar to the original content in terms of persons, scenery, and the location-specific setting. To the best of our knowledge, a comparable approach that addresses the problem of visualizing protected archive contents using similar images does not exist. A few proposals exist that facilitate the exploration of large media archives or tackle the problem of video summarization by recognizing persons, scenes or objects [7,9]. However, these approaches have not dealt with the problem of directly replacing visual contents with suitable substitute images.

G. Berget et al. (Eds.): TPDL 2021, LNCS 12866, pp. 123–127, 2021.
https://doi.org/10.1007/978-3-030-86324-1_15

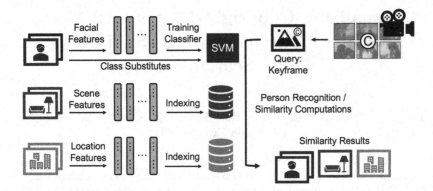

Fig. 1. Proposed system for replacing copyrighted broadcast video keyframes with similar images from publicly available datasets.

2   Visual Alternatives for Copyright-Protected Content

Figure 1 illustrates the building blocks of our system for replacing copyright-protected broadcast video keyframes with publicly accessible image data. In the first step, suitable public image collections are acquired that represent general scene setups, geolocations, and faces. While public person images are used to represent classes of a person classifier, image collections for the other modalities are fed into suitable CNN (convolutional neural network) models to extract relevant features. Subsequently, the features are indexed and constitute individual collection indexes. Finally, similarity searches with each index and face classification are performed for each given video keyframe, and keyframes are replaced with their visually nearest neighbors in terms of scene structure, location, and detected persons.

Scene Similarity Search: In order to capture the general scene structure of an image and extract meaningful features, the ResNet-152 model pre-trained on the Places365 dataset [12] is used. The dataset consists of around 1.8 million images corresponding to 365 scene categories based on urban, nature, or indoor categories. We use this dataset as our public reference collection for scenes and extract features for each image. Based on the extracted feature representations, an index is built using the FAISS library [3]. The index is based on product quantization [2]. It allows for efficient comparisons between query vectors and stored vectors based on cosine similarity and returns nearest neighbors.

Geolocation Similarity Search: For a location-based feature representation, a pre-trained ResNet-152 model for geolocation estimation [8] is used. The model was trained on the MP-16 dataset [6], which consists of 4.7 million images from all around the world. The reference dataset for the similarity search is formed from images primarily taken in area of the former GDR. For this purpose, a list of landmarks and relevant cities in the area of the former GDR is compiled using

Wikidata [11]. The resulting list is then used to crawl images from Wikimedia Commons, Flickr, and Google Images. Additionally, we use a subset of the MP-16 dataset covering the area of the GDR and worldwide landmarks. This collection results in a total number of around 915,000 images. Similar to scenes, a FAISS index is built to retrieve similar location images based on the stored features.

Person Recognition: In contrast to scenes and locations, we define a lexicon of public figures and employ a classification approach to identify faces. For the lexicon, 92 public figures of different fields of interest like politics or entertainment such as "Angela Merkel" or "Erich Honecker" are chosen. The person recognition approach consists of the following steps: face detection, face alignment, feature extraction, and face recognition. We used RetinaFace [1] to detect faces in images and aligned the detected faces using the Dlib shape predictor [4]. Face images are then represented by feature vectors extracted using FaceNet [10]. Lastly, a Support Vector Machine (SVM) classifier with a linear kernel is trained to identify the detected face. For training, face images from the GDR archive annotated by archivists are used. In contrast, the substitute images for the visualization are retrieved from Web sources. Each person from the lexicon is assigned a fixed image retrieved from Wikimedia Commons and Google Images.

Visualization of Face Recognition and Similarity Search Results: The scene, geolocation similarity search, and person recognition components are applied to available keyframes of videos from the DRA archive. After pruning results with low confidence scores, close-ups and indoor images, remaining results are used to visualize the original video content. The graphical user interface of the resulting visualization is shown in Fig. 2. The GUI allows for selecting a broadcast video (left), sliding across available keyframes for the video (bottom), displaying recognized persons and the retrieved scene, and location-specific images.

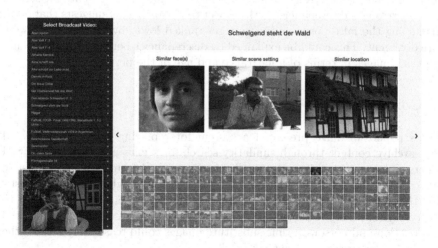

Fig. 2. Similarity results for selected frame (left bottom) of exemplary broadcast video.

Table 1. Annotation accuracies for substitute images proposed by the similarity approaches.

Participant	Face	Location	Scene	Overall
1	0.90	0.85	0.74	0.83
2	0.74	0.77	0.58	0.70
3	0.74	0.86	0.67	0.76

Table 2. Inter-coder agreement of participants measured by K's α's.

Face	Location	Scene	Overall
0.663	0.754	0.584	0.667

3 Evaluation

We evaluate the person and similarity search results of our system. The experiment examines whether the evaluators (three co-authors of the paper, non-historians), given an original keyframe and several substitute images, select the top-1 ranked reference image of the system. To ensure a fair evaluation, a list of 100 keyframes were randomly sampled from available videos for each of the similarity search tasks: scene, location, and person. The evaluators were presented with five options to choose the most similar image to the shown keyframe. In addition to the top-1 reference image, other four images were chosen from the ranking list of the respective method. In total, 300 keyframes were annotated in the study. The resulting accuracies, i.e., in how many cases the participants selected the top-1 image suggested by the similarity search and the classifier, are shown in Table 1. On average, the evaluators preferred the reference image for face and location over the other image options with high accuracies. Scene reference images were selected with lower accuracies, suggesting that the results are less accurate in representing the correct image content. We also measured the inter-coder agreements using Krippendorff's alpha (K's α) coefficient [5] as given in Table 2. K's α for the location images indicates a high agreement between evaluators. While both agreement and accuracy values are moderate for scenes, there are stronger discrepancies with respect to persons. This suggests that opinions among the false positives (i.e., images ranked lower by the classifier) were more divergent. This could be explained by discrepancies between the public and historical images in terms of appearance and age of the persons.

4 Conclusions

In this paper, we have presented a system for replacing copyright-protected video archive content through similarity search for scenes and locations as well as person recognition with image collections retrieved from publicly accessible sources. We have presented an experiment to investigate whether image substitutes through similarity search and person recognition are sufficiently accurate to replace keyframes of the protected archive videos. Outcomes of the study showed that location and person-specific substitute images could reasonably replace the historical video archive content.

References

1. Deng, J., Guo, J., Ververas, E., Kotsia, I., Zafeiriou, S.: Retinaface: Single-shot multi-level face localisation in the wild. In: 2020 IEEE/CVF Conference on Computer Vision and Pattern Recognition (CVPR 2020), Seattle, WA, USA, June 13–19, 2020, pp. 5202–5211. IEEE (2020). https://doi.org/10.1109/CVPR42600.2020.00525
2. Jégou, H., Douze, M., Schmid, C.: Product quantization for nearest neighbor search. IEEE Trans. Pattern Anal. Mach. Intell. **33**(1), 117–128 (2011). https://doi.org/10.1109/TPAMI.2010.57
3. Johnson, J., Douze, M., Jégou, H.: Billion-scale similarity search with GPUs. CoRR abs/1702.08734 (2017)
4. King, D.E.: Dlib-ml: a machine learning toolkit. J. Mach. Learn. Res. **10**, 1755–1758 (2009)
5. Krippendorff, K.: Answering the call for a standard reliability measure for coding data. Commun. Methods Meas. **1**(1), 77–89 (2007). https://doi.org/10.1080/19312450709336664
6. Larson, M.A., Soleymani, M., Gravier, G., Ionescu, B., Jones, G.J.F.: The benchmarking initiative for multimedia evaluation: mediaeval 2016. IEEE Multim. **24**(1), 93–96 (2017). https://doi.org/10.1109/MMUL.2017.9
7. Müller-Budack, E., Pustu-Iren, K., Diering, S., Ewerth, R.: Finding person relations in image data of news collections in the internet archive. In: Méndez, E., Crestani, F., Ribeiro, C., David, G., Lopes, J.C. (eds.) TPDL 2018. LNCS, vol. 11057, pp. 229–240. Springer, Cham (2018). https://doi.org/10.1007/978-3-030-00066-0_20
8. Müller-Budack, E., Pustu-Iren, K., Ewerth, R.: Geolocation estimation of photos using a hierarchical model and scene classification. In: Ferrari, V., Hebert, M., Sminchisescu, C., Weiss, Y. (eds.) ECCV 2018. LNCS, vol. 11216, pp. 575–592. Springer, Cham (2018). https://doi.org/10.1007/978-3-030-01258-8_35
9. Sahoo, A., Kaushal, V., Doctor, K., Shetty, S., Iyer, R.K., Ramakrishnan, G.: A unified multi-faceted video summarization system. CoRR abs/1704.01466 (2017)
10. Schroff, F., Kalenichenko, D., Philbin, J.: Facenet: a unified embedding for face recognition and clustering. In: IEEE Conference on Computer Vision and Pattern Recognition (CVPR 2015), Boston, MA, USA, June 7–12, 2015, pp. 815–823. IEEE Computer Society (2015). https://doi.org/10.1109/CVPR.2015.7298682
11. Vrandecic, D., Krötzsch, M.: Wikidata: a free collaborative knowledgebase. Commun. ACM **57**(10), 78–85 (2014). https://doi.org/10.1145/2629489
12. Zhou, B., Lapedriza, À., Khosla, A., Oliva, A., Torralba, A.: Places: a 10 million image database for scene recognition. IEEE Trans. Pattern Anal. Mach. Intell. **40**(6), 1452–1464 (2018). https://doi.org/10.1109/TPAMI.2017.2723009

Self-assessment and Monitoring of CHI Performance in Digital Transformation

Rasa Bocyte[1]([⊠]) [iD], Johan Oomen[1] [iD], and Fred Truyen[2] [iD]

[1] Netherlands Institute for Sound and Vision, Hilversum, The Netherlands
{rbocyte,joomen}@beeldengeluid.nl
[2] KU Leuven, Leuven, Belgium
fred.truyen@kuleuven.be

Abstract. To fully reap the benefits of digitisation and sustainably create value for their audiences, cultural heritage institutions (CHI) need to implement and monitor digital, data-driven strategies that touch upon all aspects of how organisations operate. This can range from staffing and skills development to adoption of metadata models, novel audience engagement approaches and methods for collecting and using user data. We introduce the concept for the CHI Self-Assessment Tool that enables institutions to assess their strategy and plan against several aspects of digital transformation. The tool proposes a novel approach on how CHIs can continuously gather data on their activities and use insights from this data to adjust their strategies and increase their digital maturity. Equally, this data can be used by policy-makers to implement more effective policies and support the sector with targeted capacity building.

Keywords: Digital transformation · Impact · Self-assessment

1 Introduction

Since the cultural heritage (CH) sector started engaging with large-scale digitization projects, many institutions realized that they needed to implement integrated, data-driven digital workflows and strategies in order to make the most out of digital assets [6]. It soon became clear isolated projects with digital collections often result in momentary engagement and require deeper organizational and leadership changes to deliver sustainable impact to target communities [3, 5]. The currently used concept of *digital transformation* tries to encapsulate this more comprehensive and integral digital approach. Europeana provides the following definition: "Digital transformation is both the process and the result of using digital technology to transform how an organisation operates and delivers value. It helps an organisation to thrive, fulfil its mission and meet the needs of its stakeholders" [2]. This definition implies rethinking of business models, value chains as well as participatory relationships between the CHIs and their audiences. Additionally, it highlights that digital transformation is an ongoing process with a constantly moving target rather than a set goal [4]. Thus data needs to be collected not only to define targets and track progress towards them but also to monitor trends and signals in the sector

G. Berget et al. (Eds.): TPDL 2021, LNCS 12866, pp. 128–132, 2021.
https://doi.org/10.1007/978-3-030-86324-1_16

and use them to further update digital strategies and inform decision-makers (funding bodies, European and national policy makers, networks and umbrella organisations) on appropriate actions.

The CHI Self-Assessment Tool (SAT) was conceived in this context to empower cultural heritage professionals and decision-makers to implement effective digital strategies. It presents a data-driven approach for enabling CHIs to continuously monitor their performance and become more confident in using insights from data to adjust their strategies and increase the impact of their activities. The innovation of the tool lies in its unique proposition to (1) iteratively gather data from a wide range of CHIs, (2) educate organizations on how such data can be translated into concrete actions, and (3) closely monitor trends in the sector that can inform decision makers regarding innovation, funding and capacity building needs. In this poster paper, we present the state of the art for monitoring and assessment activities in the heritage domain and describe the early concept of the SAT.

2   State of the Art in Assessment and Monitoring Strategies

Over the last few years, numerous online assessment and monitoring tools have been developed. We examined four examples that are widely adopted in the CH sector. All the tools start by asking users to fill out a survey of varying length and detail. The Tracker provides 93 questions divided into 12 areas, including Strategy & Governance, Marketing & Communications, and Finance & Operations. Microsoft's Digital Transformation Framework for libraries and museums uses 16 questions to assess digital transformation across four areas: Enhanced Visitor Experience, Advanced Discovery, Dynamic Operations and Intelligent Environments. Both tools utilize rating systems to determine the current level of digital maturity and allow users to define target goals. The Digital Transformation Framework gives very specific examples for each level of maturity. For instance, one of the advanced levels in the Advanced Discovery area is "Computer vision and optical character recognition automatically generate additional metadata for real-time tagging". Such descriptions make this framework only applicable for very specific cases and provide a snapshot of the state of technology.

A scoring system is commonly used to present the results of the survey. *Digitale Maturiteit* uses a percentage from 1–100 to assess the digital maturity of each organization. Users are given a ranking in each category and can compare their performance with other organizations. Similarly, the Quick Innovation Scan used in the DEN Academy asks users to calculate their score out of a maximum of 20 points in four categories and to compare their results to a static chart. Such strict classification creates a false impression that all CHIs need to reach very specific goals and targets in order to succeed-it does not take into account the diversity of CHIs and the different paths available to them in order to reach digital maturity. This can be particularly discouraging for smaller organizations that target niche communities and do not see the need to offer the same services as internationally established CHIs.

All the examined tools provide insight about the status quo in an organization but do not offer concrete suggestions for follow up actions, hence their applicability is limited. For example, the Quick Innovation Scan offers generic guidelines such as "Seek opportunities to find collaboration partners inside and outside the organization to gain new knowledge and find new solutions". This can be useful to initiate a conversation about the necessary operational changes but more specific pointers are needed to ensure that appropriate measures and decisions are taken to achieve the envisioned targets, as well as make use of knowledge already available in the sector.

3   CHI Self-assessment Tool

Improving on the state of the art, the SAT is conceived as an interactive environment where CH professionals can collaboratively learn how to convert digital ambitions into digital strategies and continuously monitor their performance. The concept of the tool visualized in Fig. 1 presents its four components.

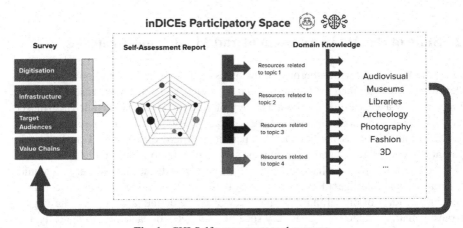

Fig. 1. CHI Self-assessment tool concept.

Survey. The users start by filling out a survey. In the first part, they are asked to answer general questions about their organization (size, target audiences, size and type of collections, participation in (inter)national networks, etc.) which help to situate each CHI in a specific context and domain. Based on these answers, the second part of the survey uses Likert scale questions to assess an organization's confidence with various aspects of digital transformation applicable to them, including adopted standards, skills and resources available in the organization, strategies for managing intellectual property rights and experience with online publication platforms. The survey sets out to give participants a rounded perspective of what digital transformation in the CH sector looks like and its many possible components. This is a learning experience in itself, and something that can be used for planning.

Self-assessment Report. The results of the survey are presented via data visualizations that showcase each CHI in relation to other organizations in the sector as well as focus on a particular domain or region/country. It is important to note that the report is not meant to give a rating or a grade on each question as this tends to favor larger, more advanced organizations with a wide outreach. Instead, the report is meant to highlight areas of high potential where further investment could lead to significant improvements. The aggregated results are available publicly for consultation by policy-makers and decision-makers to monitor the activities in the sector. All the examined already existing self-assessment tools stop at this stage.

Domain Knowledge. Based on the strengths and goals of each CHI as highlighted by the survey results, SAT provides targeted, domain-specific resources to support digital transformation processes (for instance, a media archive would be pointed to resources related to standards for audiovisual data enrichment). These resources have been either created specifically by the inDICEs project or aggregated from other web sources and CH communities. Additionally, SAT provides resources on what data collection strategies CHIs could use to monitor the impact of their activities and how to draw practical insights from this data. A complementary MOOC course will provide further guidance.

Participatory Space. SAT is embedded in the inDICEs Participatory Space that facilitates active engagement and knowledge sharing between CH professionals on topics related to digital transformation. It is specifically designed to engage participants in debates, brainstorming and community building activities. Again, a data-driven approach is used - topics discussed in the Participatory Space are visualized via embedded data visualizations that help to observe more granular trends in the sector. As new trends emerge, the initial survey questions are iteratively updated to reflect these changes.

As Fig. 1 indicates, SAT is meant to be used iteratively. Users receive notifications as new relevant resources are added and are encouraged to update the survey answer at regular intervals. Time-series data is used to visualize progress over time. Importantly, the SAT serves not only individual CHIs but also policy-makers who require monitoring tools to implement effective policies and capacity building activities [1]. Using the results of the SAT, they can monitor the effectiveness of their instruments over time and adjust them based on the data provided by the CHIs.

4   Conclusions and Future Work

This paper presented the concept of the CHI Self-Assessment Tool. During the conference, we will demonstrate the first prototype of the tool and present specific scenarios for its usage. Our further work will focus on testing this prototype with a diverse group of cultural heritage professionals as well as investigating strategies to ensure their sustained engagement with the tool.

Acknowledgements. This project has received funding from the European Union's Horizon 2020 research and innovation programme under grant agreement No 870792.

References

1. Cerreta, M., di Girasole, E.G.: Towards heritage community assessment: indicators proposal for the self-evaluation in faro convention network process. Sustainability **12**(23), 9862 (2016). https://doi.org/10.3390/su12239862
2. Europeana Pro, Building Digital Capacity. https://pro.europeana.eu/page/building-digital-cap acity#step-2-defining-digital-transformation. Accessed 19 Apr 2021
3. James, D., Royston, C.: How to be a digital leader and advocate: the changing role of the digital department. MW2015: Museums and the Web 2015. https://mw2015.museumsandth eweb.com/paper/how-to-be-a-digital-leader-and-advocate-the-changing-role-of-the-digital-department/
4. Ludden, J., Russick, J.: Digital Transformation: It's a Process and You Can Start Now. Museums and the Web 2020. https://mw20.museweb.net/paper/digital-transformation-its-a-process-and-you-can-start-now/
5. Malde, S., Kennedy, A., Parry, R.: Understanding the digital skills & literacies of UK museum people–Phase Two Report (2019). https://doi.org/10.29311/2018.02
6. Terras, M., Coleman, S., Drost, S., et al.: The value of mass-digitised cultural heritage content in creative contexts. Big Data & Society. January 2021 doi:https://doi.org/10.1177/205395172 11006165

Automatic Translation and Multilingual Cultural Heritage Retrieval: A Case Study with Transcriptions in Europeana

Mónica Marrero[1(✉)], Antoine Isaac[1,2], and Nuno Freire[3]

[1] Europeana Foundation, The Hague, The Netherlands
monica.marrero@europeana.eu
[2] Vrije Universiteit Amsterdam, Amsterdam, The Netherlands
[3] INESC-ID, Lisbon, Portugal

Abstract. Multilinguality is of particular interest for digital libraries in Cultural Heritage (CH), where the language of the data may not match users' languages. However, multilingual access is rarely implemented beyond the use of multilingual interfaces. We have run an experiment using the Europeana CH digital library as a use case. We evaluate the effectiveness of a multilingual information retrieval strategy using machine translations to English as pivot language. We conducted an indirect evaluation that should be considered preliminary. Yet, together with a manual analysis of the query translations, it already shows (or confirms) some of the benefits and challenges of deploying such systems in CH.

Keywords: Multilinguality · Cultural Heritage · Machine translation

1 Introduction and Related Work

Multilingual access to metadata and contents is of particular interest for international digital libraries (DL) in the area of Cultural Heritage (CH), which have collections in multiple languages, and users from different countries and with different cultural backgrounds. However, Multilingual Information Retrieval (MLIR) is rarely implemented in this domain beyond the interface language [9,15]. Only a few practical cases have been reported in the literature (see extensive reviews in Vassilakaki and Garoufallou [19], Diekema [3], and Chen [2]), and most of them use human translations and specialized vocabularies. This is the case for example of the World Digital Library [11], or the International Children's Digital Library[1], where contents are manually translated. In query translation, Bonet et al. [5] obtained good results using specialized dictionaries, while Kools et al. [7] obtained satisfactory results using machine translation. Matusiak et al. [9] reports an experiment using Google Translate to translate to English a collection of Chinese artworks, but they finally opted for human translation given

---

[1] http://en.childrenslibrary.org/.

© Springer Nature Switzerland AG 2021
G. Berget et al. (Eds.): TPDL 2021, LNCS 12866, pp. 133–138, 2021.
https://doi.org/10.1007/978-3-030-86324-1_17

the limitations found. In other domains machine translation seems to work well for the most widely spoken languages [4], with only a decrease of performance of 5–12% compared to the monolingual setting [13]. This lack of use of machine translation in DLs could be explained by the translation ambiguity and the insufficient lexical tools' coverage, considered to be among the most prominent problems in MLIR [12].

Europeana, a European digital library that aggregates content from libraries, archives and museums from all around Europe[2], is also a good example of this situation. It provides access to more than 60 million objects, from textual documents, like books or newspapers, to multimedia objects like audio, videos and paintings, which are primarily associated with 38 different languages. The data of these objects (i.e. metadata and content) is indexed in a search engine that provides a search functionality over all collections, however, in most cases, this data is only available in one language. Europeana performs data enrichment, adding persons, locations and concepts described in multiple languages to its metadata records. Yet the coverage of this approach is incomplete: there is no wide-spread translation of metadata, content and/or queries.

We have run an experiment using part of Europeana's collections to see the effectiveness of a MLIR system in this domain. We have focused on the content, not the metadata, and we have adopted a mixed approach where queries and object content are automatically translated to English as a pivot language, following the Europeana Multilingual Strategy [10]. Although document translation is considered more effective [12,13,17], this hybrid approach has outperformed other strategies in an experiment conducted [13], and it is more scalable when the number of different languages is considerable. Also, English is the most present language in these collections, and its effectiveness in machine translation is higher [4,13]. We have used the CEF translation service [1] as it is intended as a free, secure service for public bodies, which can be appealing for CH institutions, especially in Europe. The repository with the data of the experiment [8] and the client [6] used to get the translations are publicly available.

2   Data and Evaluation

We have selected a sample of 18,257 handwriting transcriptions of documents from the Europeana 1914–1918 thematic collection[3], obtained from the Transcribathon crowdsourcing platform [18]. This collection includes many World War I related objects contributed by members of the public all over Europe, like soldiers' diaries or letters. After removing 18 transcriptions that lacked indication of the original language, and those originally in English, we submitted 13,996 transcriptions to the service for translation to English. We received errors for 404 of them (2.9%), either because the language is not supported or because the text is too long and a different interface should then be used (this is part

---

[2] http://europeana.eu.
[3] https://www.europeana.eu/en/collections/topic/83-1914-1918.

Table 1. Original language of the transcriptions and queries (assuming for the queries it is the same as the language of the portal), and number of successful English translations.

Language tag	de	en	fr	it	ro	nl	el	lv	bs	cs	da	sl	hu	es	pl	sk	hr	Total
Transcriptions	9300	4243	1669	992	578	455	364	226	215	90	90	7	3	2	2	2	1	**18239**
Translated	9151	0	1659	973	577	454	356	226	0	90	90	7	2	2	2	2	1	**13592**
Queries	12	0	13	29	2	2	0	0	1	0	0	0	3	6	0	0	0	**68**
Translated	12	0	13	29	2	2	0	0	1	0	0	0	3	6	0	0	0	**68**

of our future work). As a result, we obtained 13,592 transcriptions translated to English from 15 different languages (see Table 1).

Regarding queries, we successfully translated a small sample of 68 queries issued in languages other than English from the logs of Europeana's 1914–1918 collection between January and August 2019.

We manually assessed the quality of translation of the queries, as they play a major role in the cross-lingual system. We also conducted a quantitative evaluation to answer the following research question: *is it possible to obtain similar results as those obtained with the original query, when searching on the same collection using translations?* Our assumption is that the results obtained in a monolingual system for a specific query and collection in that language, should also appear when searching with the translated query in the same collection translated to English. In order to answer this question, we compare two lists of retrieval results per query q in original language l: a) the set s_{qo} obtained when searching with the original query q_o in the transcriptions in l, and b) the set s_{qt} obtained when searching with the English translation of q_o, q_t, in the transcriptions in l translated to English. The precision and recall of s_{qt} with respect to s_{qo} is then computed. Finally, we calculate the additional number of transcriptions retrieved when using q_t in the whole corpus of English transcriptions (translated or not).

3   Results

After a manual assessment of the queries, we discovered that in a number of cases the input to the translation tool was wrong because the queries contain typos or have the wrong language assigned (i.e., our assumption that its language is the language of the portal is wrong). The first issue happened 6 times, while the second happened in 18 queries, with two of them having both issues at the same time. After removing them, and an additional 3 for which the user's intention was not clear to us, we manually analyzed the translation of the remaining 43 queries. In 37 cases the query was an entity that had to be left unchanged (e.g., 'Bernhard Stiens' is to be left unchanged, while 'Italia' must be translated to 'Italy'). The service correctly translated (that is, left unmodified) 20 of those entities (54%). In the remaining 6 cases, where the translation was supposed to be different from the original, the translation service did it correctly in 5 cases (83%).

The incorrect translation of named entities is the main source of problems as, setting aside other issues, there are more queries with entities than without: 42 of the 68 queries are (or include) named entities (62%). The problem is especially hard to solve as the named entities present and queried in the World War I context are very specialized (less-known authors, small villages) and sometimes incompletely referred to (e.g., 'Tonale' refering to 'Passo del Tonale'), or are formulated with typos (e.g., 'san elia' refering to Antonio Sant'Elia). In some other cases they include common nouns that are not correctly disambiguated (e.g.,'Antonio Sordi' and 'Fogliano' are translated from Italian as 'Antonio Deaf' and 'sheet' respectively). This ambiguity issue is also observed in queries not involving named entities. For example, 'carnet de route' is correctly translated from French as 'journey log' in the transcriptions, however the query 'carnet' is translated as 'notebook', so no relevant results are retrieved.

For the quantitative evaluation, we obtained precision, recall, and new translations found for the queries with search results, that is, 31 queries out of the 68 originally considered (see Table 2). The recall indicates that 67% of the objects in s_{qo} are retrieved when using the translations. As a negative counterpart, we have on average 49% of results that are not in s_{qo}. Given the poor quality of the translation of the queries, we would have to assume that those results are more likely to be noisy: in our case, on average 337 of those new transcriptions retrieved are less likely to be relevant. This could be however compensated in some cases by the new transcriptions found. When using q_t in the whole corpus of English transcriptions we retrieve an average of 687 new transcriptions per query. A quick review shows that some of those new results are relevant. For example, for the query 'domov' in Czech ('home' in English) we only retrieve 2 results, however if we search by 'home' in the English translations we retrieve more than 1500 transcriptions in 9 additional languages.

Table 2. Precision and recall obtained when comparing s_{qt} and s_{qo} per language, as well as additional transcriptions retrieved when searching on the translations of any language.

Language tag	cs	de	it	fr	ro	Average
Queries	1	8	16	4	2	**6.2**
Precision	0.15	0.57	0.44	0.74	0.5	**0.51**
Recall	1	0.87	0.57	0.70	0.5	**0.67**
New transcriptions	1527	397	823	851	1	**687**

4   Conclusions and Future Work

This experiment in a real scenario shows (or confirms) some of the benefits and the challenges of deploying MLIR systems in this specific domain. Albeit focused on a rather small set of queries, our case illustrates the problem of performing query translation in the CH context: the number of queries that we are sure the service should actually translate is way smaller than the number of queries that it should leave unmodified, so the selection of a high quality translation service is important. Additional techniques like controlled vocabularies and named entity recognition tools are also needed [16], although they need to be adapted to the specific domain and updated regularly.

We have observed a significant number of cases where the queries had typos or there was a mismatch between the language of the query and the language assigned according to the language of the portal. These cases are especially harmful as the translation service was not given appropriate input. A spelling-correction system could mitigate the first problem, while for the second, language detection based on various signals [14] could improve the results.

This work shows that without addressing these issues, the drawbacks of a multilingual system in a CH domain could easily exceed its benefits. The next step will be to address those challenges and complement the evaluation conducted with a more balanced sample of queries in terms of languages to see its impact in the results. A qualitative analysis of the retrieval results is also due to better account for additional benefits of the translation (e.g. synonyms).

References

1. CEF automated translation service: etranslation. https://ec.europa.eu/cefdigital/wiki/display/CEFDIGITAL/eTranslation
2. Chen, H.: Digital library research in the US: an overview with a knowledge management perspective. Prog. Electr. Libr. Inf. Syst. **38**(3), 157–167 (2004)
3. Diekema, A.R.: Multilinguality in the digital library: a review. Electr. Libr. **30**(2), 165–181 (2012)
4. Dolamic, L., Savoy, J.: Retrieval effectiveness of machine translated queries. J. Am. Soc. Inf. Sci. Technol. **61**, 2266–2273 (2010)
5. España-Bonet, C., Stiller, J., Ramthun, R., van Genabith, J., Petras, V.: Query translation for cross-lingual search in the academic search engine PubPsych. In: Research Conference on Metadata and Semantics Research, pp. 37–49. Limassol, Cyprus (2018)
6. Freire, N.: GitHub repository: europeana-etranslation-research. https://github.com/nfreire/europeana-etranslation-research
7. Kools, J., Lagos, N., Petras, V., Stiller, J., Vald, E.: GALATEAS project (Generalized Analysis of Logs for Automatic Translation and Episodic Analysis of Searches). D7.4 Final Evaluation of Query Translation (2013), version 2.0
8. Marrero, M., Isaac, A., Freire, N.: Automatic translation and multilingual cultural heritage retrieval: a case study with transcriptions in Europeana [Dataset], June 2021. https://doi.org/10.5281/zenodo.5045066

9. Matusiak, K.K., Meng, L., Barczyk, E., Shih, C.J.: Multilingual metadata for cultural heritage materials: the case of the Tse-Tsung Chow collection of Chinese scrolls and fan paintings. Electr. Libr. **33**(1), 136–51 (2015)
10. Neale, A., Isaac, A., Manguinas, H., Moskalenko, D.: Multilingual strategy. Tech. rep., Europeana (2020). https://pro.europeana.eu/post/europeana-dsi-4-multilingual-strategy
11. Oudenaren, J.V.: The world digital library. Uncommon Culture **3**(5/6), 65–71 (2012)
12. Peters, C., Braschler, M., Clough, P.: Multilingual Information Retrieval: From Research to Practice. Springer, Heidelberg (2012)
13. Savoy, J., Braschler, M.: Information retrieval evaluation in a changing world: lessons learned from 20 Years of CLEF, chap. Lessons Learnt from Experiments on the Ad Hoc Multilingual Test Collections at CLEF, pp. 177–200. Springer, Cham (2019)
14. Stiller, J., Gäde, M., Petras, V.: Ambiguity of queries and the challenges for query language detection. In: CLEF 2010 LABs and Workshops. Padua, Italy (2010)
15. Stiller, J., Gäde, M., Petras, V.: Multilingual access to digital libraries: the European use case. Inf. Wissenschaft Praxis **64**(2–3), 86–95 (2013)
16. Stiller, J., Petras, V.: Best practices for multilingual access. Tech. rep., Europeana (2016). https://pro.europeana.eu/post/best-practices-for-multilingual-access
17. Stiller, J., Petras, V., Lüschow, A.: CLUBS Project (Cross-Lingual Bibliographic Search). M5.3 Final Evaluation (2019), version 1.0
18. Transcribathon crowdsourcing platform. https://transcribathon.eu
19. Vassilakaki, E., Garoufallou, E.: Multilingual digital libraries: a review of issues in system-centered and user-centered studies, information retrieval and user behavior. Int. Inf. Libr. Rev. **45**, 3–19 (2013)

Linked Data and Open Data

Leveraging a Federation of Knowledge Graphs to Improve Faceted Search in Digital Libraries

Golsa Heidari[1]([✉])[iD], Ahmad Ramadan[1][iD], Markus Stocker[1,2][iD],
and Sören Auer[1,2][iD]

[1] L3S Research Center, Leibniz University of Hannover, Hannover, Germany
{golsa.heidari,ramadan}@stud.uni-hannover.de
[2] TIB Leibniz Information Centre for Science and Technology, Hannover, Germany
{markus.stocker,auer}@tib.eu
https://www.uni-hannover.de/
https://www.tib.eu/

Abstract. Scientists always look for the most accurate and relevant answers to their queries in the literature. Traditional scholarly digital libraries list documents in search results, and therefore are unable to provide precise answers to search queries. In other words, search in digital libraries is metadata search and, if available, full-text search. We present a methodology for improving a faceted search system on *structured content* by leveraging a federation of scholarly knowledge graphs. We implemented the methodology on top of a scholarly knowledge graph. This search system can leverage content from third-party knowledge graphs to improve the exploration of scholarly content. A novelty of our approach is that we use dynamic facets on diverse data types, meaning that facets can change according to the user query. The user can also adjust the granularity of dynamic facets. An additional novelty is that we leverage third-party knowledge graphs to improve exploring scholarly knowledge.

Keywords: Knowledge graph · Scholarly knowledge · Information retrieval · Search system · Faceted search · Digital libraries

1 Introduction

A knowledge graph (KG) is a knowledge base that uses a graph-structured data model or topology to combine data [3]. Knowledge graphs are often used to store interlinked information about entities with free-form semantics. In recent years, knowledge graphs have been presented and made publicly available in the scholarly field, in particular bibliographic metadata including information about entities such as publications, authors, and venues [4].

Scholarly Knowledge graphs are knowledge bases for representing scholarly knowledge [11]. If scholarly knowledge graphs represent the key content published in papers about the addressed research problem, employed materials,

G. Berget et al. (Eds.): TPDL 2021, LNCS 12866, pp. 141–152, 2021.
https://doi.org/10.1007/978-3-030-86324-1_18

methods, and obtained results, then accurate information can be retrieved from such graphs to satisfy user queries and questions. Due to the rise of knowledge graph usage among scientists, it is predictable that researchers' method of searching and exploring data is moving in that direction over the next few decades [9,10].

One of the essential applications of scholarly knowledge relies on data retrieval. Various search systems are implemented to help scientists for exploration of accurate data. An example of that is faceted search. Faceted search is a high-efficiency search method with various applications. Faceted search is a method that augments traditional search systems with a faceted exploration system, allowing users to narrow down search results by applying multiple filters based on the classification of the properties [7]. A faceted classification system lists each knowledge component along various dimensions, called facets, facilitating the classifications to be reached and managed in multiple forms. Faceted search is widely implemented on bibliographic metadata. However, on data, i.e. the actual content of a paper, it simply cannot be implemented because this data is not structured properly.

Facets are defined in two categories: Static Facets and Dynamic Facets [14]. Facets in which the values for a facet are taken from a list of predefined values are called static facets. Static facets are useful for categories such as *resource type* that have a limited number of possible values [21]. In contrast, dynamic facets in which the values for each facet category are derived from the values stored in the knowledge graph are flexible [6]. Once the system determines which values to display for each category, it will show the matching items accordingly. This means that facets are not fixed and will be defined while search [2].

The rest of the paper is organized as follows: Sect. 2 describes the background and related work; Sect. 3 illustrates our methodology, proposed conceptual model and workflow for improving dynamic faceted search to explore data in federated knowledge graphs; Sect. 4 describes our implementation of the conceptual model in ORKG[1]; In Sect. 5 we discuss our work and challenges that we faced; In Sect. 6 we propose some directions for future work; Finally, in Sect. 7 we conclude the work with a glance to the future work.

2   Related Work

Search Systems. Nowadays, many databases contribute scholarly knowledge such as papers. Although faceted search is exceptionally beneficial for knowledge retrieval, search engines have used it almost at the level of metadata for the scholarly literature. In some disciplines, people also described content in articles in a structured manner and they have built search systems, but their work is limited to one research field.

Google Scholar[2] is a well-known example that renders a huge number of results fast and most results are not precise to the user information need.

---

[1] Open Research Knowledge Graph.
[2] https://scholar.google.com/.

Although it has a vast database, static facets are just defined on the publishing date and, thus, limited support for refining queries. Furthermore, it does not search the content of a paper. Solely a full-text search on the abstract part of a paper when the full text is available.

Publishers such as IEEE[3] and Springer[4] show better results via their search system. Their search results are more accurate and using facets they can limit a huge number of unwanted papers to a more relevant set. But there are still limitations to their search system. The most prominent is that their database is limited to their publications. Therefore a large number of results would be missed. Moreover, while they offer faceted search, their facets are static and identical for all queries.

TIB portal[5] is a meta catalogue, so it provides more relevant answers to the search. Hence, the results would be more accurate. But the problem of the static facets, however, exists there.

Research on Knowledge Graphs and Search Systems. Most of the scientific discoveries depend on searching and re-using the results of former researchers. Although data and metadata of publications always have been available easily, exploring content of a paper remained inaccessible. Scientists tried to explore how developments in web technology might support that method by implementing semantic improvements to journal articles.

S. Fathalla et al. claim that research contributions must be transparent and comparable. They designated surveys for research fields in a semantic way and introduced a knowledge graph that defines the specific research problems, approaches, implementations and evaluations in a structured and comparable way. They offered an ontology to capture the content of survey papers [5]. D. Poole et al. worked on semantic science. They focused on having machine-accessible scientific theories that can be used in making data comparable [17].

Some researchers extend the current concept of nanopublications—small items of scientific results in RDF description—to expand their application range. Nanopublications have been introduced to make it more findable [12,15].

Y. Tzitzikas et al. introduced features and standards for surveying the products in the area of browsing and exploring RDF/S data sets. They introduced information requirements and structures. They provided a generalization of the main faceted exploration/browsing approaches using a small model including states and transitions between states [20].

Some researchers provide theoretical foundations for faceted search in the context of RDF-based knowledge graphs enhanced with OWL ontology [1]. Others in addition to faceted search implementation, proposed a ranking system to order facets, and filtered the answer size to avoid numerous answers on statistical properties of their data set, as well [13].

---

[3] https://www.ieee.org/.

[4] https://www.springer.com.

[5] https://www.tib.eu/de/.

Shotton et al. published downloadable spreadsheets containing data from within tables and figures and enriched them with information from other articles. They published machine-readable RDF[6] metadata both about the article and about the references it cites [19].

LINDASearch presents a middle ware structure to produce information about some of the Open Linked Data Projects such as DBpedia, GeoNames, Linked-GeoData, FOAF profiles, Global Health Observatory, Linked Movie Database (LinkedMDB) and World Bank Linked Data [18].

The next section briefly describes how implementing a faceted search over scholarly knowledge supports granular refinement of search queries and would leverage federated knowledge graphs.

3   Methodology

The main idea is to work on different data types to leverage faceted search systems on knowledge graphs. The scholarly knowledge graph which is used for the infrastructure of the faceted search system should not only contain the metadata of the publications, but also semantic, machine-readable descriptions of scholarly knowledge [16]. Therefore, the knowledge graph would represent some of the content of a publication in a structured manner using inter-linked properties i.e., *study date, study location, method, approaches, research problem,* etc. Figure 1 shows how some of the information contained in a scholarly article would be defined in a scholarly knowledge graph.

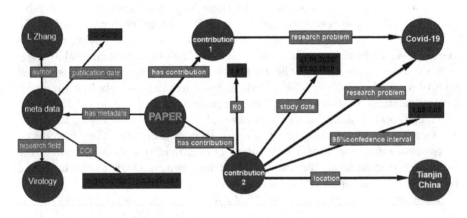

Fig. 1. An example of semantically representing some of the information contained in a paper in a scholarly knowledge graph.

---

[6] Resource Description Framework.

3.1   Exploratory Search

Our search system not only explores the exact data indicated in a paper but also processes some data to narrow down the search results by defining innovative facets. We treat each data type differently. For string data (i.e., properties that have strings for values), a user can select one or more values among all. This is also supported by an auto-complete feature to suggest candidate options. For properties such as *method* and *approach*, all methods used in the papers and all approaches related to them are proposed to the user and can be filtered. For numerical data, users may not only want to filter data by a distinct value but also by a range. Hence, different operators can be selected for the filtering process, specifically greater or smaller than a specific amount. Furthermore, a user can exclude values or even filter data for an interval. Similarly, operators can be applied for values of type date. In addition to including or excluding a date, a duration of a study can be selected as a valid filtering criterion. A date picker is activated on date properties so a user can easily select the date on a calendar.

In order to have smarter facets to better filter the search results for some data types, we need other knowledge graphs' data. Here is the point that exploration will flow from one knowledge graph to another one. For taxonomic data such as location, we search for the hierarchy in a related knowledge graph. Using API, a third-party knowledge graph can be explored to find the hierarchy of that location. Getting the hierarchy, exploration at various levels of a taxonomy can be done. In other words, different levels of facets will define.

3.2   Defining Facets

Facets are defined not only on the metadata of a paper but also on the data, which is essential for each publication. Since facets are defined according to the semantic contribution descriptions for each paper, they are not static and would differ for each query. They are defined dynamically according to the query, and their granularity level can be chosen by the user while querying. For instance, looking for a paper about Covid-19, one would find $R0^7$ amounts as a facet. Such facet would not appear when searching mathematics research contributions. As our focus is on approaching a high-quality search on taxonomic data, these facets are defined in various granularity levels. For instance, *Location* can be explored at the continent level, region level, country level, city level, or even a compound level.

Our system is supporting such dynamic facets, which are inferred automatically from the respective data types and values. Facets can be different for each query, in contrast to other search systems which use just a predefined set of static facets.

---

[7] The basic reproduction number (R0) is the average number of infections produced by a single infectious person in a population with no immunity.

4 Implementation

The Open Research Knowledge Graph (ORKG)[8] is an online resource that semantically represents research *contributions* (from papers) in the form of an interconnected knowledge graph [16]. It provides machine-actionable access to scholarly literature that habitually is written in prose [5], and enables the generation of tabular representations of contributions as *comparisons*. Given described papers and their research contributions, it is possible to compare the contributions addressing a specific problem, across the scholarly literature. Figure 2 shows a comparison in ORKG. We implemented our faceted search system for ORKG comparisons.

Some research contribution descriptions in the ORKG are specified by predefined templates. These templates support the dynamic and automated construction of facets for ORKG comparisons. Facets are defined on the different properties in a comparison.

In order to illustrate how we can leverage other knowledge graphs, we use Geonames[9] for the *Location* property. Each instance of the *Location class* in ORKG has a link to the corresponding resource in the Geonames knowledge graph. Querying Geonames is done via this link. According to its schema, the Geonames knowledge graph offers a variety of relations for the described resources. We are interested in the *parent feature* which annotates the parent entity of any given other entity (i.e., show the hierarchy of locations in Geonames). We propose to implement the solution, using API request to find the hierarchy of the location. Getting the hierarchy, exploration at various levels of a region taxonomy can be done. Figure 3 shows a subset of RDF triples from the Geonames representation of the *City of Bonn* entity indicating the *parent feature* as well. By querying the Geonames graph, the hierarchy of locations can be discovered. After obtaining this hierarchy, the information can be leveraged in a faceted search system to support searching on broader locations and thus support a form of qualitative spatial reasoning[10]. Figure 4 demonstrates the workflow between the ORKG and Geonames knowledge graphs.

For instance, if a user filters a contribution comparison for studies conducted in Europe (e.g., studies involving a European population or an ecosystem in Europe), for each paper's *study location*, our system checks the (RDF) description of the study location in Geonames. After evaluating in the hierarchy, whether the location has Europe in its parent features, the location is shown as a facet. If now a user chooses this facet, the correspondingly matching contribution descriptions would be displayed in the results. Therefore, a query for exploring paper contribution descriptions that refer to a special method of research and have specific values in a specific duration of a particular region, can easily be answered.

---

[8] https://www.orkg.org/orkg/.

[9] https://www.geonames.org.

[10] Hierarchy of Geonames: https://www.geonames.org/export/place-hierarchy.html#hierarchy.

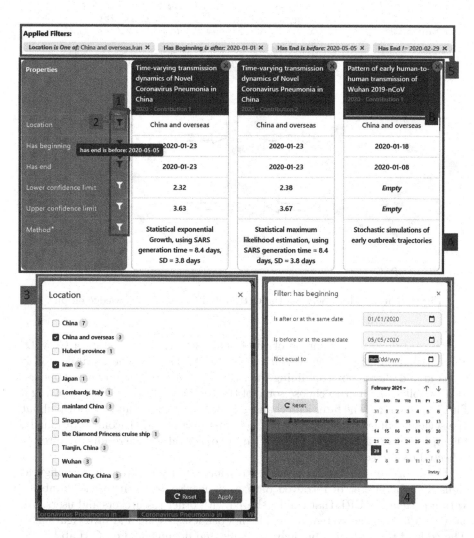

Fig. 2. Comparison and faceted search UI showing a comparison of studies on the COVID-19 reproductive number estimates and corresponding scholarly knowledge managed by the ORKG. The upper part (A) highlights the tabular comparison of the individual contribution descriptions (B) extracted from scientific papers that employ knowledge graph properties shown on the left-most side of box A. Numbered bounding boxes illustrate the search facilities that are available to users. 1) Filter icons to select the value for the properties. 2) Upon clicking a filter icon certain dialogue boxes like (3) or (4) appear. 3) A selection prompt of location candidate facets. 4) A selection prompt of study date facets. Different facet types call for different selection options. 5) Currently activated filters on the comparison.

```
<gn:parentFeature rdf:resource="https://sws.geonames.org/2861876/"/>
<gn:parentCountry rdf:resource="https://sws.geonames.org/2921044/"/>
<gn:parentADM1 rdf:resource="https://sws.geonames.org/2861876/"/>
<gn:parentADM1 rdf:resource="https://sws.geonames.org/2861876/"/>
```

Fig. 3. A subset of RDF triples from the Geonames representation of the *City of Bonn* entity indicating the *parent feature* as well.

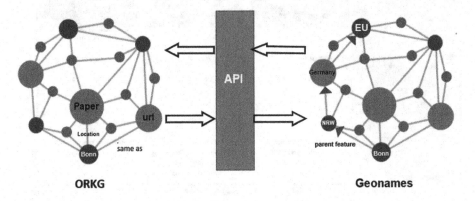

Fig. 4. The workflow between the ORKG and Geonames knowledge graphs.

Figure 2 depicts an example of the faceted search performed on a COVID-19 contribution comparison, which consists of 31 papers. When a filter icon is selected, a dialogue box containing the relevant values for the property appears, thus enabling the user to choose some of the candidate values. When applying a filter, the colour of the filter icon changes to be recognizable, and a tool-tip about the selected values is displayed when hovering over the filter icon. Additionally, all applied filters are indicated clearly on top of the table. The results are directly reflected on the screen.

Furthermore, the system provides the opportunity to save these configurations and the subset of retrieved data as a new comparison to the database, with a permanent URL that can be shared with other researchers and users. We provide a link to the system to enable independent testing and investigation.[11] The code of the system is publicly available and documented on GitLab.[12]

5 Discussion

Faceted search, as a search system, became popular with e-commerce services. During recent years, this search and exploration paradigm was increasingly used for developing scholarly knowledge databases, since it could better filter the search results and support the retrieval of more relevant data. It also improves data findability and reduces null-result searches. However, these benefits are not

---

[11] https://www.orkg.org/orkg/comparisons.
[12] https://gitlab.com/TIBHannover/orkg/orkg-frontend.

enough for a researcher who is looking for knowledge. We discuss next the key factors in evaluating a search system.

Precision matters. The problem with the knowledge graphs mentioned in the related work section is that despite having a huge database, the data indicated in a paper is not searchable. Therefore, scientists mostly would not achieve an accurate and relevant answer to their scientific queries. The key point is that, search on structured content, rather than full text, is likely to result in higher precision. However, it makes formulating queries also more complicated.

Recall is essential. The few knowledge graphs with structured content have limited databases and struggle to satisfy recall (e.g., limited to a particular research field and missing potentially relevant work outside the particular field). Hence, relevant answers to a query may not appear in the results.

Moreover, facets are normally defined on the metadata of a publication. Few knowledge graphs with a limited database defined facets on the content of a paper. Also, the facets are fixed and static and have no flexibility according to the users' query.

While the Scholarly knowledge graph describes papers in a structured manner, the content of each paper is explorable to discover the accurate data related to a search. As the number of contributions described in a knowledge graph increases so does recall.

Our faceted search system leverages a federation of knowledge graphs. That's why the facets are defined dynamically according to the users' query. So the results of a query can be narrowed down into a precise set of answers.

Challenges. What made the problem of faceted search challenging for us are the following points:

- Knowledge graphs are heterogeneous by nature. Different knowledge graphs have different structure. Thus, they are not compatible with a strict search system. Various schemas and APIs make the exploration of federated systems even harder.
- Completeness matters. The more complete the database is, the more data would be discovered. Unfortunately, some well-structured systems suffer from an incomplete data source [8].
- Each paper could be related to one or more research fields. Therefore, finding the appropriate facet according to the user's search expression is challenging.
- Facets which are defined according to the data obtained from other knowledge graphs e.g., *location* facets, could be defined on two different occasions. The first one was during the search process. We could run an API request when a user searches for a location. The advantage of this approach is that the data is current and there is no need to prepare data beforehand. However, the disadvantage is the increase in the response time and the fragility in regard to network connectivity and service availability. The second option is to cache data from the second knowledge graph to allow for faster processing. An important advantage of this approach is better performance. We propose to implement the first approach not to cache unnecessary data.

6   Future Work

For future work, we plan to evaluate the proposed approach with user study (precision and recall), in particular user friendliness. We also plan to leverage more knowledge graphs for even smarter faceted search. We suggest that smart faceting may be defined for numerous data types, e.g., taxonomies, units, space and time, and numeric ranges which we briefly discuss next. Similarly to the approach described here with Geonames locations, for taxonomic data more generally we can leverage corresponding knowledge graphs to obtain hierarchies, e.g., about species, materials, chemicals, ecosystems, language, etc.

Also we plan to integrate a smart unit conversion. For example, if the user is looking for the data in *meter* and the data in the knowledge graph is defined in *kilometre*, an automatic conversion would be applied before processing and displaying the results.

Our focus here was on demonstrating how knowledge graphs can be leveraged to improve faceted search for the special case of qualitative spatial data. In future work, we will extend the approach to quantitative spatial data in order to enable users filtering by regions on a map and support quantitative spatial reasoning in faceted search.

Of interest are also smart faceting on numeric ranges, such as *Confidence Interval (CI)* or types with well-defined boundaries, such as time intervals, pH or degree Kelvin. Smart faceting is aware of such constraints and prompts users accordingly with additional functionality (e.g., filtering by duration) or warnings (e.g., if a given value is invalid such as -300 degrees Kelvin).

Finally, we will explore applying ontologies for resolving the synonyms of the queries and defining facets according to them. For instance, if somebody is looking for the word *covid*, data using synonymous terms such as *corona*, *covid-19*, *sars-cov-2*, etc. should appear in results.

7   Conclusion

Nowadays, knowledge graphs are central to the successful exploitation of knowledge available as a steadily growing amount of digital data on the web. Such technologies are essential to lift traditional search systems from a keyword search to smart knowledge retrieval, which is crucial for obtaining the most relevant answers for a user query, especially in digital libraries. Despite improvements of scholarly search engines, traditional full-text search remains ineffective in many use cases. In this paper, we demonstrate a methodology for developing a faceted search system leveraging a federation of scholarly knowledge graphs. This search system can dynamically integrate content from further remote knowledge graphs to achieve a higher order of exploration usability on scholarly content, which can be matched and filtered to better satisfy user information needs. In future work, we will implement better support for various taxonomies and data types. In addition, we will work on integration query expansion features for discovering abbreviations and synonyms of terms in a query to further improve dynamic faceted search.

Acknowledgements. This work was co-funded by the European Research Council for the project ScienceGRAPH (Grant agreement ID: 819536) and the TIB Leibniz Information Centre for Science and Technology. The authors would like to thank Mohamad Yaser Jaradeh for helpful comments.

References

1. Arenas, M., Grau, B.C., Kharlamov, E., Marciuška, Š, Zheleznyakov, D.: Faceted search over RDF-based knowledge graphs. J. Web Semant. **37**, 55–74 (2016)
2. Basu Roy, S., Wang, H., Das, G., Nambiar, U., Mohania, M.: Minimum-effort driven dynamic faceted search in structured databases. In: Proceedings of the 17th ACM Conference on Information and Knowledge Management, pp. 13–22 (2008)
3. Ehrlinger, L., Wöß, W.: Towards a definition of knowledge graphs. SEMANTiCS (Posters Demos SuCCESS) **48**, 1–4 (2016)
4. Färber, M., Ao, L.: Enhancing the Microsoft academic knowledge graph via author name disambiguation, publication classification, and embeddings
5. Fathalla, S., Vahdati, S., Auer, S., Lange, C.: Towards a knowledge graph representing research findings by semantifying survey articles. In: Kamps, J., Tsakonas, G., Manolopoulos, Y., Iliadis, L., Karydis, I. (eds.) TPDL 2017. LNCS, vol. 10450, pp. 315–327. Springer, Cham (2017). https://doi.org/10.1007/978-3-319-67008-9_25
6. Feddoul, L., Schindler, S., Löffler, F.: Automatic facet generation and selection over knowledge graphs. In: Acosta, M., Cudré-Mauroux, P., Maleshkova, M., Pellegrini, T., Sack, H., Sure-Vetter, Y. (eds.) SEMANTiCS 2019. LNCS, vol. 11702, pp. 310–325. Springer, Cham (2019). https://doi.org/10.1007/978-3-030-33220-4_23
7. Feddoul, L., Schindler, S., Löffler, F.: Semantic relatedness as an inter-facet metric for facet selection over knowledge graphs. In: Hitzler, P., et al. (eds.) ESWC 2019. LNCS, vol. 11762, pp. 47–51. Springer, Cham (2019). https://doi.org/10.1007/978-3-030-32327-1_10
8. Heist, N., Hertling, S., Ringler, D., Paulheim, H.: Knowledge graphs on the web - an overview (2020)
9. Hoffman, M.R., Ibáñez, L.-D., Fryer, H., Simperl, E.: Smart papers: dynamic publications on the blockchain. In: Gangemi, A., et al. (eds.) ESWC 2018. LNCS, vol. 10843, pp. 304–318. Springer, Cham (2018). https://doi.org/10.1007/978-3-319-93417-4_20
10. Jaradeh, M.Y., et al.: Open research knowledge graph: next generation infrastructure for semantic scholarly knowledge. In: Proceedings of the 10th International Conference on Knowledge Capture, pp. 243–246 (2019)
11. Jaradeh, M.Y., Oelen, A., Prinz, M., Stocker, M., Auer, S.: Open research knowledge graph: a system walkthrough. In: Doucet, A., Isaac, A., Golub, K., Aalberg, T., Jatowt, A. (eds.) TPDL 2019. LNCS, vol. 11799, pp. 348–351. Springer, Cham (2019). https://doi.org/10.1007/978-3-030-30760-8_31
12. Kuhn, T., Barbano, P.E., Nagy, M.L., Krauthammer, M.: Broadening the scope of nanopublications. In: Cimiano, P., Corcho, O., Presutti, V., Hollink, L., Rudolph, S. (eds.) ESWC 2013. LNCS, vol. 7882, pp. 487–501. Springer, Heidelberg (2013). https://doi.org/10.1007/978-3-642-38288-8_33
13. Manioudakis, K., Tzitzikas, Y.: Faceted search with object ranking and answer size constraints. ACM Trans. Inf. Syst. (TOIS) **39**(1), 1–33 (2020)

14. Mihindukulasooriya, N., et al.: Dynamic faceted search for technical support exploiting induced knowledge. In: Pan, J.Z., et al. (eds.) ISWC 2020. LNCS, vol. 12507, pp. 683–699. Springer, Cham (2020). https://doi.org/10.1007/978-3-030-62466-8_42

15. Mons, B., Velterop, J.: Nano-publication in the e-science era. In: Workshop on Semantic Web Applications in Scientific Discourse (SWASD 2009), pp. 14–15. sn (2009)

16. Oelen, A., Stocker, M., Auer, S.: Creating a scholarly knowledge graph from survey article tables. In: Ishita, E., Pang, N.L.S., Zhou, L. (eds.) ICADL 2020. LNCS, vol. 12504, pp. 373–389. Springer, Cham (2020). https://doi.org/10.1007/978-3-030-64452-9_35

17. Poole, D., Smyth, C., Sharma, R.: Semantic science: ontologies, data and probabilistic theories. In: da Costa, P.C.G., et al. (eds.) URSW 2005-2007. LNCS (LNAI), vol. 5327, pp. 26–40. Springer, Heidelberg (2008). https://doi.org/10.1007/978-3-540-89765-1_2

18. Sánchez-Cervantes, J.L., Colombo-Mendoza, L.O., Alor-Hernández, G., García-Alcaráz, J.L., Álvarez-Rodríguez, J.M., Rodríguez-González, A.: LINDASearch: a faceted search system for linked open datasets. Wireless Netw. 26(8), 5645–5663 (2020). https://doi.org/10.1007/s11276-019-02029-z

19. Shotton, D., Portwin, K., Klyne, G., Miles, A.: Adventures in semantic publishing: exemplar semantic enhancements of a research article. PLoS Comput. Biol. 5(4), e1000361 (2009)

20. Tzitzikas, Y., Manolis, N., Papadakos, P.: Faceted exploration of RDF/S datasets: a survey. J. Intell. Inf. Syst. 48(2), 329–364 (2017). https://doi.org/10.1007/s10844-016-0413-8

21. Zheng, B., Zhang, W., Feng, X.F.B.: A survey of faceted search. J. Web Eng. 12(1 & 2), 041–064 (2013)

A Comprehensive Extraction of Relevant Real-World-Event Qualifiers for Semantic Search Engines

Guillaume Bernard[(✉)] ⓘ, Cyrille Suire, Cyril Faucher, and Antoine Doucet ⓘ

Université de La Rochelle, Laboratoire L3i, 17000 La Rochelle, France
{guillaume.bernard,cyrille.suire,cyril.faucher,antoine.doucet}@univ-lr.fr
https://l3i.univ-larochelle.fr/

Abstract. In this paper, we present an efficient and accurate method to represent events from numerous public sources, such as Wikidata or more specific knowledge bases. We focus on events happening in the real world, such as festivals or assassinations. Our method merges knowledge from Wikidata and Wikipedia article summaries to gather entities involved in events, dates, types and labels. This event characterization procedure is extended by including vernacular languages. Our method is evaluated by a comparative experiment on two datasets that shows that events are represented more accurately and exhaustively with vernacular languages. This can help to extend the research that mainly exploits hub languages, or biggest language editions of Wikipedia. This method and the tool we release will for instance enhance event-centered semantic search engines, a context in which we already use it. An additional contribution of this paper is the public release of the source code of the tool, as well as the corresponding datasets.

Keywords: Event · Information retrieval · Linked and open data

1 Introduction

Analysing and characterising events in natural language processing has multiple applications. One of them is semantic search engines, used to browse large digital libraries or press articles [1,2,24]. To build an efficient event based query, the event representation and description are crucial. It is necessary to collect exhaustive information from data sources in order to be as precise as possible when qualifying events. This means being able to answer some simple questions, such as where the event happened, and when and who or what was involved [5,25]. The answers to these questions are often named entities [33], and considered as event qualifiers. To the best of our knowledge, the state of the art is missing a method to extract an as comprehensive as possible representation of real-world-events. Research projects often propose their own definition of events and adopt their own representation that fulfill their needs. Reference data sources are numerous and nothing exists to exploit them in a unified way.

© Springer Nature Switzerland AG 2021
G. Berget et al. (Eds.): TPDL 2021, LNCS 12866, pp. 153–164, 2021.
https://doi.org/10.1007/978-3-030-86324-1_19

The purpose of this paper is to overcome these limitations by taking advantage of past experiments and to provide an efficient representation of events by addressing two different issues. We first wish to know how to qualify, in any language, real-world-events based on publicly available resources. Subsequently, we propose an approach to obtain an almost comprehensive event qualification by exploiting vernacular languages, that is to say, the languages spoken where the events happened. We try to demonstrate the most spoken languages are not sufficient to accurately extract event qualifiers and that vernacular languages must be processed as well.

2   Related Work

In the recent years, a lot of publicly available data sources emerged to provide a universal access to multilingual information. A lot of them took benefit from Wikipedia, the largest knowledge base in the history of human kind. Through the years, many ontologies projects aimed at extracting the semantic knowledge of Wikipedia articles. Back in 2007, the DBPedia project [16] was the first knowledge graph (KG) to gather data from Wikipedia articles, infoboxes and lists. Released a few years after, YAGO2 [11] inherits the same characteristics. It is built from Wikipedia and supplemented with WordNet [19] and GeoNames information. YAGO2 is linked to DBPedia entities. A year after, the Wikimedia Foundation unveiled Wikidata [31], a community maintained knowledge graph. This one is used as a reference graph to harmonize content across versions of Wikipedia. Recent projects investigate automatic writing of Wikipedia articles in low endowed Wikipedia linguistic versions [30]. The AbstractWikipedia project aims at solving an automated text generation task from semantic knowledge hosted on Wikidata. This is made possible as Wikidata is one of the highest qualitative multilingual knowledge repository, even if the amount and quality of its knowledge is not always connected to the number of worldwide native speakers [13]. A survey [6] compared these knowledge graphs in terms of quality according to many metrics and gives criteria to find the most suitable graph for the needs of researchers.

None of these graphs is dedicated to events. EventKG [10] fills this gap. It is based on the Simple Event Model [29] (SEM) ontology and intended to store events. SEM focuses on events elementary characteristics: types, dates, locations and participants. It defines a simple model to represent real-world-events. The role of entities associated to events is to point out who, what, where and when the event happened [32]. EventKG aggregates data from multiple sources and connects them in a graph to ensure easy communication through the semantic web. EventKG is good to represent major events such as happenings, festivals and disasters [21].

Characterizing real world events has become an important research issue for a few years. While a lot of work has been made to detect and extract events from news articles [15,17], another trend consists of extracting the semantic knowledge from data sources in order to connect real world events to news and press articles.

This purpose is striven towards the usage for digital libraries by providing for instance semantic or event based search engines to explore historical news [24]. Wikipedia articles lead sections offer qualitative data and give an overall picture of events [21]. They often contain elementary event information: dates, places, and participating entities. The latter have also been used to extract events from real time news, with a particular focus on people, organisations, places and dates when semantically enriching documents [14]. Semantic labeling thanks to Wikidata and Wikipedia [5] has been proven useful in semantic search engines [22] with annotated press articles.

We notice in the state of the art that exploiting Wikidata and Wikipedia entities and elementary event knowledge is useful, especially with specific use cases as exploring digital libraries. We propose to associate Wikidata and Wikipedia to exhaustively collect real-world-event qualifiers which are dates, places and participating entities. Ontologies such as EventKG do not provide comprehensive data, some entities may miss. We propose to collect knowledge where it is: from encyclopedias. On another hand, we know Wikimedia projects are multilingual. Some studies on event mentions tracking suggested to focus on hub languages [23] (languages with a high number of articles and significant overlap in article coverage) to qualify events, we will propose another approach, based on vernacular languages.

3   Representing Events from Wikidata and Wikipedia

At first, we address the first question: we wish to qualify, in any language, real-world-events based on publicly available resources. We present the method we developed to collect event qualifiers from Wikidata and Wikipedia. We consider they both provide sufficient data to characterize real world events. We act in the continuation of the Automated Content Extraction program [3] and existing event ontologies [25,29]. Our event qualifiers are used in the same context as ACE's event arguments. We benefit from Wikidata to extract elementary event information and use Wikipedia to aggregate all the entities involved in it.

3.1   The Extraction of Elementary Event Information

Wikidata supplies two different event identifiers, which point subtleties: some apply for breaking events, others for event with premises. In this paper, we conform to the Wikidata Event Type (WET) [22] definition which accepts both. We refer to events as *happenings in the real world which have spatio-temporal anchors and additional entities involved in it.* From Wikidata entities, we only collect the event type and date, the locations, participants and labels. We consider these properties discriminate two events: it is unlikely that two distinct events have the same label, type, and occurred at the same place at the same time. As a community project, Wikidata is not an exhaustive data source. Table 1 shows that expecting a comprehensive event qualifiers collection is not possible when only capitalizing on Wikidata. For instance, almost all events miss the *involved participant* property.

Table 1. The proportion of WETs with location, date and participants qualifiers. There is a total of 952.351 events.

Named entities category [28]	Wikidata property	Number of events	Percentage
PER[SON]	Participant (*P710*)	58,885	6.18%
DATE	Time (*P585, P580, P582*)	511,312	53.69%
LOC[ATION]	Location (*P7, P276*)	524.532	55.08%

Table 2. Properties of the different language editions of Wikipedia. Sorted by decreasing number of articles (*Data collected in Oct. 2020*).

Language	Articles *in millions*	Modified pages *in thousands*	Contributors	Active contributors	Article depth
English	6.151	1200	386	32	1026.81
German	2.475	241	50	5.5	93.6
French	2.246	280	54	5.1	237.67
Russian	1.657	173	40	3.4	135.94
Italian	1.631	183	44	2.5	169.03
Spanish	1.622	270	87	4.2	208.81
Polish	1425	113	14	1.3	30.99

3.2 Entities Involved in the Event

To go beyond, we propose to analyze Wikipedia lead sections in search of participating entities. A lead section (i.e., a summary) on Wikipedia contains a lot of important information, a synthesis of the article itself and reports the main topic [9]. On Wikipedia, internal links connect articles to Wikidata. We use Wikipedia lead section internal links to detect entities involved in the event. We assume it is possible to add time, location and participant information, when they are absent from Wikidata.

There are, in April 2021, 310 active language editions of Wikipedia. First, and in the interest of efficiency, we presume we can only focus on some languages with the most articles, hub languages (Table 2). In addition to the number of articles, we included the number of modified pages, of contributors (and active ones) and the Wikipedia article depth [8]. The latter is a Wikipedia article quality indicator based on content edits. From the top-ten language list, Cebuano (2nd), Swedish (3rd) and Dutch (6th) are mainly bot written and therefore excluded. In case of conflict, the higher Wikipedia depth, the higher priority. We decided to arbitrarily select five languages. Following the criteria mentioned earlier, we kept English, German, French, Italian and Spanish, covering native languages of 30% of the world's population [4] and 25.14% of all Wikipedia articles (14.125 [7] over 56.615 million articles). We suppose this set of Wikipedia editions is sufficient to accurately gather event qualifiers. Nevertheless, this selection is biased and excludes most Asian and African languages with large speaker communities, as Mandarin and Hindi, whose Wikipedia versions are smaller. They respectively gather 1.120 billion and 128 thousands of articles [7].

From articles lead sections, we keep people, locations and organisations or geopolitical entities. The number of occurrences found for each entity in all lead sections is counted and represents the entity weight in relation to the event. This weight shows the relevance of the entity in relation to the event. We assume the entities found in multiple lead sections are important entities in the event description.

Let us take the example of the *assassination of Rasputin* event on Wikidata (identified by *Q2882749*). From Wikidata, we retain the date, locations, participants and entity labels in multiple languages. We ignore, for the time being, other properties associated with the event type, such as the *target* for a *political assassination*. Participants and locations are linked entities and identified by their URIs in the ontology. We supplement the event characterization with entities found in Wikipedia articles. There only exists Wikipedia articles written in French and Spanish for this event. After processing, we obtain, among others, these triples: *(PER, Q312997 [Felix Yusupov, perpetrator], 3), (PER, Q43989 [Grigori Rasputin, target], 2), (PER, Q34266 [Stanislas Lazovert], 1)*. The weights, respectively 3, 2 and 1 show that *Yusupov* is a major player in the event, while *Lavozert* has a limited implication, even if he is a known plotter. Weights synthesize historical knowledge and give an unbiased information about entities implication in the event. The *Lavozert* entity is absent from Wikidata and was extracted from the French lead section.

3.3 Localizing Event Qualifiers

The event description consists of an association of absolute properties such as the date and labels with links to knowledge bases. The description is fundamentally multi-lingual. In most cases, Wikidata provides multiple names in different languages (*i.e.* with different spellings) for each entity. To continue with the previous example, in French the entity *Q312997* on Wikidata is equally written *Félix Youssoupoff* or *Felix Youssoupov*.

This final step transforms abstract entities, identified by their Wikidata URIs to a language-dependent description. It takes all the alternative spellings for every entity involved in the event and saves them in the targeted language. Our approach makes it possible to get the event description in Italian even if, in this example, only French and Spanish Wikipedias were analyzed.

3.4 Conclusion

In this section, we proposed a method to characterize real-world events with qualifiers. Our method relies on the Wikidata ontology and Wikipedia to extract all the event participating entities. Our approach is multi-lingual: entities are identified by URIs but can be turned into any existing language. By selecting a subset of all the available Wikipedia languages, we assume we can efficiently collect most of the event entities. With this paper, we release the wikivents tool[1]

---

[1] The package is a Python 3 library called wikivents on Pypi.org and available on the Software Heritage repository at https://archive.softwareheritage.org/swh:1:dir: ef325a054ba6f7eb1121807da7b1c92b9ecde8f8.

that implements the method described in this section. It is able to automatically extract the event representation and participating entities with a Wikidata identifier as input. The package can be customized in order to gather data from other resources, out of Wikimedia projects. More information about its API and tutorials are available in the project archive.

4   Enhancing the Event Representation with Vernacular Languages

Although we introduced in Sect. 3 our method to collect most of the event qualifiers, the arbitrary selection of some hub languages is biased. Widely spoken languages that are less present on Wikipedia are ignored. Numerous languages (*i.e.* Arabic, Mandarin, Hindi, Bengali, Portuguese or Russian) are concerned. We intend to discover whether the language influences the event representation when processing Wikipedia articles. To answer this second question, we propose to extend the list of processed languages with vernacular languages.

In this section, we carry out a comparative experiment to know how useful and pertinent it is to benefit from vernacular language when processing Wikipedia articles. First, we introduce the dataset we built, then the evaluation process and our results. We conclude with a short error analysis.

4.1   Datasets Description

Selected Events. In order to compare the influence of language, we built two distinct datasets with the same events. As the nature of an event is ambiguous [27], we qualify of indisputable an event that is considered as such for people with various backgrounds (history scholars [26], psychologists [20] or NLP reseachers [18], for instance). This led us to restrict events to only three categories, taken as examples: assassinations and attacks, natural disasters and political happenings. On Wikidata, the first two concern breaking events while the last gathers events with premisses. We randomly selected two event types for each category.

- **Assassination and attacks**: political murder (*Q1139665*) and terrorist attack (*Q2223653*).
- **Natural disasters**: earthquake (*Q7944*) and volcanic eruption (*Q7692360*).
- **Political happenings**: ceremony (*Q2627975*) and election (*Q40231*).

We express the same reserve about the exhaustiveness of Wikidata. The number of events reported is not uniform over the years but tends to grow since the beginning of the 21st century. This increase must not be interpreted as an increase of events happening in the world but as a better data quality, especially with events now better anchored in time [22]. Therefore, we decided to only focus on events happening in the last fifty years, from January 1970 to December 2019. This ensures to exclude poorly documented events. For the sake of the experiment, it is necessary to process events which are described in at

Table 3. The number and ratio of events with at least one Wikipedia article in any language (even not a hub language), from 1970 to 2019.

Category	Event type	Events	With an article	Ratio
Assassinations and attacks	Political murder	44	24	54.55%
	Terrorist attack	905	806	89.06%
Natural disasters	Earthquake	1,102	987	89.56%
	Volcanic eruption	23	18	78.26%
Political happenings	Ceremony	11,428	11,233	98.29%
	Election	29,236	24.488	82.10%

least one Wikipedia article. Thus, we exclude events without any articles. The number of found events is reported in Table 3.

The process of gathering participating entities described in Sect. 3 may be slow for some events. It produces numerous API calls and can take from a few seconds to a significant amount of time depending on the number of lead sections to be processed. Consequently, we randomly select a maximum of fifty events for every event type. Selected events all satisfy the previously mentioned requirements: they have a date property and at least one related article.

Vernacular Languages. The difference between the two datasets resides in the number of languages processed to gather participating entities. The first one is called "base language" and built from the five languages mentioned above. We call the other one "all languages" for which vernacular languages are processed in addition to those from the base dataset. In case a Wikipedia project in this language is missing, we fall back to its standard dialect. For instance, American English is "en-us" which does not exist on Wikipedia, but is a dialect of "en".

This process introduces another bias: temporality. French was an official language in Algeria before 1950. This information is missing from Wikidata which only provides current information. Moreover, the ontology sometimes provides the languages spoken in the countries, including the non official ones. We state the hypothesis that if an event occurs somewhere, the event will be better reported on Wikipedia in one of the languages spoken where it happened.

It may happen that the political entity changed through the years: the Easter Rising occurred in the *United Kingdom of Great Britain and Ireland*. This country does no longer exist, as the current *United Kingdom* exists since 1922. This is not an issue as Wikidata still informs about official or spoken languages. In any case, our dataset comprises events from 1970 to 2019, which limits this risk.

Table 4. The four metrics for the selected languages about the assassination of JFK.

Characteristic	Language				
	Italian	Spanish	German	English	French
M1: participating entities in the lead section	40	42	13	**47**	35
M2: tokens found in the lead section	218	125	179	**316**	279
M3: ratio between the two previous metrics	0.183	**0.336**	0.073	0.149	0.125
M4: alternative names for each Wikidata entity	83	130	166	**224**	115

Conclusion. With this paper, we release the datasets we built.[2,3] They comprise 241 events divided up among six events types, in three categories. The first dataset is produced with selected languages, the other with selected and vernacular languages. Events were processed using the `wikivents` tool we described in Sect. 3. For each of them, we also provide the content of the lead section that was used to extract entities and we saved each event in all the processed languages to simplify any further analysis.

4.2 Experimental Metrics

The comparison between the two datasets is based on four metrics we consider as relevant to evaluate our hypothesis: processing vernacular languages on Wikipedia supplies additional and more precise information about participating entities. Metrics respectively are the number of participating entities found in the lead section of Wikipedia articles (**M1**), the number of tokens in the lead section, to the exclusion of tokens shorter than two characters (**M2**), the ratio between the two previous metrics (**M3**) and the number of alternative names found for each Wikidata entity, as mentioned in Sect. 3.3 (**M4**).

Table 4 records the results for the assassination of John Fitzgerald Kennedy in 1963. As the assassination took place in the USA, an English speaking country, no additional language gets processed in addition to the five default ones. We notice the English version of Wikipedia provides more information about this event. More entities are found in the lead section, the lead section length is longer and we have more alternative names in English than in order languages.

In a second phase, languages are sorted in decreasing order, the higher value in Table 4, the first. Sorts for this events are shown in Table 5 and demonstrate the English version of Wikipedia is the most accurate to describe the event participating entities. English is in first place in terms of participating entities, tokens and number of alternative names found. The ratio is sometimes erroneous due to the different writing styles adopted by the multiple language Wikipedia communities. This may explain why Spanish is in first place for this metric.

---

[2] The dataset is hosted on Zenodo: https://doi.org/10.5281/zenodo.4733506.

[3] Available on the Software Heritage repository at https://archive.softwareheritage.org/swh:1:dir:ef325a054ba6f7eb1121807da7b1c92b9ecde8f8.

Table 5. Ranked languages that best represent the assassination of JFK

Characteristic	1st	2nd	3rd	4th	5th
Participating entities	**en**	es	it	fr	de
Tokens in the lead section	**en**	fr	it	de	es
Ratio	es	it	**en**	fr	de
Alternative names	**en**	de	es	fr	it

Table 6. Number of events excluded because of a missing spoken language, or because of missing Wikipedia articles.

Event type	Events	Without spoken language given	Without article	
			Base language	*All languages*
Political murder	24	0	1	0
Terrorist attack	50	13	5	2
Earthquake	50	11	17	11
Volcanic eruption	17	1	3	2
Ceremony	50	29	9	6
Election	50	10	11	2

4.3 Experiment Evaluation

Although when building the dataset in Sect. 4.1 we excluded events without any Wikipedia article, it may happen that some selected events do not exist on Wikipedia in any of the processed languages. They were not filtered out in the first step because they have at least an article, but written in a language which is not a hub or a vernacular language, which we were unaware of at the first step. It is also a necessity to exclude events for which we do not know either any official or spoken language. The two overlap in most cases. We report in Table 6 the number of events excluded by this final selection. When considering vernacular languages, the number of events to analyze increases. This is the first argument in favour of our hypothesis that events are better described in their vernacular languages.

In order to compare the description of events in the two datasets, we apply, for each event, the same computations as shown in Table 4 and Table 5. For each metric, we check whether one of the official languages spoken in the event place is in the best three languages to characterize it. Results shown in Table 7 show, for each metric, for how many events a vernacular language is in the top three of language that best represent the event. Results are significant with only the first language but selecting the best third languages tends to limit the issue described with the Kennedy's assassination example. By doing so, we state that the five languages we previously identified as core languages are not sufficient to accurately extract event qualifiers. This statement refutes the hypothesis we assumed in Sect. 3 that led us to only consider only five hub languages.

162   G. Bernard et al.

Table 7. Comparison of how many events are better described by a vernacular language. The top-three languages that best represent the event are taken into account.

Event type	Dataset	Number of events	Events better described by a vernacular language			
			M1: entities	M2: tokens	M3: ratio	M4: alt. names
Political murder	Base	23	14	14	13	12
	All		22	22	20	18
Terrorist attacks	Base	34	25	25	25	27
	All		30	30	29	28
Earthquake	Base	25	13	13	12	11
	All		24	24	23	20
Volcanic eruption	Base	14	12	12	12	12
	All		13	13	13	13
Ceremony	Base	18	12	13	13	15
	All		15	15	15	17
Election	Base	31	27	27	26	26
	All		30	30	29	26

4.4 Error Analysis

For the majority of events that contradict the hypothesis, the main reason is a lack of resources in the vernacular languages: we miss Wikipedia articles so cannot extract any lead section. Missing articles are due to a small community of speakers and then results in a small Wikipedia edition or may be explained by cultural bias. The latter is mainly true for assassination and attacks events which are treated, or not, differently in the Wikipedia language editions. For few events, the vernacular language is in fourth position or even further away and is not the best at representing the given event.

We mainly processed Indo-European languages for which the tokenization procedure is quite uniform, then comparable. This is a noticeable limit of our analysis regarding some of our metrics.

5 Conclusion

In this paper, we described a method to gather event qualifiers coming from Wikidata and Wikipedia. We analysed and described its shortcomings and proposed to include vernacular languages. Our experiments demonstrate that this approach is greatly beneficial when describing events. We release an implementation of our approaches, and actually hereby make publicly available the source code, the analysis as well as the datasets, to be updated regularly. In the near future, we will add features to encode the event model into SEM [29] or LODE [25]. Researchers working on real-world events may already take advantage of our tool to fulfil their needs. It can be used to qualify events for their semantic search engines. We already use the library as the entry point of an event based search engine for a historical news digital library. It uses the event representation from the `wikivents` library in order to forge queries to retrieve documents associated to events [12].

References

1. Brank, J., Leban, G., Grobelnik, M.: Semantic annotation of documents. Informatica **42**, 23–32 (2017)
2. Cybulska, A.K., Vossen, P.: Historical event extraction from text. In: Proceedings of the 5th ACL-HLT Workshop on Language Technology for Cultural Heritage, Social Sciences, and Humanities, Portland, Oregon, USA, pp. 39–43, June 2011. https://www.aclweb.org/anthology/W11-1506
3. Doddington, G., Mitchell, A., Przybocki, M., Ramshaw, L., Strassel, S., Weischedel, R.: The Automatic Content Extraction (ACE) program. Tasks, data and evaluation. In: Proceedings of the Fourth International Conference on Language Resources and Evaluation (LREC 2004), Lisbon, Portugal, pp. 837–840, May 2004. http://www.lrec-conf.org/proceedings/lrec2004/pdf/5.pdf
4. Eberhard, D.M., Simons, G.F., Fennig, C.D.: Ethnologue: Languages of the World (2021). https://www.ethnologue.com/
5. Exner, P., Nugues, P.: Using semantic role labeling to extract events from Wikipedia. In: DeRiVE@ ISWC, pp. 38–47 (2011)
6. Färber, M., Bartscherer, F., Menne, C., Rettinger, A.: Linked data quality of DBpedia, Freebase, OpenCyc, Wikidata, and YAGO. Semantic Web **9**(1), 77–129 (2017). https://doi.org/10.3233/SW-170275
7. The Wikimedia Foundation: List of Wikipedias. Wikipedia, April 2021. https://en.wikipedia.org/w/index.php?title=List_of_Wikipedias&oldid=1016309550
8. The Wikimedia Foundation: Wikipedia article depth - Meta, April 2021. https://meta.wikimedia.org/wiki/Wikipedia_article_depth
9. The Wikimedia Foundation: Wikipedia: Summary style. Wikipedia, April 2021. https://en.wikipedia.org/w/index.php?title=Wikipedia:Summary_style&oldid=1015628666
10. Gottschalk, S., Demidova, E.: EventKG - the hub of event knowledge on the web - and biographical timeline generation. Semantic Web **10**(6), 1039–1070 (2019). https://doi.org/10.3233/SW-190355
11. Hoffart, J., Suchanek, F.M., Berberich, K., Weikum, G.: YAGO2: a spatially and temporally enhanced knowledge base from Wikipedia. Artif. Intell. **194**, 28–61 (2013). https://doi.org/10.1016/j.artint.2012.06.001
12. Jean-Caurant, A., Doucet, A.: Accessing and investigating large collections of historical newspapers with the Newseye platform. In: Proceedings of the ACM/IEEE Joint Conference on Digital Libraries in 2020, pp. 531–532 (2020)
13. Kaffee, L.A., Piscopo, A., Vougiouklis, P., Simperl, E., Carr, L., Pintscher, L.: A glimpse into babel: an analysis of multilinguality in Wikidata. In: Proceedings of the 13th International Symposium on Open Collaboration - OpenSym 2017, Galway, Ireland, pp. 1–5 (2017). https://doi.org/10.1145/3125433.3125465
14. La Fleur, A., Teymourian, K., Paschke, A.: Complex event extraction from realtime news streams. In: Proceedings of the 11th International Conference on Semantic Systems, Vienna Austria, pp. 9–16, September 2015. https://doi.org/10.1145/2814864.2814870
15. Leban, G., Fortuna, B., Brank, J., Grobelnik, M.: Event registry: learning about world events from news. In: Proceedings of the 23rd International Conference on World Wide Web - WWW 2014 Companion, Seoul, Korea, pp. 107–110 (2014). https://doi.org/10.1145/2567948.2577024
16. Lehmann, J., et al.: DBpedia – a large-scale, multilingual knowledge base extracted from Wikipedia. Semantic Web **6**(2), 167–195 (2015). https://doi.org/10.3233/SW-140134

17. Mele, I., Bahrainian, S.A., Crestani, F.: Event mining and timeliness analysis from heterogeneous news streams. Inf. Process. Manage. **56**(3), 969–993 (2019). https://doi.org/10.1016/j.ipm.2019.02.003

18. Mele, I., Crestani, F.: A multi-source collection of event-labeled news documents. In: Proceedings of the 2019 ACM SIGIR International Conference on Theory of Information Retrieval - ICTIR 2019, Santa Clara, CA, USA, pp. 205–208 (2019). https://doi.org/10.1145/3341981.3344253

19. Miller, G.A.: WordNet: a lexical database for English. Commun. ACM **38**(11), 3 (1995)

20. Minsky, M.: A framework for representing knowledge. The Psychology of Computer Vision (1975)

21. Mishra, A., Berberich, K.: EXPOSÉ: exploring past news for seminal events. In: Proceedings of the 24th International Conference on World Wide Web - WWW 2015 Companion, Florence, Italy, pp. 223–226 (2015). https://doi.org/10.1145/2740908.2742844

22. Rudnik, C., Ehrhart, T., Ferret, O., Teyssou, D., Troncy, R., Tannier, X.: Searching news articles using an event knowledge graph leveraged by Wikidata. In: Companion Proceedings of The 2019 World Wide Web Conference on - WWW 2019, San Francisco, USA, pp. 1232–1239 (2019). https://doi.org/10.1145/3308560.3316761

23. Rupnik, J., Muhic, A., Leban, G., Skraba, P., Fortuna, B., Grobelnik, M.: News across languages - cross-lingual document similarity and event tracking. J. Artif. Intell. Res. **55**, 283–316 (2016). https://doi.org/10.1613/jair.4780

24. Shaw, R.: A semantic tool for historical events. In: Proceedings of the The 1st Workshop on EVENTS: Definition, Detection, Coreference, and Representation, Atlanta, Georgia, USA, pp. 38–46, June 2013

25. Shaw, R., Troncy, R., Hardman, L.: LODE: linking open descriptions of events. In: Gómez-Pérez, A., Yu, Y., Ding, Y. (eds.) ASWC 2009. LNCS, vol. 5926, pp. 153–167. Springer, Heidelberg (2009). https://doi.org/10.1007/978-3-642-10871-6_11

26. Shaw, R.B.: Events and periods as concepts for organizing historical knowledge. Ph.D. thesis, UC Berkeley (2010). https://escholarship.org/uc/item/4111f1fw

27. Sprugnoli, R.: Event detection and classification for the digital humanities. Ph.D. thesis, Università degli Studi di Trento, Trento, Italia, April 2018. http://eprints-phd.biblio.unitn.it/2865/

28. Sundheim, B.M.: Overview of results of the MUC-6 Evaluation. In: Proceedings of the 6th Conference on Message Understanding, pp. 13–31, November 1995. https://doi.org/10.3115/1072399.1072402

29. van Hage, W.R., Malaisé, V., Segers, R., Hollink, L., Schreiber, G.: Design and use of the Simple Event Model (SEM). J. Web Semant. **9**(2), 128–136 (2011). https://doi.org/10.1016/j.websem.2011.03.003

30. Vrandečić, D.: Architecture for a multilingual Wikipedia. arXiv:2004.04733 [cs], April 2020. http://arxiv.org/abs/2004.04733

31. Vrandečić, D., Krötzsch, M.: Wikidata: a free collaborative knowledgebase. Commun. ACM **57**(10), 78–85 (2014). https://doi.org/10.1145/2629489

32. Xiang, W., Wang, B.: A survey of event extraction from text. IEEE Access **7**, 173111–173137 (2019). https://doi.org/10.1109/ACCESS.2019.2956831

33. Yadav, V., Bethard, S.: A survey on recent advances in named entity recognition from deep learning models. In: Proceedings of the 27th International Conference on Computational Linguistics, p. 14, August 2018

Citation Recommendation for Research Papers via Knowledge Graphs

Arthur Brack[1](✉)(iD), Anett Hoppe[1](✉)(iD), and Ralph Ewerth[1,2](✉)(iD)

[1] TIB – Leibniz Information Centre for Science and Technology, Hannover, Germany
{arthur.brack,anett.hoppe,ralph.ewerth}@tib.eu
[2] L3S Research Center, Leibniz University Hannover, Hannover, Germany

Abstract. Citation recommendation for research papers is a valuable task that can help researchers improve the quality of their work by suggesting relevant related work. Current approaches for this task rely primarily on the text of the papers and the citation network. In this paper, we propose to exploit an additional source of information, namely research knowledge graphs (KGs) that interlink research papers based on mentioned scientific concepts. Our experimental results demonstrate that the combination of information from research KGs with existing state-of-the-art approaches is beneficial. Experimental results are presented for the STM-KG (STM: Science, Technology, Medicine), which is an automatically populated knowledge graph based on the scientific concepts extracted from papers of ten domains. The proposed approach outperforms the state of the art with a mean average precision of 20.6% (+0.8) for the top-50 retrieved results.

Keywords: Information retrieval · Research knowledge graph · Research paper citation recommendation

1 Introduction

Citations are a core part of research articles as they enable the reader to position the novel contribution in the scientific context. Moreover, relating own contributions with relevant research via references can also improve visibility. In consequence, it is in the interest of authors to provide complete and high-quality citation links to existing research. However, this task becomes ever more complicated since the number of published research articles has been growing exponentially in the recent years [5].

Consequently, the recommendation of suitable references for a piece of scientific writing is an important task to (a) improve the quality of future publications, (b) help authors and reviewers to point out additional relevant related work, and (c) discover interesting links to other areas of research. Färber and Jatowt [14] distinguish between *local citation recommendation* which aims to provide citations for a short passage of text, and *global citation recommendation* which uses

© Springer Nature Switzerland AG 2021
G. Berget et al. (Eds.): TPDL 2021, LNCS 12866, pp. 165–174, 2021.
https://doi.org/10.1007/978-3-030-86324-1_20

the documents' full text or abstract as the input. Here, we focus on the task of global citation recommendation.

Current best-performing approaches for global citation recommendation [4,9,32] leverage primarily the articles' text and the citation network as information sources. In this paper, we explore another source of information, that is the set of scientific concepts which are mentioned in the article. The assumptions are (1) that additionally to the article's text, these provide condensed evidence to the described problem statement, used methodology or evaluation metrics, and (2) that research papers which should be citing each other usually share a similar set of concepts. Consequently, we investigate whether research KGs interconnecting research papers based on the mentioned scientific concepts are instrumental in improving citation recommendation. For this purpose, we propose an approach which combines automatically extracted scientific concepts from the research articles with existing approaches for citation recommendation. The approach is evaluated on a KG that has been automatically populated from papers of ten scientific domains [6]. The experimental results demonstrate that our proposed approach consistently improves the state of the art with a MAP@50 (mean average precision of top-50 results) of 20.6% (+0.8). To facilitate further research, we release all our corpora and source code: https://github.com/arthurbra/citation-recommendation-kg.

The remaining of the paper is organised as follows: Sect. 2 reviews existing research KGs and approaches for citation recommendation. In Sect. 3 we describe our proposed approach. The experimental setup and results are reported in Sect. 4 and 5, while Sect. 6 concludes the paper and outlines future work.

2   Related Work

Here, we briefly review research KGs and approaches for citation recommendation.

2.1   Research Knowledge Graphs

Various KGs interlink research papers through metadata (e.g. authors, venues) and citations [13,22], or through research artefacts (e.g. datasets) [1,23]. Other initiatives organise scientific knowledge in a structured manner with community effort, such as Gene Ontology [10], WikiData [28] with encyclopaedic knowledge, or Papers With Code [24] and Open Research Knowledge Graph [16] for research contributions.

Furthermore, various KGs have been populated automatically from research articles. Computer Science Ontology (CSO) is a taxonomy for computer science research areas [27]. Kannan et al. [19] create a multimodal KG for deep learning papers from text and images and the corresponding source code. The AI-KG has been generated from 333,000 research papers in the field of artificial intelligence (AI) [11]. It contains five concept types (*tasks, methods, metrics, materials, others*) linked by 27 relations types. The COVID-19 KG [30] has been populated from the Covid-19 Open Research Dataset [29] and contains various biological concept entities. Brack et al. [6] generate a KG for ten science domains with the concept types *material, method, process,* and *data*.

2.2   Citation Recommendation

In the following, we outline recent approaches for global citation recommendation. For local recommendation, we refer to the survey of Färber and Jatowt [14].

Bhagavatula et al. [4] propose a neural network-based document embedding model to retrieve candidate documents for a query document via similarity search [18] and a ranking model to rerank the top-k candidates. The document embedding model is trained via a triplet loss with the papers' abstract and title using a Siamese architecture. It learns a high cosine similarity between embeddings of papers citing each other. The reranker estimates the probability that a query document should cite a candidate document using the abstract, title, and optional metadata (e.g. author, venue) as features. Cohan et al. [9] propose a document embedding model named SPECTER (Scientific Paper Embeddings using Citationinformed TransformERs). It is trained with an approach similar to Bhagavatula et al. [4]. However, they use a BERT encoder [12] pre-initialised with SciBERT embeddings [3]. Furthermore, Cohan et al. omit the reranking step and obtain the ranked results directly via the document embeddings' cosine similarity.

Graph-based approaches learn document embeddings via graph convolution networks on the citation graph [15,20,31]. However, they require the citation network also at inference time. Other approaches [7,17,32] frame citation recommendation as a binary classification task: given a query and a candidate paper, the model learns to predict whether the query paper should cite the candidate paper. The models learn rich relationships between the contents of the two documents via various cross-document attention mechanisms. However, in contrast to the document embedding models [4,9], such binary classification models can not be used for retrieval but only for reranking the top k results, since a query paper has to be compared with all other documents [8].

To the best of our knowledge, approaches for citation recommendation that exploit KGs with scientific concepts have not been proposed yet.

3   Citation Recommendation via a Research Knowledge Graph

As the discussion of related work shows citation recommendation approaches have not exploited research KGs yet. To leverage research KGs, we propose an approach to combine document embeddings learned from textual content and the citation graph together with scientific concepts mentioned in the document.

Let $KG = (D, E, V)$ be a KG, D the set of documents, E the set of concepts, $V \subseteq D \times E$ the set of links between papers and concepts, and $E_d \subseteq E$ the set of concepts mentioned in a paper $d \in D$. Let $one\_hot(e_i) \in \mathbb{R}^{|E|}$ be the one-hot vector for concept e_i in which the i-th component equals 1 and all remaining components are 0. Now, we construct the *concept vector* $c_d \in \mathbb{R}^{|E|}$ for a paper $d \in D$ as follows:

$$c_d = \sum_{e_i \in E_d} one\_hot(e_i) \qquad (1)$$

Furthermore, let s_d be a document embedding of a paper d obtained via an existing document embedding model (e.g. SPECTER [9]). The *vector representation* $\vec{d}$ of a paper d is the concatenation of the concept vector c_d and the document embedding s_d:

$$\vec{d} = [c_d, s_d] \qquad (2)$$

For a query paper $q \in D$ the task is to retrieve the top k results such that papers to be cited appear at the top of the list. We use cosine similarity for retrieval and ranking where $\vec{q}$ for the query paper q is constructed in the same way as $\vec{d}$ for a paper d:

$$rank(q, d) = \cos(\vec{q}, \vec{d}) = \frac{\vec{q}^{\mathsf{T}} \cdot \vec{d}}{||\vec{q}|| \cdot ||\vec{d}||} \qquad (3)$$

4   Experimental Setup

In this section, we describe the experimental setup, i.e. the used benchmark dataset, baseline approaches, and the evaluation procedure.

Benchmark Dataset: Existing benchmark datasets for research paper citation recommendation (e.g. [4,9,22]) do not provide a research KG that interlinks papers with scientific concepts. Therefore, we use the STM-KG [6] as our benchmark dataset whose characteristics are depicted in Table 1. It has been populated from 55,485 abstracts in ten different scientific, technical, and medical domains and comes in two variants: (1) in-domain KG that shares scientific concepts only between papers of the same domain to avoid ambiguity of scientific terms (e.g. neural network in medicine vs. computer science), and (2) cross-domain KG that shares scientific concepts also between domains.

The KG contains 15,395 citation links within the KG in total, of which 2,200 citation links are across papers from different domains. For evaluation, analogous to related work [4,9], we use only papers that cite at least four papers within the KG which results in 720 query documents and 4,069 citations links. In contrast to Cohan et al. [9], we pursue a realistic approach like Bhagavatula et al. [4], i.e. we retrieve top-k documents from *all* documents in the corpus instead of using predefined candidate sets of 30 documents (5 cited and 25 uncited papers) for each query document.

Baseline Approaches: We compare our approach with two simple (1 & 2) and three strong baselines (3, 4 & 5):

1. **Random:** We use randomly initialised document embeddings with dimension 200.
2. **Concept vector:** Only the concept vector is used for ranking (see Eq. 1).

Table 1. Characteristics of the STM-KG [6] per domain in terms of number of abstracts, the number of citation links within the KG, and the number of scientific concepts in the cross-domain and in-domain KG. The number of concepts used across multiple domains are denoted as MIX. The domains are: Agriculture (Agr), Astronomy (Ast), Biology (Bio), Chemistry (Che), Computer Science (CS), Earth Science (ES), Engineering (Eng), Materials Science (MS), Mathematics (Mat), and Medicine (Med).

	Agr	Ast	Bio	CS	Che	ES	Eng	MS	Mat	Med	MIX	Total
# abstracts	7,731	15,053	11,109	1,216	1,234	2,352	3,049	2,258	665	10,818	–	55,485
# citations	1,670	1,853	1,347	171	151	477	677	375	65	2,116	–	15,395
Cross-domain KG												
KG concepts	138,342	173,027	177,043	20,474	21,298	62,674	55,494	39,211	9,275	227,690	70,044	994,572
In-domain KG												
KG concepts	180,135	197,605	229,201	30,736	32,191	81,584	78,417	55,358	14,567	278,686	–	1,178,480

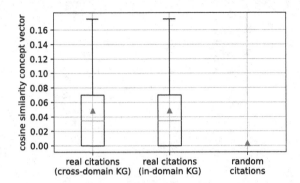

Fig. 1. Boxplot for cosine similarities between concept vectors of papers citing each other (15,395 links) for cross-domain and in-domain KG, respectively, and papers citing random papers (15,395 links). The green triangles depict the mean values. (Color figure online)

3. **GloVe:** Document embedding of a paper is the average of GloVe [25] word embeddings obtained from the abstract of the paper.
4. **SciBERT:** Document embedding is also the average of the contextual word embeddings obtained from the abstract of the paper via SciBERT [3] that is based on BERT [12] and has been pre-trained on scientific text. It has demonstrated superior performance in various downstream tasks on research papers [3].
5. **SPECTER:** Document embedding is obtained via SPECTER [9] from the title and the abstract. The SPECTER model has been trained on the textual content and the citation graph of research papers, and is the current state of the art.

To compute GloVe and SciBERT document embeddings, we use the *sentence transformers* library [26]. For SPECTER we use the implementation of Cohan et al. [9].

Evaluation: To evaluate the quality of the ranking results for the top k citation recommendations, we use *Mean Average Precision* (MAP@k) [2, 21] as in related work [9]. MAP@k is the mean of the *Average Precision at k* (AP@k) scores over the query documents. The metric AP@k assumes that a user is interested in finding many relevant documents and is thus an appropriate evaluation metric for citation recommendation:

$$AP@k(q) = \frac{\sum_{k'=1}^{k} Precision@k'(q) \cdot rel(k')}{\# \text{ relevant documents for } q} \tag{4}$$

Precision@k is the fraction of relevant documents among the top k retrieved documents, and $rel(k)$ equals 1 if the document at position k is relevant, 0 otherwise.

Table 2. Experimental results (in percent) for citation recommendation with random vectors, only the concept vector as well as document embeddings obtained from GloVe, SciBERT and SPECTER with and without using the concept vector.

	MAP@10	MAP@20	MAP@50
Random	0.0	0.0	0.0
Concept vector (cross-domain KG)	7.5	8.0	8.5
Concept vector (in-domain KG)	8.1	8.7	9.3
– Material	3.7	4.1	4.4
– Process	3.6	3.9	4.2
– Data	1.9	2.1	2.2
– Method	1.1	1.2	1.4
GloVe	9.1	10.0	10.8
GloVe + concept vector (cross-domain KG)	11.4 (+2.3)	12.5 (+2.5)	13.4 (+2.6)
GloVe + concept vector (in-domain KG)	11.3 (+2.2)	12.5 (+2.5)	13.5 (+2.7)
SciBERT	10.2	11.5	12.6
SciBERT + concept vector (cross-domain KG)	12.1 (+1.9)	13.3 (+1.8)	14.4 (+1.8)
SciBERT + concept vector (in-domain KG)	11.9 (+1.7)	13.2 (+1.7)	14.4 (+1.8)
SPECTER	16.5	18.3	19.8
SPECTER + concept vector (cross-domain KG)	16.9 (+0.4)	18.9 (+0.6)	20.5 (+0.7)
SPECTER + concept vector (in-domain KG)	**17.0** (+0.5)	**19.0** (+0.7)	**20.6** (+0.8)

5 Results and Discussion

The boxplots in Fig. 1 depict the distribution of cosine similarities of concept vectors between citing and non-citing papers. It can be seen that papers citing each other have on average a higher cosine similarity than papers not citing each other. This underlines our hypothesis that papers citing each other share a common set of scientific concepts.

Table 2 shows the results of the evaluated approaches. Using only the concept vectors for ranking outperforms the random baseline noticeably. When using only certain concept types (i.e. *process, method, material,* or *data*), we can observe that *material* and *process* concept types contribute most to the results. However, using all concept types together yields the best results.

Baseline ranking approaches via document embeddings learned from the text (GloVe and SciBERT), or text and the citation graph (SPECTER) outperform the ranking only via concept vectors noticeably, while SPECTER performs best as expected. This indicates that concept vectors alone do not contain enough information for the task of citation recommendation. However, our proposed approach combining document embeddings and concept vectors consistently improves all baseline approaches. For SPECTER, the in-domain KG yields slightly better results than the cross-domain KG. However, in our error analysis we found out that concept vectors from the cross-domain KG provide more accurate rankings for cross-domain citations.

Our results indicate that the exploitation of a research KG as an additional source of information can improve the task of citation recommendation.

6   Conclusions

In this paper, we have investigated whether an automatically populated research KG can enhance the task of citation recommendation. For this purpose, we have combined document embeddings that have been learned from text and the citation graph together with concept vectors representing scientific concepts mentioned in a paper. The experimental results demonstrate that the concept vectors provide meaningful features for the task of citation recommendation. In future work, we plan to evaluate our approach on further datasets and develop approaches that can learn document embeddings jointly from text, the citation graph, *and* the research KG. Another possible direction of future research is to optimise for particular research fields.

References

1. Aryani, A., Wang, J.: Research graph: building a distributed graph of scholarly works using research data switchboard. In: Open Repositories CONFER-ENCE (2017). https://doi.org/10.4225/03/58c696655af8a. https://figshare.com/articles/Research_Graph_Building_a_Distributed_Graph_of_Scholarly_Works_using_Research_Data_Switchboard/4742413
2. Bassani, E.: Rank_eval: blazing fast ranking evaluation metrics in python (2021). https://github.com/AmenRa/rank_eval
3. Beltagy, I., Lo, K., Cohan, A.: SciBERT: a pretrained language model for scientific text. In: Inui, K., Jiang, J., Ng, V., Wan, X. (eds.) Proceedings of the 2019 Conference on Empirical Methods in Natural Language Processing and the 9th International Joint Conference on Natural Language Processing, EMNLP-IJCNLP 2019, Hong Kong, China, 3–7 November 2019, pp. 3613–3618. Association for Computational Linguistics (2019). https://doi.org/10.18653/v1/D19-1371
4. Bhagavatula, C., Feldman, S., Power, R., Ammar, W.: Content-based citation recommendation. In: Walker, M.A., Ji, H., Stent, A. (eds.) Proceedings of the 2018 Conference of the North American Chapter of the Association for Computational Linguistics: Human Language Technologies, NAACL-HLT 2018, New Orleans, Louisiana, USA, 1–6 June 2018, Volume 1 (Long Papers), pp. 238–251. Association for Computational Linguistics (2018). https://doi.org/10.18653/v1/n18-1022
5. Bornmann, L., Mutz, R.: Growth rates of modern science: a bibliometric analysis based on the number of publications and cited references. J. Assoc. Inf. Sci. Technol. **66**(11), 2215–2222 (2015). https://doi.org/10.1002/asi.23329
6. Brack, A., Müller, D.U., Hoppe, A., Ewerth, R.: Coreference resolution in research papers from multiple domains. In: Hiemstra, D., Moens, M.-F., Mothe, J., Perego, R., Potthast, M., Sebastiani, F. (eds.) ECIR 2021. LNCS, vol. 12656, pp. 79–97. Springer, Cham (2021). https://doi.org/10.1007/978-3-030-72113-8_6
7. Caciularu, A., Cohan, A., Beltagy, I., Peters, M.E., Cattan, A., Dagan, I.: Cross-document language modeling. CoRR abs/2101.00406 (2021). https://arxiv.org/abs/2101.00406

8. Chang, W., Yu, F.X., Chang, Y., Yang, Y., Kumar, S.: Pre-training tasks for embedding-based large-scale retrieval. In: 8th International Conference on Learning Representations, ICLR 2020, Addis Ababa, Ethiopia, 26–30 April 2020. OpenReview.net (2020). https://openreview.net/forum?id=rkg-mA4FDr
9. Cohan, A., Feldman, S., Beltagy, I., Downey, D., Weld, D.S.: SPECTER: document-level representation learning using citation-informed transformers. In: Jurafsky, D., Chai, J., Schluter, N., Tetreault, J.R. (eds.) Proceedings of the 58th Annual Meeting of the Association for Computational Linguistics, ACL 2020, Online, 5–10 July 2020, pp. 2270–2282. Association for Computational Linguistics (2020). https://doi.org/10.18653/v1/2020.acl-main.207
10. Consortium, T.G.O.: The gene ontology resource: 20 years and still going strong. Nucleic Acids Res. **47**(Database-Issue), D330–D338 (2019). https://doi.org/10.1093/nar/gky1055
11. Dessì, D., Osborne, F., Reforgiato Recupero, D., Buscaldi, D., Motta, E., Sack, H.: AI-KG: an automatically generated knowledge graph of artificial intelligence. In: Pan, J.Z., et al. (eds.) ISWC 2020, Part II. LNCS, vol. 12507, pp. 127–143. Springer, Cham (2020). https://doi.org/10.1007/978-3-030-62466-8_9
12. Devlin, J., Chang, M., Lee, K., Toutanova, K.: BERT: pre-training of deep bidirectional transformers for language understanding. In: Burstein, J., Doran, C., Solorio, T. (eds.) Proceedings of the 2019 Conference of the North American Chapter of the Association for Computational Linguistics: Human Language Technologies, NAACL-HLT 2019, Minneapolis, MN, USA, 2–7 June 2019, Volume 1 (Long and Short Papers), pp. 4171–4186. Association for Computational Linguistics (2019). https://doi.org/10.18653/v1/n19-1423
13. Färber, M.: The microsoft academic knowledge graph: a linked data source with 8 billion triples of scholarly data. In: Ghidini, C., et al. (eds.) ISWC 2019, Part II. LNCS, vol. 11779, pp. 113–129. Springer, Cham (2019). https://doi.org/10.1007/978-3-030-30796-7_8
14. Färber, M., Jatowt, A.: Citation recommendation: approaches and datasets. Int. J. Digit. Libr. **21**(4), 375–405 (2020). https://doi.org/10.1007/s00799-020-00288-2
15. Hamilton, W.L., Ying, Z., Leskovec, J.: Inductive representation learning on large graphs. In: Guyon, I., et al. (eds.) Advances in Neural Information Processing Systems 30: Annual Conference on Neural Information Processing Systems 2017, Long Beach, CA, USA, 4–9 December 2017, pp. 1024–1034 (2017). https://proceedings.neurips.cc/paper/2017/hash/5dd9db5e033da9c6fb5ba83c7a7ebea9-Abstract.html
16. Jaradeh, M.Y., Oelen, A., Prinz, M., Stocker, M., Auer, S.: Open research knowledge graph: a system walkthrough. In: Doucet, A., Isaac, A., Golub, K., Aalberg, T., Jatowt, A. (eds.) TPDL 2019. LNCS, vol. 11799, pp. 348–351. Springer, Cham (2019). https://doi.org/10.1007/978-3-030-30760-8_31
17. Jiang, J., Zhang, M., Li, C., Bendersky, M., Golbandi, N., Najork, M.: Semantic text matching for long-form documents. In: Liu, L., et al. (eds.) The World Wide Web Conference, WWW 2019, San Francisco, CA, USA, 13–17 May 2019, pp. 795–806. ACM (2019). https://doi.org/10.1145/3308558.3313707
18. Johnson, J., Douze, M., Jégou, H.: Billion-scale similarity search with GPUS. CoRR abs/1702.08734 (2017). http://arxiv.org/abs/1702.08734
19. Kannan, A.V., et al.: Multimodal knowledge graph for deep learning papers and code. In: d'Aquin, M., Dietze, S., Hauff, C., Curry, E., Cudré-Mauroux, P. (eds.) CIKM 2020: The 29th ACM International Conference on Information and Knowledge Management, Virtual Event, Ireland, 19–23 October 2020, pp. 3417–3420. ACM (2020). https://doi.org/10.1145/3340531.3417439

20. Kipf, T.N., Welling, M.: Semi-supervised classification with graph convolutional networks. In: 5th International Conference on Learning Representations, ICLR 2017, Toulon, France, 24–26 April 2017, Conference Track Proceedings. OpenReview.net (2017). https://openreview.net/forum?id=SJU4ayYgl
21. Liu, L., Özsu, M.T. (eds.): Mean Average Precision, p. 1703. Springer, Boston (2009). https://doi.org/10.1007/978-0-387-39940-9_3032
22. Lo, K., Wang, L.L., Neumann, M., Kinney, R., Weld, D.S.: S2ORC: the semantic scholar open research corpus. In: Jurafsky, D., Chai, J., Schluter, N., Tetreault, J.R. (eds.) Proceedings of the 58th Annual Meeting of the Association for Computational Linguistics, ACL 2020, Online, 5–10 July 2020, pp. 4969–4983. Association for Computational Linguistics (2020). https://doi.org/10.18653/v1/2020.acl-main.447
23. Manghi, P., et al.: The openaire research graph data model, April 2019. https://doi.org/10.5281/zenodo.2643199
24. Papers with code. https://paperswithcode.com/. Accessed 10 Apr 2021
25. Pennington, J., Socher, R., Manning, C.D.: Glove: global vectors for word representation. In: Moschitti, A., Pang, B., Daelemans, W. (eds.) Proceedings of the 2014 Conference on Empirical Methods in Natural Language Processing, EMNLP 2014, Doha, Qatar, 25–29 October 2014, A meeting of SIGDAT, a Special Interest Group of the ACL, pp. 1532–1543. ACL (2014). https://doi.org/10.3115/v1/d14-1162
26. Reimers, N., Gurevych, I.: Sentence-BERT: sentence embeddings using Siamese BERT-networks. In: Inui, K., Jiang, J., Ng, V., Wan, X. (eds.) Proceedings of the 2019 Conference on Empirical Methods in Natural Language Processing and the 9th International Joint Conference on Natural Language Processing, EMNLP-IJCNLP 2019, Hong Kong, China, 3–7 November 2019, pp. 3980–3990. Association for Computational Linguistics (2019). https://doi.org/10.18653/v1/D19-1410
27. Salatino, A.A., Thanapalasingam, T., Mannocci, A., Birukou, A., Osborne, F., Motta, E.: The computer science ontology: a comprehensive automatically-generated taxonomy of research areas. Data Intell. **2**(3), 379–416 (2020). https://doi.org/10.1162/dint_a_00055
28. Vrandecic, D., Krötzsch, M.: Wikidata: a free collaborative knowledgebase. Commun. ACM **57**(10), 78–85 (2014). https://doi.org/10.1145/2629489
29. Wang, L.L., et al.: CORD-19: the COVID-19 open research dataset. CoRR abs/2004.10706 (2020). https://arxiv.org/abs/2004.10706
30. Wise, C., et al.: COVID-19 knowledge graph: accelerating information retrieval and discovery for scientific literature. CoRR abs/2007.12731 (2020). https://arxiv.org/abs/2007.12731
31. Wu, F., Souza, A., Zhang, T., Fifty, C., Yu, T., Weinberger, K.Q.: Simplifying graph convolutional networks. In: Chaudhuri, K., Salakhutdinov, R. (eds.) Proceedings of the 36th International Conference on Machine Learning, ICML 2019, Long Beach, California, USA, 9–15 June 2019. Proceedings of Machine Learning Research, vol. 97, pp. 6861–6871. PMLR (2019). http://proceedings.mlr.press/v97/wu19e.html
32. Zhou, X., Pappas, N., Smith, N.A.: Multilevel text alignment with cross-document attention. In: Webber, B., Cohn, T., He, Y., Liu, Y. (eds.) Proceedings of the 2020 Conference on Empirical Methods in Natural Language Processing, EMNLP 2020, Online, 16–20 November 2020, pp. 5012–5025. Association for Computational Linguistics (2020). https://doi.org/10.18653/v1/2020.emnlp-main.407

AnnoTag: Concise Content Annotation via LOD Tags derived from Entity-Level Analytics

Amit Kumar(✉) and Marc Spaniol(✉)

Department of Computer Science, Université de Caen Normandie,
Campus Côte de Nacre, 14032 Caen Cedex, France
{amit.kumar,marc.spaniol}@unicaen.fr

Abstract. Digital libraries build on classifying contents by capturing their semantics and (optionally) aligning the description with an underlying categorization scheme. This process is usually based on human intervention, either by the content creator or a curator. As such, this procedure is highly time-consuming and - thus - expensive. In order to support the human in data curation, we introduce an annotation tagging system called "AnnoTag". AnnoTag aims at providing concise content annotations by employing entity-level analytics in order to derive semantic descriptions in the form of tags. In particular, we are generating "Semantic LOD Tags" (linked open data) that allow an interlinking of the derived tags with the LOD cloud. Based on a qualitative evaluation on Web news articles we prove the viability of our approach and the high-quality of the automatically extracted information.

Keywords: Data curation · Linked open data · Entity-level analytics

1 Introduction

Tagging is a widely adopted and popular method of content classification [14], e.g., in cataloging books online[1] or for classifying Web news articles[2]. Its success can be summarized by its simplicity as well as due to its intuitive human interpret-ability. Nevertheless, the main drawback is the required effort in creating the annotations. In parallel automatically generated knowledge bases knowledge (KBs) such as DBpedia [1] or YAGO [17] have been developed. Conceptually, these approaches are located on the other side of the "spectrum". Here, information are highly structured and based on a predefined ontology. From an annotation point of view this implies that data annotation is very concise, but requires a non-negligible expertise about the underlying ontology.

In order to bridge the gap between both worlds we introduce AnnoTag: a system that provides automatically generated concise content annotation via LOD

---

[1] LibraryThing Tags https://blog.librarything.com/main/category/tags/.
[2] BBC Tags https://www.bbc.co.uk/blogs/aboutthebbc/tags.

© Springer Nature Switzerland AG 2021
G. Berget et al. (Eds.): TPDL 2021, LNCS 12866, pp. 175–180, 2021.
https://doi.org/10.1007/978-3-030-86324-1_21

tags derived from entity-level analytics. For that purpose, AnnoTag addresses two problems at the same time: it provides concise human-interpretable content annotations by simultaneously providing links with semantic concepts of the LOD cloud.

2   Related Work

Semantic content annotation has been widely investigated in the digital libraries (DL), information retrieval (IR) and natural language processing (NLP) communities [13]. In the following, we give an overview on those approaches that offer public interfaces for automatic content annotation. GoNTogle [2,6] generates semantic annotation of the document based on the ACM ontology classes. WebAnno [3], ANNIE [4] and GATE [5] are tools that support annotation such as tokenization, named entity recognition, part-of-speech tagging and semantic tagging of annotated entities, but do not provide type-specific content annotation with links to the LOD cloud. Open Calais [16] and AIDA [10] mainly focus on named entity recognition and disambiguation, but are not suitable for concise document annotation. STICS [8], however, supports semantic retrieval via named entities, but does not provide typed annotations. TagTheWeb [15] and CALVADOS [7] aim at generating semantic fingerprints of Web documents for analysis and comparison, only. Semantator [18] serves for the conversion of text to linked data in the biomedical domain.

Annotations by the approaches mentioned before are either highly application specific (e.g. limited to a specific domain) or extremely generic (i.e. part-of-speech tags or named entities). In contrast, our approach is generally applicable (no domain constraints by employing YAGO as a general purpose knowledge base) and concise (focus on the most relevant type(s) derived from entity-level analytics) at the same time. Furthermore, we provide the annotation as an RDF file in order to allow a seamless linkage via sameAS links with the LOD cloud.

3   Conceptual Approach

In the following, we introduce the conceptual approach of AnnoTag. Figure 1 presents the four consecutive stages in the annotation pipeline of AnnoTag employing state-of-the approaches in named entity disambiguation and concise entity classification. The first step is the document upload (cf. ① in Fig. 1). Here, we allow either the provisioning of a URL or a set of documents to be uploaded to the server for subsequent processing. In the second step, we derive the document's semantics from the named entities contained. In order to do so, we utilize the named entity disambiguation tool AIDA [10] (cf. ② in Fig. 1). As a result, we obtain the canonicalized named entities in YAGO [9,17] and a plenitude of information about them contained in the KB via the computation of the transitive closure. For instance, there are 42 types for *Emmanuel Macron* or 14 for the *European Banking Authority (EBA)* stored in YAGO. In order to ensure a highly concise tagging, we focus on the most "representative" type(s) only. To this end, we employ as a third step the PURE (Pattern Utilization for Representative Entity type classification) framework [11] (cf. ③ in Fig. 1), which builds upon more than 300 types structured by the 5 top-level types from the YAGO ontology. By doing so, we derive the most representative types of each named entity. In a final step (cf. ④ in Fig. 1), the LOD Tags are generated. These tags are generated in RDF and provide a reference of each representative type in DBpedia and YAGO. As a result, the document can now be linked to the LOD cloud and the underlying ontology may be used for a fine-grained classification.

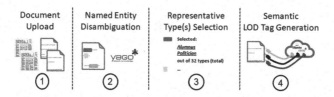

Fig. 1. Conceptual approach of the AnnoTag pipeline

4 Demonstration

4.1 AnnoTag Demonstration

The AnnoTag demo presents the concise annotation of documents with semantic LOD tags. Figure 2 depicts the steps of the AnnoTag demonstration. Figure 2a shows the initial interface for document upload (cf. step ① in Fig. 1). Here, a choice can be made between uploading a local file to the server and providing a URL. In addition, two configurations can be chosen: an annotation with LOD tags (only) or an annotation with LOD tags including the named entities. After that, the document is processed and the named entities contained are identified by employing AIDA [10] (cf. step ② in Fig. 1). The result of this process is then shown as an overview (cf. Fig. 2b). Subsequently, the concise tags per entity are extracted, for which we employ our PURE framework [11]. Figure 2c shows the obtained types in the AnnoTag user interface. Finally, the semantic LOD tags are generated and exported as RDF triples (cf. step ④ in Fig. 1). An example excerpt of a resulting document is highlighted in Fig. 3. It can be observed, that the RDF triples provide links of the assigned concise types to the LOD cloud, in particular, to the corresponding concepts in YAGO and (exploiting the sameAs link also directly to) DBpedia. The overall process including a demonstration video, live demonstrator and the assessed documents can be found at the AnnoTag Website[3].

4.2 Evaluation

We assessed AnnoTag through a comparative qualitative and quantitative analysis of the automatically generated semantic LOD tags (cf. [12] for details).

---

[3] AnnoTag Website https://spaniol.users.greyc.fr/research/AnnoTag/.

(a) AnnoTag User Interface for Document Upload

(b) Listing of the Named Entities   (c) Concise Types per Entity

Fig. 2. Steps of the AnnoTag demonstration

```
<My_Document_123> <http://www.w3.org/2000/01/rdf-schema#member> <capital>.
<My_Document_123> <http://www.w3.org/2000/01/rdf-schema#member> <company>.
...
<capital> <http://www.w3.org/2002/07/owl#sameas> yago3:<wordnet_capital_108518505>.
<capital> <http://www.w3.org/2002/07/owl#sameas> <http://dbpedia.org/class/yago/Capital108518505>.
<company> <http://www.w3.org/2002/07/owl#sameas> yago3:<wordnet_company_108058098>.
<company> <http://www.w3.org/2002/07/owl#sameas> <http://dbpedia.org/class/yago/Company108058098>.
```

Fig. 3. Excerpt of a file annotated by AnnoTag

We report here our qualitative results on Precision and Mean Reciprocal Rank (MRR), which are "de facto standards" measures in information retrieval. The study was performed by utilizing a large data set[4] consisting of 3,824 articles for annotation. Out of the aforementioned documents, we drew a random sample of 50 documents and performed manually an individual assessment (accessible via the AnnoTag Website) based on a three-level grading scheme (2: "highly concise annotation(s)", 1: "concise annotation(s)", 0: "unsuitable annotation(s)"). Based on these evaluations, we computed the following measures:

---

[4] Harvard Dataverse News Articles https://doi.org/10.7910/DVN/GMFCTR.

1) "Hard" Precision: $2 \rightsquigarrow$ relevant, 1 or $0 \rightsquigarrow$ irrelevant
2) "Soft" Precision: 2 or $1 \rightsquigarrow$ relevant, $0 \rightsquigarrow$ irrelevant
3) "Emulated" MRR: $2 \rightsquigarrow 1^{st}$ rank, score $= 1$
$\qquad\qquad\qquad 1 \rightsquigarrow 2^{nd}$ rank, score $= 0.5$
$\qquad\qquad\qquad 0 \rightsquigarrow$ no rank, score $= 0$

The evaluation results are summarized in Table 1. AnnoTag shows very good performance for both, Precision and emulated MRR. In particular, the results of "Soft" Precision achieve 92%. Considering the fact, that the automatically generated semantic tags are supposed to be used as an assistance in a (semi-) automatic data curation process involving a human curator, the remaining annotation errors might be easily corrected while saving valuable human time and labor due to the high quality of the automatically generated annotations.

Table 1. Qualitative assessment over 50 randomly sampled documents

Measure	Score
"Hard" Precision	0.72
"Soft" Precision	0.92
"Emulated" MRR	0.82

References

1. Auer, S., Bizer, C., Kobilarov, G., Lehmann, J., Cyganiak, R., Ives, Z.: DBpedia: a nucleus for a web of open data. In: ISWC/ASWC, pp. 722–735 (2007)
2. Bikakis, N., Giannopoulos, G., Dalamagas, T., Sellis, T.: Integrating keywords and semantics on document annotation and search. In: Meersman, R., Dillon, T., Herrero, P. (eds.) OTM 2010. LNCS, vol. 6427, pp. 921–938. Springer, Heidelberg (2010). https://doi.org/10.1007/978-3-642-16949-6_19
3. Eckart de Castilho, R., et al.: A web-based tool for the integrated annotation of semantic and syntactic structures. In: Proceedings of the Workshop on Language Technology Resources and Tools for Digital Humanities (LT4DH), pp. 76–84. The COLING 2016 Organizing Committee, Osaka (2016). https://www.aclweb.org/anthology/W16-4011
4. Cunningham, H., Maynard, D., Bontcheva, K., Tablan, V.: GATE: a framework and graphical development environment for robust NLP tools and applications. In: Proceedings of the 40th Anniversary Meeting of the Association for Computational Linguistics (ACL'02) (2002)
5. Cunningham, H., et al.: Text Processing with GATE (Version 6) (2011). http://tinyurl.com/gatebook
6. Giannopoulos, Giorgos, Bikakis, Nikos, Dalamagas, Theodore, Sellis, Timos: GoNTogle: a tool for semantic annotation and search. In: Aroyo, Lora, et al. (eds.) ESWC 2010. LNCS, vol. 6089, pp. 376–380. Springer, Heidelberg (2010). https://doi.org/10.1007/978-3-642-13489-0_27

7. Govind, Kumar, A., Alec, C., Spaniol, M.: CALVADOS: a tool for the semantic analysis and digestion of web contents. In: Proceedings of the 16th Extended Semantic Web Conference (ESWC 2019), Portorož, Slovenia, 2–6 June, pp. 84–89 (2019)
8. Hoffart, J., Milchevski, D., Weikum, G.: STICS: searching with strings, things, and cats, p. 1247–1248 (2014). https://doi.org/10.1145/2600428.2611177
9. Hoffart, J., Suchanek, F.M., Berberich, K., Weikum, G.: YAGO2: a spatially and temporally enhanced knowledge base from Wikipedia. Artif. Intell. **194**, 28–61 (2013)
10. Hoffart, J., et al.: Robust disambiguation of named entities in text. In: Conference on Empirical Methods in Natural Language Processing, Edinburgh, Scotland, UK, pp. 782–792 (2011)
11. Kumar, A., Govind, Alec, C., Spaniol, M.: Blogger or president? Exploitation of patterns in entity type graphs for representative entity type classification. In: Proceedings of the 12th International ACM Web Science Conference (WebSci '20), pp. 59–68 (2020)
12. Kumar, A., Spaniol, M.: Semantic tagging via entity-level analytics: assessment of concise content tagging. In: Proceedings of the 25th International Conference on Theory and Practice of Digital Libraries (TPDL 2021), 8 p. (2021, to appear)
13. Liao, X., Zhao, Z.: Unsupervised approaches for textual semantic annotation, a survey. ACM Comput. Surv. **52**(4), 66:1–66:45 (2019). https://doi.org/10.1145/3324473
14. Macgregor, G., McCulloch, E.: Collaborative tagging as a knowledge organisation and resource discovery tool. Libr. Rev. **55**(5), 291–300 (2006)
15. Medeiros, J.F., Pereira Nunes, B., Siqueira, S.W.M., Portes Paes Leme, L.A.: TagTheWeb: using Wikipedia categories to automatically categorize resources on the web. In: Gangemi, A., et al. (eds.) ESWC 2018. LNCS, vol. 11155, pp. 153–157. Springer, Cham (2018). https://doi.org/10.1007/978-3-319-98192-5_29
16. REFINITIV: Open Calais. http://www.opencalais.com (2021). Accessed 26 Apr 2021
17. Suchanek, F.M., Kasneci, G., Weikum, G.: YAGO: a core of semantic knowledge unifying WordNet and Wikipedia. In: 16th International World Wide Web Conference (WWW 2007), pp. 697–706. ACM (2007)
18. Tao, C., Song, D., Sharma, D.K., Chute, C.G.: Semantator: semantic annotator for converting biomedical text to linked data. J. Biomed. Inform. **46**(5), 882–893 (2013). https://doi.org/10.1016/j.jbi.2013.07.003

SmartReviews: Towards Human- and Machine-Actionable Reviews

Allard Oelen[1,2]([✉]) [iD], Markus Stocker[2] [iD], and Sören Auer[1,2] [iD]

[1] L3S Research Center, Leibniz University of Hannover, Hannover, Germany
oelen@l3s.de
[2] TIB Leibniz Information Centre for Science and Technology, Hannover, Germany
{markus.stocker,soeren.auer}@tib.eu

Abstract. Review articles summarize state-of-the-art work and provide a means to organize the growing number of scholarly publications. However, the current review method and publication mechanisms hinder the impact review articles can potentially have. Among other limitations, reviews only provide a snapshot of the current literature and are generally not readable by machines. In this work, we identify the weaknesses of the current review method. Afterwards, we present the *SmartReview* approach addressing those weaknesses. The approach pushes towards semantic community-maintained review articles. At the core of our approach, knowledge graphs are employed to make articles more machine-actionable and maintainable.

Keywords: Article authoring · Knowledge graphs · Living documents · Review articles · Scholarly communication

1 Introduction

The number of published scholarly articles remains to grow steadily [5]. Scholarly communication mainly relies on document-based methods, often using PDF files to communicate and share knowledge. This traditional document-based communication method has several limitations either caused by the PDF format itself or by the document-based approach in general [7]. We distinguish research articles and review articles. The former presents original research contributions while the latter reviews contributions from other work [18]. Review articles, in particular, are severely limited in their scope and reach due to the static nature of publications. They give extensive overviews of research for a particular domain, but do so merely for a period of time up to when the review is conducted. Because of the static nature of published articles, updating reviews is either cumbersome or not possible at all [11,19]. This results in review articles being outdated soon after they are published, especially in research domains that face rapid (technology) evolution. In this work, we reimagine scholarly publishing for reviews by presenting a collaborative and community-maintained approach that aims to address the limitations and weaknesses of document-based communication.

© Springer Nature Switzerland AG 2021
G. Berget et al. (Eds.): TPDL 2021, LNCS 12866, pp. 181–186, 2021.
https://doi.org/10.1007/978-3-030-86324-1_22

At the core of our approach, we leverage knowledge graphs for representing content of articles in a semantic machine-actionable manner. The approach and its main concepts are summarized in Fig. 1. A prototype of the approach is implemented in the Open Research Knowledge Graph (ORKG) [4] and is available online[1]. In summary, this work makes the following research contributions: (i) Analysis of the limitations and weaknesses of the current review method. (ii) Presentation of the SmartReview concept and approach to address the limitations.

Fig. 1. Overview of key concepts of the SmartReview approach. Review articles are built on top of a knowledge graph.

2   Weaknesses of Current Approach

The current approach of authoring and publishing review articles has multiple weaknesses. The weaknesses are identified based on previous work, in particular from [12].

Lacking Updates. Once an article is published, it is generally not updated [9]. This is caused either by lacking incentives from the author's perspective or due to technical limitations. For most research articles, this is acceptable. After all, if new results are available, it provides an opportunity to publish a new article building upon previous work. However, specifically for review articles this implies that the articles are outdated soon after they are published.

Lacking Collaboration. Reviews include research articles created by numerous authors. With the current review method, only the viewpoint of the review authors is considered and not from the community as a whole. This potentially imposes biases and hinders the objectiveness of the discussion of the reviewed work. Schmidt et al. found that a considerable amount of evaluated narrative review articles for the medical domain was severely biased [13].

---

[1] https://www.orkg.org/orkg/smart-reviews.

Limited Coverage. Authoring review articles is a resource intensive activity, which is generally more cumbersome than writing a research article [18]. Therefore, reviews are often only conducted for relatively popular domains and are lacking for less popular domains. Since review articles are an important factor for the development of research domains [17], the lack of review articles can potentially hinder the evolution of a domain.

Lacking Machine-Actionability. The most frequently used format for publishing scholarly articles is PDF, which is hard to process for machines [6]. PDF files focus on visual presentation specifically designed for human consumption. Nowadays, machine consumption of PDF files relies on machine learning techniques and is often limited to parsing the article's metadata [8,10].

Limited Accessibility. Documents published in PDF format are often inaccessible to readers with disabilities [1]. PDF documents focus on the visual representation of documents instead of a structured representation, which hinders accessibility [3].

Lacking Overarching Systematic Representation. Generally, there is no systematic representation of concepts used in articles, which means scholarly publishing does not use related web technologies to their full potential [15]. This has several implications and potentially causes redundancy and ambiguity across scholarly articles.

3 The SmartReview Approach

Based on the identified weaknesses, we devise the SmartReview approach and determine its six definitorial dimensions. Each dimension presents system requirements that define how the dimension is addressed. Requirements are formulated using the FunctionalMASTeR template [16].

Article Updates. It should be possible to update review articles once published, resulting in "living" documents [14]. The individual versions should be citable and it should be clear which version of the article is cited. Additionally, readers should be able to see which parts of the articles have changed across versions. Based on these criteria, we formulate the following requirements:

R1 SmartReviews shall provide researchers the ability to update articles.
R2 SmartReviews shall persist all versions of published articles.
R3 SmartReviews shall provide researchers with the ability to compare different versions of the same article (i.e., diff view).

Collaboration. To fully support community collaboration for review articles, they should be editable by anyone within the community. To ensure no work is getting lost (e.g., removed by another author), it should be possible to go back in time and compare different versions (as described in R3).

R4 SmartReviews shall provide any researcher with the ability to contribute to articles.

R5 SmartReviews shall list all contributors in the acknowledgements.

Coverage. To increase the review coverage for less popular domains, the entry barrier for creating and updating SmartReviews should be low (related to R4). SmartReviews can be created even if only a limited amount of articles are reviewed. This is achieved by decoupling publishing (i.e., peer-reviewed publishing in a journal or conference) and authoring of articles.

R6 SmartReviews shall provide researchers with the ability to create articles without the need for an a priori peer review.

Machine-Actionability. In order to improve machine-actionability, a systematic and structured representation in a knowledge graph should be used for knowledge representation. The resources defined within the knowledge graph serve as building blocks to create the article. This structured data is supplemented by natural text sections. To improve machine-actionability, natural text sections are complemented by types describing their contents.

R7 SmartReviews shall use a knowledge graph as data source for articles.

R8 SmartReviews shall semantically type and structure natural language text sections.

R9 SmartReviews shall provide machine-actionable formats (i.e., RDF, JSON-LD).

Accessibility. Most accessibility issues originate from the PDF format in which most articles are published. By publishing the articles in HTML instead, the article is already more accessible. Furthermore, by adhering to the Web Content Accessibility Guidelines (WCAG) [2], the accessibility is further improved.

R10 SmartReviews shall publish articles in HTML format.

R11 SmartReviews shall follow WCAG guidelines.

Systematic Representation. Review articles often use tabular representations for comparing research contributions from different articles. SmartReviews should focus on these comparison tables, and encourage researchers to use these tables to devise a structured description of the reviewed articles.

R12 SmartReviews shall devise a structured comparison of reviewed work.

R13 SmartReviews shall support linking existing resources and properties from the knowledge graph.

4 Conclusion

The current review method suffers from numerous weaknesses which we described in this work. Based on the identified weaknesses, we devised the SmartReview approach. This approach proposes a collaborative community-maintained method for authoring review articles. It employs a knowledge graph to support machine-actionable articles. Future work will focus on evaluation and implementation of the SmartReview approach.

Acknowledgements. This work was co-funded by the European Research Council for the project ScienceGRAPH (Grant agreement ID: 819536) and the TIB Leibniz Information Centre for Science and Technology.

References

1. Ahmetovic, D., et al.: Axessibility: a LaTeX package for mathematical formulae accessibility in PDF documents. In: ASSETS 2018 - Proceedings of the 20th International ACM SIGACCESS Conference on Computers and Accessibility, pp. 352–354 (2018). https://doi.org/10.1145/3234695.3241029
2. Caldwell, B., Cooper, M., Reid, L.G., Vanderheiden, G.: Web Content Accessibility Guidelines (WCAG) 2.0. W3C Recommendation 11 December 2008, 33 (2008). http://www.w3.org/TR/WCAG20/
3. Darvishy, A.: PDF accessibility: tools and challenges. In: Miesenberger, K., Kouroupetroglou, G. (eds.) ICCHP 2018. LNCS, vol. 10896, pp. 113–116. Springer, Cham (2018). https://doi.org/10.1007/978-3-319-94277-3_20
4. Jaradeh, M.Y., et al.: Open research knowledge graph: next generation infrastructure for semantic scholarly knowledge. In: Proceedings of the 10th International Conference on Knowledge Capture, pp. 243–246 (2019). https://doi.org/10.1145/3360901.3364435
5. Jinha, A.: Article 50 million: an estimate of the number of scholarly articles in existence. Learned Publishing **23**(3), 258–263 (2010). https://doi.org/10.1087/20100308
6. Klampfl, S., Granitzer, M., Jack, K., Kern, R.: Unsupervised document structure analysis of digital scientific articles. Int. J. Digit. Libr., 83–99 (2014). https://doi.org/10.1007/s00799-014-0115-1
7. Kuhn, T., Chichester, C., Krauthammer, M., Queralt-rosinach, N., Verborgh, R., Giannakopoulos, G.: Decentralized provenance-aware publishing with nanopublications, pp. 1–29 (2016). https://doi.org/10.7717/peerj-cs.78
8. Lipinski, M., Yao, K., Breitinger, C., Beel, J., Gipp, B.: Evaluation of header metadata extraction approaches and tools for scientific PDF documents. In: Proceedings of the ACM/IEEE Joint Conference on Digital Libraries, pp. 385–386 (2013). https://doi.org/10.1145/2467696.2467753
9. Mendes, E., Wohlin, C., Felizardo, K., Kalinowski, M.: When to update systematic literature reviews in software engineering. J. Syst. Softw. **167**, 110607 (2020). https://doi.org/10.1016/j.jss.2020.110607
10. Nasar, Z., Jaffry, S.W., Malik, M.K.: Information extraction from scientific articles: a survey. Scientometrics **117**(3), 1931–1990 (2018). https://doi.org/10.1007/s11192-018-2921-5
11. Nepomuceno, V., Soares, S.: On the need to update systematic literature reviews. Inf. Softw. Technol. **109**, 40–42 (2019). https://doi.org/10.1016/j.infsof.2019.01.005
12. Oelen, A., Jaradeh, M.Y., Stocker, M., Auer, S.: Generate FAIR literature surveys with scholarly knowledge graphs. In: JCDL 2020: Proceedings of the ACM/IEEE Joint Conference on Digital Libraries in 2020, pp. 97–106 (2020). https://doi.org/10.1145/3383583.3398520
13. Schmidt, L.M., Gotzsche, P.C.: Of mites and men: reference bias in narrative review articles; a systematic review. J. Fam. Pract. **54**(4), 334–339 (2005)
14. Shanahan, D.R.: A living document: reincarnating the research article. Trials **16**(1), 151 (2015). https://doi.org/10.1186/s13063-015-0666-5

15. Shotton, D.: Semantic publishing: the coming revolution in Scientific journal publishing. Learned Publishing **22**(2), 85–94 (2009). https://doi.org/10.1087/2009202
16. TheSophists: Requirements Engineering - A short RE Primer (2016). https://www.sophist.de/fileadmin/user_upload/Bilder_zu_Seiten/Publikationen/Wissen_for_free/RE-Broschuere_Englisch_-_Online.pdf
17. Webster, J., Watson, R.T.: Analyzing the past to prepare for the future: writing a literature review. MIS Q. **26**(2), xiii–xxiii (2002). https://doi.org/10.1.1.104.6570
18. Wee, B.V., Banister, D.: How to write a literature review paper? Transp. Rev. **36**(2), 278–288 (2016). https://doi.org/10.1080/01441647.2015.1065456
19. Wohlin, C., Mendes, E., Felizardo, K.R., Kalinowski, M.: Guidelines for the search strategy to update systematic literature reviews in software engineering. Inf. Softw. Technol. **127**, 106366 (2020). https://doi.org/10.1016/j.infsof.2020.106366

User Interfaces and Experience

Comparing Methods for Finding Search Sessions on a Specified Topic: A Double Case Study

Tessel Bogaard[1]([📧])(iD), Aysenur Bilgin[1](iD), Jan Wielemaker[1,2](iD),
Laura Hollink[1](iD), Kees Ribbens[3,4](iD), and Jacco van Ossenbruggen[1,2](iD)

[1] Centrum Wiskunde & Informatica, Amsterdam, The Netherlands
tessel.bogaard@cwi.nl
[2] Vrije Universiteit Amsterdam, Amsterdam, The Netherlands
[3] NIOD Institute for War, Holocaust and Genocide Studies,
Amsterdam, The Netherlands
[4] Erasmus School of History, Culture and Communication,
Rotterdam, The Netherlands

Abstract. Users searching for different topics in a collection may show distinct search patterns. To analyze search behavior of users searching for a specific topic, we need to retrieve the sessions containing this topic. In this paper, we compare different topic representations and approaches to find topic-specific sessions. We conduct our research in a double case study of two topics, World War II and feminism, using search logs of a historical newspaper collection. We evaluate the results using manually created ground truths of over 600 sessions per topic. The two case studies show similar results: The query-based methods yield high precision, at the expense of recall. The document-based methods find more sessions, at the expense of precision. In both approaches, precision improves significantly by manually curating the topic representations. This study demonstrates how different methods to find sessions containing specific topics can be applied by digital humanities scholars and practitioners.

Keywords: Digital libraries · User interests · Log analysis

1 Introduction

Analysis of search logs is an unobtrusive technique for large-scale investigations into user behavior in digital libraries. Users interested in different topics might display different search behaviors. For example, the work presented in [34] demonstrated different search patterns of users searching for five major religions. In a previous study, we observed a distinct search pattern for users searching for documents related to World War II (WWII) [5]. For these types of studies, we need to be able to retrieve those user interactions from the search logs that relate to a user interest in a specified topic. In this paper, we propose and compare generally applicable methods to find user interactions that relate to a specified topic from

G. Berget et al. (Eds.): TPDL 2021, LNCS 12866, pp. 189–201, 2021.
https://doi.org/10.1007/978-3-030-86324-1_23

a larger set of logged search interactions. We work at the level of sessions (coherent sequences of user interactions with the collection) as they capture the context in which individual user actions occurred and connect search actions to clicks on documents. We address two research questions:

(**RQ1**) How can we represent a specified topic?

(**RQ2**) How can we use the topic representation to retrieve relevant sessions? To answer the first research question, we look into different, consecutive ways to build a term list as a representation of a topic: i) using semantic relations in an explicit knowledge resource, ii) applying local word embeddings trained on the documents in the collection, and iii) in each step, by manual curation of the term lists by domain experts. To answer the second research question, we look into matching the different term lists to user sessions. We match them to either a) the user queries, or b) the contents of the clicked documents. We compare and discuss the combined methods in terms of number of retrieved sessions as well as estimated precision scores. We conduct our research using data from the National Library of the Netherlands, focusing on search in their historical newspaper collection[1]. In previous work [4,5], the search logs of the digital library were already split into user sessions, and we consider this session identification step outside the scope of this paper. We present a double case study in the context of two historical topics with societal relevance: WWII (a pivotal period in Dutch and global history), and feminism (a movement that has had and still has an impact on Dutch society). We evaluate our methods on a ground truth of over 600 manually assessed sessions per topic.

This study contributes insights into how different topic representations and matching approaches perform when retrieving topic-specific sessions. Our results show that when sessions are retrieved based solely on user queries, the precision is high, however, the set of sessions remains small. When the document-based matching approach is used, the set of sessions retrieved increases, but at the expense of precision. Moreover, we find that by manually curating the term lists we improve precision while still preserving a larger set of sessions. The two topics investigated in this paper show similar general patterns in their results, however, we observe a higher overall precision for the more popular topic (WWII). Finally, our study demonstrates how different methods can be applied and combined by digital humanities scholars and practitioners to retrieve topic-specific sessions.

2   Related Work

We discuss work on detection and analysis of user interests; and how knowledge resources and word embeddings have been used to enrich queries and documents.

---

[1] The National Library of the Netherlands has granted us access to user logs from their search platform https://www.delpher.nl, providing access to collections from the National Library of the Netherlands and other heritage institutions.

2.1 Topic-Specific Search Log Analysis

Search behavior in digital libraries and archives has been studied frequently, e.g., [7,10,18,21,29,33]. Topics have been detected in search logs for various reasons; for example, to determine user interests [16,19,23,26], to uncover topic-specific search patterns [4,34], or to recognize changes in topic within a session [17]. Other studies observe topic-specific search patterns by analyzing logs from a specific search interface, such as a health portal [8], or a media archive [19,20].

In most cases, topics are detected in search logs by investigating the queries that users entered. Sometimes, in addition to the query, the contents of what was clicked in sessions is also taken into account. For example, query analysis has been combined with mouse-fixation behavior and the metadata of clicked documents [16]. In previous work, we used the metadata of clicked documents, as well as the use of facets to filter search results, to understand search behavior in different parts of a digital library collection [4,5]. In this study, we investigate and compare how query-based and content-based approaches perform.

We represent a topic as a list of terms. This is similar to the work presented in [34], where users searching for five large religions were identified by matching queries to five respective lists of professionally curated terms. The authors of [13] used a list of terms and phrases that signify specific types of questions, and matched these to queries in order to analyze how people learn within sessions.

2.2 External Resources to Enrich Queries or Documents

In previous work, knowledge resources have been used to classify documents in collections, e.g., by finding relevant Wikipedia categories [35]; or by finding relevant concepts [24] for the documents in the collection. In other cases, knowledge resources have provided a semantic enrichment of user queries, e.g., to categorize queries [20,26,36]; or for query expansion during search, e.g., by searching related concepts in Wikipedia [1,2,15]. In the present study, we use Wikipedia as a knowledge resource to expand a single term topic representation. Wikipedia is widely used, publicly available and has a broad coverage, making it applicable to many use cases beyond the ones studied in this paper. This makes Wikipedia an attractive option, even though we are aware of the fact that Wikipedia is biased both with respect to which topics are represented in the articles and the contents of the articles [9,30].

Word embeddings have been used by researchers in several query expansion applications, such as search, text classification, plagiarism detection [3]. In this type of distributed representation, words with similar meanings are more likely to be close together [28]. The semantic associations between words that thus emerge, have been shown to be effective in tackling the query-document vocabulary mismatch problem [14]. We use word embeddings to expand on the terms representing a topic, and as such to be able to increase the number of sessions found. Specifically, we use local embeddings, following [12], where it was demonstrated that corpus-specific embeddings perform better than global embeddings for query expansion.

3   Data

We use collection and log data from the National Library of the Netherlands. As a knowledge resource for the topic representations we use Wikipedia.

3.1   Document Collection and Search Logs

Our research is conducted using a document collection and search logs from the National Library of the Netherlands. The library maintains a number of digitized historic collections, our focus is on the historical newspaper collection spanning almost four hundred years (1618–1995). Within this collection, users can search using full-text search and facets (filters based on the metadata attributes of the collection). The logs used in this study were collected between October 2015 and March 2016 (raw data 200M records). They record the user interactions with the search system. These interactions have previously been grouped in sessions, to be able to study search behavior in context. The log records have been cleaned and processed, and sessions have been identified based on a *clickstream* model as described in [4,5], using the IP address as identifier and connecting sequential HTTP requests to follow a user navigating the search system. For this study, we have retained all sessions which include clicked documents within the newspaper collection, resulting in a total of 204,266 sessions over the six month period. In addition, we received the full text digitization and metadata records of the historical newspaper collection (103M documents at the time).

3.2   Knowledge Sources for Topic Representations

In this double case study, the topics of interest are WWII ("Tweede Wereldoorlog" in Dutch), and feminism ("feminisme" in Dutch). These topics are selected based on their societal relevance, and thus their value to digital humanities scholars. For example, professional historians from the Dutch NIOD Institute for War, Holocaust and Genocide Studies are interested in understanding how people search for topics related to World War II (WWII) in the media, and how this changes over time. We represent the two topics using lists of relevant terms. In the first expansion of the list of relevant terms, we use Wikipedia. As this is a publicly available knowledge resource, with many possible applications in different domains for different topics, it contributes to the general applicability of our methods. Our topics of interest correspond to the existing Wikipedia categories for WWII[2] and for feminism[3]. We have selected the top-300 Wikipedia articles in these categories, based on the popularity within the same period as the logs (October 2015–March 2016). To collect these Wikipedia articles, we have used the tool Massview Analysis[4], including the subcategories. The top-300 most

---

[2] https://nl.wikipedia.org/wiki/Categorie:Tweede_Wereldoorlog.

[3] https://nl.wikipedia.org/wiki/Categorie:Feminisme.

[4] https://pageviews.toolforge.org/massviews/, by MusikAnimal, Kaldari, and Marcel Ruiz Forns.

popular Wikipedia articles within the WWII category counted to of a total of 4.7 million views, compared to 1.2 million views within the feminism category. The assessed Wikipedia articles for the topics are available online[5]. We use the popularity ranking as an indicator for public interest in the topics described in the articles as the use of Wikipedia is a strong indicator for how this interest is composed in a country such as the Netherlands.

4   Method

We describe the different methods we compare to find topic-specific sessions. First, we explain the consecutive steps to build term lists representing the topics. Second, we describe how to use the term lists to find topic-specific sessions in a larger set of sessions. Third, we explain how we evaluate the different methods.

4.1   Creating Term Lists

We compare five ways of creating terms lists to represent the topics, where each list builds on the previous list.

List 1. Single term: List 1 contains a single term or phrase to represent the topic, in our case "Tweede Wereldoorlog" (WWII) or "feminisme" (feminism).

List 2. Wikipedia: For this list, we leverage the semantic relations in Wikipedia to find additional terms to represent the topic. First, we match the term in List 1 to their corresponding Wikipedia category and add them to List 2. Then, we take the article titles of pages within that category or any of its sub-categories. To increase the likelihood that these article titles are indeed relevant terms, we select only the top-300 most popular titles based on Wikipedia page view data. Some Wikipedia article titles require preprocessing. Where the title only consists of a named entity, it is used as-is. In the case of a title consisting of a named entity and a class between parentheses, for example, "The Color Purple (film)", we separate the class from the named entity. In the case of a title consisting of a classifying noun, preposition, named entity title phrase, for example "Bombardement op Rotterdam" (Bombing of Rotterdam), we leave out the preposition when it is not part of a named entity.

List 3. Wikipedia curated: For List 3, we ask domain experts to manually assess the terms in List 2 and remove those that are less relevant, in the assumption that this will improve the quality of the terms on the list and thus improve the precision of the matched sessions. For the WWII terms, experts from the NIOD Institute for War, Holocaust and Genocide Studies were involved in the assessment; for the feminism terms, two of the authors of this paper familiar with the topic. The assessment is based on the question whether it is plausible that someone with a specific interest in WWII or in feminism would consult the subject described in the corresponding Wikipedia article. Articles in which our main topic of interest (WWII or feminism) is only of minor importance – for example,

---

[5] https://edu.nl/4arxw and https://edu.nl/9qbfr.

in biographies of politicians, actors and professional sportsmen for whom the WWII period was not pivotal in their lives – were removed from the lists. Similarly, articles referring to a topic occurring outside the time period of the historical newspaper collection (1618–1995) – for example, movies or books published after 1995 – were also removed. We note that in the case of the WWII topics, most of these are topics from the war period itself or from the period leading to the war, but also included are issues that are part of the post-war remembrance culture and therefore refer to the period after WWII.

List 4. Wikipedia expanded: We expand the terms in List 3 using local word embeddings to create the larger List 4. We describe this process in detail in Sect. 4.2.

List 5. Wikipedia expanded and curated: To create List 5, we ask domain experts to asses the terms in List 4, using the same process as for List 3.

This results in five term lists for our topics (see Table 1).

Table 1. Number of terms in each term list

	1: single	2: wiki	3: wiki curated	4: wiki expanded	5: wiki exp&cur
WWII	1	300	200	728	364
Feminism	1	300	199	703	327

4.2 Term Expansion Based on Local Word Embeddings

To expand the term lists, we employ a widely used technique based on word embeddings [27], vector representations of words where words that appear close together in the vector space are likely to have a similar meaning. We use local embeddings instead of global embeddings, training on a selected set of topically relevant documents, as we expect term similarity to be highly dependent on the context of the topic, as was shown in [12]. For this purpose, we query the library's newspaper collection for documents that contain the terms in List 3, and use those as a topically-constrained training corpus. We work with the Indri search engine [32], using default Dirichlet smoothing [31]. The terms are translated to Indri queries, searching for an exact phrase match, or in the case of a title and a class description an exact phrase match and a Boolean AND for the class. We use the gensim library[6] for both preprocessing and to train the embeddings. To preprocess the digitized text in the training corpus, we first identify the combination of symbols and characters that mark the beginning and end of each article, and remove them. Next, we extract the sentences to be broken down into tokens, and lowercase the text. For the configuration of the hyper-parameters of gensim's word embedding algorithm, we refer to the *set expansion* solution proposed by [25] where the authors suggest setting the word vector size to 100

---

[6] https://radimrehurek.com/gensim/.

and the window size to 10^7. The reason to use a window size as large as 10, is the empirical evidence that larger window sizes are good at providing more topical similarity [22]. Since we are interested in identifying phrases that can be made up of multiple words (e.g., "Nationaal-Socialistische Beweging", "Tweede Wereldoorlog"), we instruct the model to learn bigrams and trigrams (phrases that contain two and three words). With these settings the model is expected to find associations for the single or multi-word target phrase, and suggest related words (made up of phrases consisting of one or more words). Once the model is trained, we query it using the terms in List 3 as seeds. We retain the top-3 most similar words for each term, and add them as expanded terms to List 4.

4.3   Matching Terms to Sessions

We match the terms of the five lists to sessions in two ways: matching the terms to (a) the user queries and to (b) the clicked documents.

In the **query-based** approach, user queries in the sessions are compared to the terms in the lists using exact phrase matching. As there is little context in a user query, we only include the named entity and not any information included in brackets (such as a class or publication year for the terms based on the Wikipedia article titles). Sessions are considered relevant to a topic if they contain at least one query that contains words matching a term from the topical term list.

In the **document-based** approach, we leverage the contents of the documents clicked in the sessions. For the matching of a term with the content of clicked documents, we include – where present – the class or the noun in the set of terms. This results in for example, the terms *"A Bridge Too Far" AND film*, or *Bombing AND Rotterdam*. For the WWII matching we include an extra step: we remove all matched clicked documents published before 1920, as WWII is a topic based on a historical period, and any documents from before 1920 are considered not relevant. Thus, we retrieve all sessions in which at least one matching document has been clicked.

4.4   Manually Evaluating Retrieved Sessions

The different methods provide us with sets of sessions for each of the five term lists based on either the query matching, and the document matching, with a total of ten sets of sessions for each topic. To estimate the precision of the resulting ten sets of sessions for each topic, human raters assess samples drawn from these sets. The raters judge whether one of the information needs of the user in that session is to find newspaper documents about a topic that is directly related to the topic of interest. To do this, the rater can inspect the session, using a visualization that includes the search interactions with the queries and selected facets [6], and the clicked documents and their metadata and content. We use inter-rater reliability to check the agreement among the raters.

---

[7] https://github.com/NervanaSystems/nlp-architect/tree/master/nlp_architect/ solutions/set_expansion.

5   Results

We apply the ten methods described in Sect. 4 – five ways to represent a topic as a term list, combined with two approaches to match the terms to a session – to the full set of sessions. This results in ten retrieved sets of sessions per topic.

To estimate precision, we draw samples from each set and manually assess a total of 1243 sessions. We compute the inter-rater agreement using Cohen's κ [11] based on a dual assessment of about 50 sessions per topic. We observe a κ of 0.90 for WWII and 0.84 for feminism, demonstrating good agreement.

Table 2. Size (count) and precision (percentage) for the retrieved session sets

topic representation	query-based matching				document-based matching			
	WWII	Feminism	WWII	Feminism	WWII	Feminism	WWII	Feminism
1: single	89	26	100%	100%	116	37	95%	100%
2: wiki	667	702	83%	44%	10,001	8,260	66%	37%
3: wiki curated	471	222	100%	100%	7,434	5,341	81%	56%
4: wiki expanded	4,977	6,064	52%	20%	103,833	126,656	22%	9%
5: wiki exp&cur	626	339	100%	97%	12,044	10,519	74%	63%

Size and Precision. Table 2 shows the number of sessions and the precision of each set. As expected, the use of a single term to represent a topic (List 1) results in almost perfect precision but a low number of retrieved sessions. Precision remains high (97% to 100%) when using the longer, curated lists (Lists 3 and 5) in a query-based matching. This method increases the number of retrieved sessions significantly (5 to 13 times as many, in our case). When these lists (3 and 5) are used for document-based matching, the number of retrieved documents increases even more; however, precision is lower. On the WWII topic, precision of this method may still be acceptable (74% to 81%) but on feminism it is probably not (56% and 63%). For the expanded term lists in their un-curated form (Lists 2 and 4), precision drops depending on matching method and topic. When List 2 is used for query-based matching, precision is 83% on the WWII topic, which may still be acceptable. For document-based matching, and/or when applied to feminism, precision will be too low for most applications (37% to 66%). List 4 results in low precision in all cases (9% to 52%).

Note that Lists 4 and 5 were created by expanding List 3. In theory, the same local embedding-based expansion method could be applied to Lists 1 and 2. However, in practice, this is not promising, as List 1 consists of a single term and List 2 has relatively low precision. For that reason, expansions of List 1 and 2 were not included in our experiment.

Combining Two Matching Methods. Table 3 shows the number of sessions that appear in both the query-based and document-based session sets, i.e., the intersection of the two sets. For List 1, the intersection is relatively small: e.g., for

WWII, only 23 of the 89 sessions retrieved with the query based method are also in the document-based set. We conclude that when using a single term topic representation, a combination of query-based and document based matching is a good way to increase the number of retrieved sessions. For List 2, 3, 4 and 5, on the other hand, the intersection is relatively large; the majority of the sessions retrieved with the query-based methods are also retrieved with the document-based methods. Combining the two methods is less worthwhile here.

Table 3. Intersection of query- and document-based session sets

Topic representation	WWII			Feminism		
	Query only	Both	Doc only	Query only	Both	Doc only
1: single	66	**23**	93	9	**17**	20
2: wiki	142	**525**	9,476	386	**316**	7,944
3: wiki curated	116	**355**	7,079	39	**183**	5,158
4: wiki expanded	107	**4,870**	98,963	390	**5,674**	120,982
5: wiki exp&cur	114	**512**	11,532	45	**294**	10,225

Error Analysis. Our manual annotation effort gave us insight into the types of errors that occur. Some sessions were incorrectly retrieved because of terms in the term lists that are not unique to the two topics, WWII and feminism. For example "concentration camps" may also occur in documents about the Indonesian Independence War; "emancipation" may occur in documents about slavery or religion; the term "gas chamber" is now almost uniquely associated with WWII, but had a different meaning historically; Anne Frank's last name is common in the Netherlands and appears in sessions of family historians unrelated to Anne Frank, and in many documents throughout the collection that are not related to WWII. This type of error happens with all methods but is more frequent when using the document-based matching. We hypothesize that users act as a "smart filter", as they are less likely to use generic or ambiguous query terms without adding meaningful modifying terms. A future direction of research could be to investigate if only selecting terms that users used in their queries might increase precision for a document-based matching.

Another cause for errors in the document-based matching is brought on by mistakes in the digitization process, such as incorrectly set document boundaries, or when the newspaper document contains multiple topics, such as articles summarizing local news or presenting a cultural calendar.

6   Lessons Learned

In general, query-based matching results in higher precision than document-based matching. Document-based matching, on the other hand, results in more retrieved sessions (up to 20 times more, in our experiments) at the loss of precision. We have experimented with a more narrow inclusion of document-based matched sessions (e.g., matching more than one document in a session), but a preliminary inspection did not seem to increase precision. Future work, though, could investigate this further. A combination of query- and document-based matching is useful when a topic is represented as a single term. In this case, the combination retrieves significantly more sessions without loosing precision. We hypothesize that the combination is similarly worthwhile when topics are represented as relatively short terms lists.

When a topic representation is expanded to a longer term list, manual curation of the terms is key. This holds for both our expansion methods (using a knowledge resource or local word embeddings). Curation is especially critical for document-based matching. In this work, we leveraged the category structure of Wikipedia. Future work will have to determine how other knowledge resources and other semantic relations perform.

All our methods perform better on the WWII topic than on the feminism topic. This could in part be due to the fact that WWII is a less abstract topic than feminism and as such may be easier to detect. Even so, we hypothesize the prevalence of the topic in our data plays a large part as well: WWII is not only the more popular topic on Wikipedia, the retrieved session sets (both query- and document-based) are larger than the respective sets containing topics related to feminism. It would be interesting to investigate this further using topics at different abstraction and popularity levels. In general, we expect that both knowledge-based and corpus-based expansion methods work better on more popular topics.

7   Conclusion

Understanding search behavior for topics with societal relevance can provide digital humanities scholars insights into the interest in these topics within a collection, and the research presented in this paper supports this objective. We compared different methods on how to retrieve user sessions containing specified topics, using different term lists to represent the topics and applying term matching to user queries and to clicked documents. We observed that when retrieving sessions is based solely on user queries, the precision is high, but the number of sessions retrieved small. Using the document-based matching approach, more sessions are retrieved, at the expense of precision. We found that manual curation is essential, without this step the expanded lists (using a knowledge resource or local word embeddings) perform poorly in terms of precision. This effect was particular strong for the document-based matching. Furthermore, we observed a higher overall precision for the more popular, WWII topic. In conclusion, we believe this research helps to pave the way for a better understanding and communication of topic-specific user interests within collections for digital humanities scholars as well as collection owners and practitioners.

Acknowledgements. We would like to thank the National Library of the Netherlands, and Lynda Hardman (Centrum Wiskunde & Informatica) for their support. The Wikipedia articles related to WWII were assessed by Kees Ribbens with the assistance of Caroline Schoofs and Koen Smilde. This research is partially supported by the VRE4EIC project, a project that has received funding from the European Union's Horizon 2020 research and innovation program under grant agreement No 676247.

References

1. Aggarwal, N., Buitelaar, P.: Query expansion using Wikipedia and DBpedia. In: Forner, P., Karlgren, J., Womser-Hacker, C. (eds.) CLEF 2012 Evaluation Labs and Workshop, Online Working Notes, Rome, Italy, 17–20 September 2012. CEUR Workshop Proceedings, vol. 1178. CEUR-WS.org (2012). http://ceur-ws.org/Vol-1178/CLEF2012wn-CHiC-AggarwalEt2012.pdf
2. ALMasri, M., Berrut, C., Chevallet, J.P.: Wikipedia-based semantic query enrichment. In: Proceedings of the Sixth International Workshop on Exploiting Semantic Annotations in Information Retrieval, ESAIR 2013, pp. 5–8. ACM, New York (2013). https://doi.org/10.1145/2513204.2513209. http://doi.acm.org/10.1145/2513204.2513209
3. Azad, H.K., Deepak, A.: Query expansion techniques for information retrieval: a survey. Inf. Process. Manage. (2019). https://doi.org/10.1016/j.ipm.2019.05.009
4. Bogaard, T., Hollink, L., Wielemaker, J., Hardman, L., van Ossenbruggen, J.: Searching for old news: user interests and behavior within a national collection. In: Proceedings of the 2019 Conference on Human Information Interaction and Retrieval, CHIIR 2019, pp. 113–121. ACM, New York (2019). https://doi.org/10.1145/3295750.3298925
5. Bogaard, T., Hollink, L., Wielemaker, J., van Ossenbruggen, J., Hardman, L.: Metadata categorization for identifying search patterns in a digital library. J. Doc. **75**(2), 270–286 (2019). https://doi.org/10.1108/JD-06-2018-0087
6. Bogaard, T., Wielemaker, J., Hollink, L., Hardman, L., van Ossenbruggen, J.: Understanding user behavior in digital libraries using the MAGUS session visualization tool. In: Hall, M., Merčun, T., Risse, T., Duchateau, F. (eds.) TPDL 2020. LNCS, vol. 12246, pp. 171–184. Springer, Cham (2020). https://doi.org/10.1007/978-3-030-54956-5_13
7. Borgman, C.L., et al.: Comparing faculty information seeking in teaching and research: implications for the design of digital libraries. J. Am. Soc. Inf. Sci. Technol. **56**(6), 636–657 (2005). https://doi.org/10.1002/asi.20154. https://onlinelibrary.wiley.com/doi/abs/10.1002/asi.20154
8. Callahan, A., Pernek, I., Stiglic, G., Leskovec, J., Strasberg, H.R., Shah, N.H.: Analyzing information seeking and drug-safety alert response by health care professionals as new methods for surveillance. J. Med. Internet Res. **17**(8), e204 (2015). https://doi.org/10.2196/jmir.4427. http://www.pubmedcentral.nih.gov/articlerender.fcgi?artid=4642796&tool=pmcentrez&rendertype=abstract
9. Callahan, E.S., Herring, S.C.: Cultural bias in Wikipedia content on famous persons. J. Am. Soc. Inf. Sci. Technol. **62**(10), 1899–1915 (2011). https://doi.org/10.1002/asi.21577. https://onlinelibrary.wiley.com/doi/abs/10.1002/asi.21577
10. Clough, P., Hill, T., Paramita, M.L., Goodale, P.: Europeana: what users search for and why. In: Kamps, J., Tsakonas, G., Manolopoulos, Y., Iliadis, L., Karydis, I. (eds.) TPDL 2017. LNCS, vol. 10450, pp. 207–219. Springer, Cham (2017). https://doi.org/10.1007/978-3-319-67008-9_17

11. Cohen, J.: A coefficient of agreement for nominal scales. Educ. Psychol. Measur. **20**(1), 37–46 (1960). https://doi.org/10.1177/001316446002000104

12. Diaz, F., Mitra, B., Craswell, N.: Query expansion with locally-trained word embeddings. In: Proceedings of the 54th Annual Meeting of the Association for Computational Linguistics (Volume 1: Long Papers), pp. 367–377. Association for Computational Linguistics, Berlin, August 2016. https://doi.org/10.18653/v1/P16-1035. https://www.aclweb.org/anthology/P16-1035

13. Eickhoff, C., Teevan, J., White, R., Dumais, S.: Lessons from the journey: a query log analysis of within-session learning. In: Proceedings of the 7th ACM International Conference on Web Search and Data Mining, WSDM 2014, pp. 223–232. ACM, New York (2014). https://doi.org/10.1145/2556195.2556217. http://doi.acm.org/10.1145/2556195.2556217

14. Fernández-Reyes, F.C., Hermosillo-Valadez, J., Montes-y Gómez, M.: A prospect-guided global query expansion strategy using word embeddings. Inf. Process. Manage. (2018). https://doi.org/10.1016/j.ipm.2017.09.001

15. Guisado-Gámez, J., Prat-Pérez, A., Larriba-Pey, J.L.: Query Expansion via Structural Motifs in Wikipedia Graph. CoRR abs/1602.07217, February 2016. http://arxiv.org/abs/1602.07217

16. Hienert, D., Kern, D.: Term-mouse-fixations as an additional indicator for topical user interests in domain-specific search. In: Proceedings of the ACM SIGIR International Conference on Theory of Information Retrieval, ICTIR 2017, pp. 249–252. ACM, New York (2017). https://doi.org/10.1145/3121050.3121088. http://doi.acm.org/10.1145/3121050.3121088

17. Hienert, D., Kern, D.: Recognizing topic change in search sessions of digital libraries based on thesaurus and classification system. In: Bonn, M., Wu, D., Downie, J.S., Martaus, A. (eds.) 19th ACM/IEEE Joint Conference on Digital Libraries, JCDL 2019, Champaign, IL, USA, 2–6 June 2019, pp. 297–300. IEEE (2019). https://doi.org/10.1109/JCDL.2019.00049

18. Hollink, L., Mika, P., Blanco, R.: Web usage mining with semantic analysis. In: Proceedings of the 22nd International Conference on World Wide Web, WWW 2013, pp. 561–570. ACM, New York (2013). https://doi.org/10.1145/2488388.2488438. http://doi.acm.org/10.1145/2488388.2488438

19. Hollink, V., Tsikrika, T., Vries, A.P.d.: Semantic search log analysis: a method and a study on professional image search. J. Am. Soc. Inf. Sci. Technol. **62**(4), 691–713 (2011). https://doi.org/10.1002/asi.21484. http://dx.doi.org/10.1002/asi.21484

20. Huurnink, B., Hollink, L., Van Heuvel, W.D., De Rijke, M.: Search behavior of media professionals at an audiovisual archive: a transaction log analysis. J. Am. Soc. Inform. Sci. Technol. (2010). https://doi.org/10.1002/asi.21327

21. Kules, B., Capra, R.: Designing exploratory search tasks for user studies of information seeking support systems. In: Proceedings of the 9th ACM/IEEE-CS Joint Conference on Digital Libraries, JCDL 2009, pp. 419–420. ACM, New York (2009). https://doi.org/10.1145/1555400.1555492. http://doi.acm.org/10.1145/1555400.1555492

22. Levy, O., Goldberg, Y.: dependency-based word embeddings. In: Proceedings of the 52nd Annual Meeting of the Association for Computational Linguistics (Volume 2: Short Papers), pp. 302–308. Association for Computational Linguistics, Baltimore, June 2014. https://doi.org/10.3115/v1/P14-2050

23. Liu, H., Kešelj, V.: Combined mining of web server logs and web contents for classifying user navigation patterns and predicting users' future requests. Data Knowl. Eng. **61**(2), 304–330 (2007). https://doi.org/10.1016/j.datak.2006.06.001

24. Malo, P., Sinha, A., Wallenius, J., Korhonen, P.: Concept-based document classification using Wikipedia and value function. J. Am. Soc. Inf. Sci. Technol. **62**(12), 2496–2511 (2011). https://doi.org/10.1002/asi.21596
25. Mamou, J., et al.: Term set expansion based on multi-context term embeddings: an end-to-end workflow. arXiv preprint arXiv:1807.10104 (2018)
26. Meij, E., Bron, M., Hollink, L., Huurnink, B., de Rijke, M.: Mapping queries to the linking open data cloud: a case study using DBpedia. Web Semant. Sci. Serv. Agents World Wide Web **9**(4), 418–433 (2011). https://doi.org/10.1016/j.websem.2011.04.001. http://www.sciencedirect.com/science/article/pii/S1570826811000187
27. Mikolov, T., Chen, K., Corrado, G., Dean, J.: Efficient estimation of word representations in vector space. In: 1st International Conference on Learning Representations, ICLR 2013, Scottsdale, Arizona, USA, 2–4 May 2013, Workshop Track Proceedings, January 2013. http://arxiv.org/abs/1301.3781
28. Nematzadeh, A., Meylan, S.C., Griffiths, T.L.: Evaluating vector-space models of word representation, or, the unreasonable effectiveness of counting words near other words. In: CogSci (2017)
29. Niu, X., Hemminger, B.M.: Analyzing the interaction patterns in a faceted search interface. J. Assoc. Inf. Sci. Technol. **66**(5), 1030–1047 (2015). https://doi.org/10.1002/asi.23227
30. Shane Greenstein, B., Zhu, F.: Is Wikipedia biased? Am. Econ. Rev. **102**(3), 343–48 (2012). https://doi.org/10.1257/aer.102.3.343
31. Smucker, M.D., Allan, J.: An investigation of Dirichlet prior smoothing's performance advantage. Technical report, The University of Massachusetts, The Center for Intelligent Information Retrieval (2006)
32. Strohman, T., Metzler, D., Turtle, H., Croft, W.B.: Indri: a language model-based search engine for complex queries (extended version). CIIR technical report (2005)
33. Walsh, D., Clough, P., Hall, M.M., Hopfgartner, F., Foster, J., Kontonatsios, G.: Analysis of transaction logs from national museums Liverpool. In: Doucet, A., Isaac, A., Golub, K., Aalberg, T., Jatowt, A. (eds.) TPDL 2019. LNCS, vol. 11799, pp. 84–98. Springer, Cham (2019). https://doi.org/10.1007/978-3-030-30760-8_7
34. Wan-Chik, R., Clough, P., Sanderson, M.: Investigating religious information searching through analysis of a search engine log. J. Am. Soc. Inf. Sci. Technol. **64**(12), 2492–2506 (2013). https://doi.org/10.1002/asi.22945. https://onlinelibrary.wiley.com/doi/abs/10.1002/asi.22945
35. Weale, T.: Utilizing Wikipedia Categories for Document Classification (2006)
36. Xu, Y., Jones, G.J.F., Wang, B.: Query dependent pseudo-relevance feedback based on Wikipedia. In: Proceedings of the 32nd International ACM SIGIR Conference on Research and Development in Information Retrieval, SIGIR 2009, pp. 59–66. ACM, New York (2009). https://doi.org/10.1145/1571941.1571954. http://doi.acm.org/10.1145/1571941.1571954

Clustering and Classifying Users from the National Museums Liverpool Website

David Walsh[1,3]($\boxtimes$) , Paul Clough[3,4] , Mark Michael Hall[2] ,
Frank Hopfgartner[3] , and Jonathan Foster[3]

[1] Edge Hill University, Ormskirk, Lancashire, UK
[2] The Open University, Milton Keynes, UK
walshd@edgehill.ac.uk
[3] University of Sheffield, Sheffield, UK
[4] Peak Indicators, Chesterfield, UK

Abstract. Museum websites have been designed to provide access for
different types of users, such as museum staff, teachers and the general public. Therefore, understanding user needs and demographics is
paramount to the provision of user-centred features, services and design.
Various approaches exist for studying and grouping users, with a more
recent emphasis on data-driven and automated methods. In this paper,
we investigate user groups of a large national museum's website using
multivariate analysis and machine learning methods to cluster and categorise users based on an existing user survey. In particular, we apply the
methods to the dominant group - general public - and show that subgroups exist, although they share similarities with clusters for all users.
We find that clusters provide better results for categorising users than
the self-assigned groups from the survey, potentially helping museums
develop new and improved services.

Keywords: Digital cultural heritage · Museum website · User groups ·
Cluster analysis

1 Introduction

Due to the COVID-19 pandemic, museums and galleries around the world had
to temporarily close their physical sites, leading to an increased need to provide online access to their content. This was possible thanks to prior investments in online presences, i.e., websites and the curation of digital collections
[1]. Such resources are indeed popular amongst users from diverse backgrounds
with increasingly varied goals, tasks and information needs [2]. However, users'
individual differences (e.g., age and domain knowledge), search task and context
(e.g., location and time), are known to affect the ways in which people search for
information [3]. It has, therefore, been long recognised that information systems
and services must be developed from the perspective of human actors and their
environment [4] and support information seeking behaviours beyond keyword-based search [5,6]. Since the first museums were made available online, there

© Springer Nature Switzerland AG 2021
G. Berget et al. (Eds.): TPDL 2021, LNCS 12866, pp. 202–214, 2021.
https://doi.org/10.1007/978-3-030-86324-1_24

have been attempts to grow and enhance the use of the online collections, generally based on a categorisation of their users. The diversity in users of digital cultural heritage has resulted in a strategy that simplifies the virtually unlimited possibilities of user-profiles by creating generic groups or categories of users - 'stereotypes' [7]. These groups are sometimes as abstract as *novice* or *expert* [5], but more commonly, user groups are created based on profession (e.g., curator, librarian, researcher, teacher or student). Alternative groups have been based on user interest or motivations (e.g., tourist, explorer, general user) or age group (e.g., adult, child) [8].

Manually defining user groups can be time-consuming and difficult; therefore, approaches to automate the process, such as clustering and automated persona generation [9], must be applied. In this paper, we use multivariate analysis and machine learning methods to study groups at The National Museum Liverpool (NML), a collection of seven museums that cover a wide range of areas from art galleries to natural history and slavery. The NML provide a publicly accessible website, allowing users to access information about the physical museums, as well as digital collections. In a previous study of NML users, Walsh et al. [10,11] conducted an online survey to gather information about users and their purpose of visiting the museum website. They identified that a large proportion of the NML website users (49% n = 253 from 514 respondents) considered themselves as 'General Public' [12], a finding common in other studies [13]. In this paper, as well as studying groups across the population as a whole, we focus on analysing users who describe themselves as General Public to better understand the homogeneity of this group and whether sub-groups exist. This study addresses the following research questions:

RQ1 How do cluster analysis results compare with the self-assigned groups?
RQ2 Do sub-groups exist within the self-assigned General Public group?
RQ3 Can we classify the users based on the identified clusters?

The remainder of this paper is structured as follows: In Sect. 2, we discuss existing work to understand and classify digital cultural heritage users, particularly using cluster analysis; in Sect. 3, we describe the study we undertook and our methodology. Sections 4 and 5 present and discusses the results, and Sect. 6 concludes the paper and provides directions for future work.

2   Related Work

There have been numerous past studies on categorising users of cultural heritage resources (see, e.g., [14]). Often the focus has been on users connected to the museum in either a professional/expert capacity or the lay user/non-expert/novice [5]. Groups, such as the General Public (GP) [10], present an opportunity to explore more nuanced categorisations, thereby expanding the field of study to include potential sub-categories or even new groups.

Fundamentally, the characteristics of professional users have been linked to high levels of training and experience, a good knowledge base of required tasks and systems, and expertise in the field of cultural heritage [15]. Recognition of this particular user group culminated in the term MIP *(Museum Information Professional)* as someone working with information resources, and a goal of meeting user needs both internally and externally to the museum [16]. There are sub-categories within the expert/professional category, often based on role/occupation, such as academic, archivist, student and hobbyist. At the other end of the spectrum are novices/non-experts or lay-users who have limited or no formal training in either the systems [15] or subject knowledge [17,18] but visit the museum and/or its website for personal interest. Cifter [8] states that "knowledge of the task, information needs and system expectations" are the expert's main distinction.

The hobbyist or non-professional users fit between the extremes of expert and novice [2,19–22], sharing with the expert a knowledge of cultural heritage, but mainly in specific domains and being like the lay user with a focus on personal reasons. Casual-leisure users are closely related to novice or hobbyist groups. However, they are typically only "first and short-time visitors" [23] who have stumbled upon [the digital] collection. In this respect, they are similar to Falk's experience seekers [24], who wander into the physical museum just for the experience. Villaespesa [13] studied the Metropolitan Museum of Art's collection users and found that non-specialist users needed better clues to navigate and explore the collection, highlighting thus a lack of knowledge of the collection(s) and the system/website.

In Booth's study of visitors at the London Science Museum [25], the category of 'general visitors' was identified as those seeking general information (e.g., museum opening hours or prices); whilst all other user groups (educational visitors and specialist visitors) were seeking more detailed information. Similarly, the CULTURA project identified 3 groups (professional researchers, apprentice investigators, informed users) who shared some level of domain knowledge. All other visitors were categorised as general public [26].

Although work on identifying user groups has tended to be mostly manual, there has also been use of computational approaches (mainly using cluster analysis) to identify representative users. For example, Krantz et al. [27] used a k-means method to explore and segment a number of museum audiences. Nyaupane et al. [28] identified 3 clusters based on motives for learning cultural heritage of the visitors to Native American heritage sites. These clusters were identified as 'culture-focused', 'culture-attentive' and 'culture-appreciative' with each showing distinct behaviours and experiences. There are many algorithms for doing this, with their use based on the types of data being used, as well as the desired outcome [29–32]. In our work, we use cluster analysis to group 'similar' users and identify the characteristics of the groups.

3 Methodology

The methodology used in this paper comprised the following main steps (similar to [33]): (i) data collection and preparation; (ii) multivariate analysis; (iii) cluster analysis (assess cluster tendency, run algorithms, validate cluster quality and stability, profile clusters); and (iv) classification of user groups. The steps are described in more detail below.

3.1 Data Collection and Preparation

The dataset was collected in 2016 using an intercept pop-up survey on the NML website. The survey comprised 21 questions to gather information around users' demographics (e.g., age, gender, education, location, cultural heritage knowledge/experience and employment status), interactions with the NML website (e.g., frequency of use), and context of their visit to the website (e.g., purpose and motivation) when answering the survey. More information can be found in [14]. Overall, we obtained 514 complete responses that are used in this study.

From the 21 possible questions to use as variables in the study, 9 were deemed important in profiling users based on the results of our previous analysis [12]. All selected variables were categorical (nominal and ordinal): website visit reason (nom, 4 levels), website visit purpose (nom, 9 levels), frequency of website visit (ord, 5 levels), level of domain knowledge (ord, 4 levels), level of general CH knowledge (ord, 5 levels), location (nom, 5 levels), age group (ord, 5 levels), employment status (nom, 8 levels) and user group (nom, 8 levels). The last variable reflects a self-assigned user group: Academic (25), General Public (253), Museum Staff (10), Non-Professional (137), Other (26), Professional (5), Student (33), Teacher (25).

Further preprocessing included removing cases with 'unknown' responses (e.g. for levels of knowledge). We also merged categories (e.g. those with low counts) to reduce the number of variable categories. For example, we combined 'daily', 'weekly' and 'monthly' frequency of visit into a single 'regular' category. The resulting dataset was reduced to 487 cases. For the purposes of cluster analysis, the sample size is adequate, according to Qiu and Joe [34] who suggest that the sample size should be a minimum of 10 times the number of variables.

3.2 Multivariate Analysis

Prior to further analysis, dimensionality reduction was run with categorical variables. In particular, Multiple Correspondence Analysis (MCA), an extension of Correspondence Analysis, was used to identify potential relationships between variables and a lower number of dimensions that can represent the variability in the dataset without losing important information [35]. MCA is similar to PCA; however, it can be used on multiple categorical variables. The use of multivariate analysis enables insight and also helps to confirm our understanding of the data.

We find that the first 5 dimensions account for 34.8% of the variance in the data. Figure 1 shows an MCA plot for individual variable categories on the first 2 dimensions (representing 16.2% of variance), with the shading of the points representing their squared cosine (cos2) score - this measures the degree of association between variable categories and a particular axis. The plot confirms what we might expect to see: that variable categories with a similar profile are

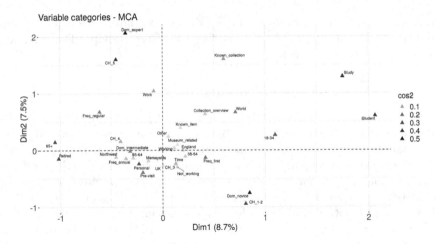

Fig. 1. MCA plot showing grouping of individual variable categories on first 2 dimensions

grouped (e.g., 65+ and retired), that some variables are well represented on the dimensions (e.g., student, study, retired) and that some variables are negatively correlated and positioned in opposing quadrants (e.g., expert and CH_5 vs novice and CH_1-2). The results of this initial analysis also confirmed the findings of our previous analysis to distinguish characteristics of self-assigned groups [12].

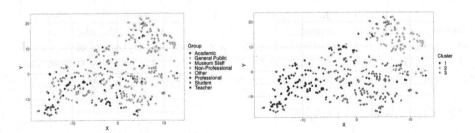

Fig. 2. 2D t-SNE plots showing users by self-assigned groups (left) and PAM clusters (right)

We also applied non-linear dimensionality reduction using t-SNE that allows the visualisation of data in a lower-dimensional space, such as 2D, to identify patterns and trends [36]. Figure 2 shows example t-SNE plots for users by self-assigned group (left) and assigned cluster (right). We observe that points for the self-assigned groups are not as clearly separated as compared to those based on the cluster number.

3.3 Cluster Analysis

The overall approach to clustering followed the 4 steps in [37]: (i) data prepro-cessing; (ii) clusterability evaluation; (iii) select and run algorithms; and (iv) cluster evaluation. In addition to the data preprocessing already described, we also computed a dissimilarity matrix using Gower distance. For assessing cluster-ability, we computed the Hopkins statistic and manually inspected a visualisation of the dissimilarity matrix, looking for blocks of similar colour.

To perform cluster analysis, we reviewed approaches that could be used on nominal and ordinal categorical data (e.g., [38]). One group of methods is based on using a dissimilarity matrix (distance-based); another group can be applied directly to the data and model class probabilities (model-based). We opted for the simpler first approach whereby a dissimilarity matrix is first computed using the Gower distance that can handle multiple data types (in this case, using an adapted version of Manhattan distance for ordinal and the Dice coefficient for nominal categories). The dissimilarity matrix can then be used with standard clustering methods. In our case, we used PAM (Partitioning Around Medoids) [39], a partition-based algorithm that works similarly to k-means clustering, but cluster centres are restricted to be the observations themselves (i.e., medoids). Compared to k-means, the algorithm is more robust to noise and outliers and also has the benefit of having an observation serve as the exemplar for each cluster, thereby making cluster interpretation easier. Different approaches were used to determine the optimum number of clusters and evaluate cluster quality.

3.4 Classification

In this work for classification, we use a Random Forest (RF) classifier, a popular learning algorithm that builds many trees on bootstrapped copies of the training data [40]. Bagging aggregates the predictions across all trees and commonly gives good predictive performance with little hyperparameter tuning. For training the RF model, we split the data into train and test sets (70:30) and apply 5-fold cross-validation repeatedly (3 times). The Gini coefficient is used as the split rule for building the trees, and we also apply tuning using a grid search over the hyperparameter space, varying the *mtry* and *min.node.size* parameters. Feature importance is assessed using impurity. We also experimented with varying the *num.trees* parameter (starting with the suggested 10 × number of features) and settled on 400. The trained model is applied to the test data, and reported accuracy scores are based on these predictions.

4 Results and Analysis

4.1 Analysing the Self-assigned Groups

We first analysed the data to determine whether the self-assigned groups are separable. By inspecting the left-hand t-SNE plot in Fig. 2 we can see that the self-assigned groups, on the whole, tend to spread across the plot, suggesting high overlap (including the General Public group). To further test this, we compared the output of PAM clustering (with $k = 8$) against the self-assigned groups using the Adjusted Rand Index (ARI). The result is a very low score of 0.021, indicating almost no overlap. Classifying the users by their self-assigned group results in an overall accuracy of 0.5315 (No Information Rate, NIR = 0.4895) on the test data, which is not that high. However, since a significant fraction is correctly classified, we hypothesised that using clustering it should be possible to create a potentially, smaller set of more distinguishable user groups, which would be easier to cater to.

4.2 Clustering and Classifying All Users

We first checked for cluster tendency using the Hopkins statistic. A resulting score of 0.1826 is well below 0.5 suggesting the data is clusterable and therefore suitable for cluster analysis. We next perform cluster analysis on all users to investigate what groups emerge from the data. Using the *fviz_nbclust* package, we compute total WSS, average silhouette width and the gap statistic to identify the optimum number of clusters for PAM. The metrics suggest 3, 3, and 9 cluster solutions respectively. Opting for the majority solution we perform PAM with $k = 3$. The average silhouette width is 0.16 and cluster medoids are shown in Table 1. The representatives reflect the mode value for each of the categories and therefore hide some of the variation within the groups.

Table 1. Cluster representatives for PAM clustering ($k = 3$) of all users

Cluster	Visit reason	Visit purpose	Freq	Domain know	CH know	Location	Age	Emp status
1	Personal	Other	First	Intermediate	3	World	35–54	Working
2	Personal	Pre-visit*	First	Intermediate	4	Northwest	65+	Retired
3	Personal	Pre-visit*	Annual	Intermediate	3	Merseyside	35–54	Working

Pre-visit refers to website visitors preparing or planning for a physical museum visit.

However, inspecting the distribution of individual categories and exemplars within the clusters, we can summarise the clusters as follows:

- **Cluster 1 - Online Researchers:** part- and full-time workers (including students) visiting the website for a wide mix of reasons (including work or study), mainly seeking known items or collections and information about the museum, often first-time visitors with a range of domain knowledge (mostly intermediate) but higher CH knowledge, mostly aged between 18 and 54 and from outside the UK, therefore less likely to visit the museum in person (125 users).
- **Cluster 2 - CH Enthusiasts:** mostly first-time and annual visitors to the website for personal reasons, perhaps preparing for a physical visit but also a range of other museum-related and other purposes, generally intermediate levels of domain and CH knowledge, predominately working or retired and aged 55+ and located in the Northwest of England and Merseyside (126 users).

– **Cluster 3 - Local Visiting Workers:** Typically, regular users, visiting the website for personal reasons and to pass time (although in a working capacity), mostly preparing for a visit to the museum, generally lower level of domain knowledge but an intermediate level of CH knowledge, mainly in the 35–64 age range and working from the local Merseyside area (236 users).

Inspecting the t-SNE plot (right) for the PAM clustering in Fig. 2 would suggest that the clustering forms clear groups - the top right set of points is clearly representing Cluster 2, which seems to map onto mostly the retired and CH enthusiasts user group. Cluster 1 at the bottom left includes the student user group (amongst others). To check the stability of the clusters, we apply bootstrapping using the R *clusterboot* package. This runs PAM multiple times on samples of the data and compares the cluster outputs to determine how many points remain in the sample. The mean scores (1 = all points remain in the same cluster) for the 3 clusters are 0.7432, 0.6770 and 0.8044, suggesting the first and third clusters are the most stable.

Training the Random Forest classifier on clusters from PAM, we obtain an accuracy of 0.9306 (NIR = 0.4861) on the test data (0.9086 on the training data). Assessing global feature importance, variables are ranked as follows (by impurity): location (100), age (66.4), visit purpose (58.6), frequency (52.6), employment (52.5), CH knowledge (14.8), visit reason (6.2) and domain knowledge (0).

4.3 Clustering and Classifying General Public Users

In this section, we focus on the users who have identified themselves as General Public (or General Users) for the purposes of the survey. As this is a dominant group for NML (and DCH more generally [13,25]), we wanted to establish the homogeneity of this group, any sub-clusters and their defining characteristics. In prior work [12], we found that general users could often be distinguished as using the museum for personal use, often visiting for the first time, novice/intermediate domain knowledge, medium levels of CH knowledge, mainly from Merseyside/Northwest and generally in the mid-life age range.

In Sect. 4.1 we find that when classifying based on all self-assigned groups, the overall classification accuracy is low (0.5315). Furthermore, performing binary classification for GP vs Other, we obtain an overall accuracy of 0.6966 (NIR = 0.5172) on the test data. Inspecting the GP class only, we obtain an accuracy of 0.83. Overall, we find the GP group shares similarities with other groups (see the t-SNE plot in Fig. 2), although there are still potential differences that can be

Table 2. Cluster representatives for PAM clustering ($k = 3$)

Cluster	Visit reason	Visit purpose	Freq	Domain know	CH know	Location	Age	Emp status
1	Personal	Pre-visit	Annual	Intermediate	4	Merseyside	35–54	Working
2	Personal	Pre-visit	First	Intermediate	3	Northwest	65+	Retired
3	Personal	Pre-visit	First	Novice	3	England	35–54	Working

used to automatically distinguish this group, suggesting that the group is fairly homogeneous.

Prior to performing clustering to identify potential subgroups within the general public users (236 users), we first check for clusterability using the Hopkins statistic (0.20) and visual inspection of a visualisation of the dissimilarity matrix. We conclude that this sub-group may contain clusters. Similarly to clustering all users with PAM, we start by computing a dissimilarity matrix using the Gower distance (using *daisy*). We then seek to identify the optimum number of clusters using the total within-cluster sum of square (WSS), average silhouette score and gap statistic. This time all metrics output $k = 3$, which we use for clustering with PAM. The resulting clustering has an average silhouette width of 0.18. The cluster medoids are shown in Table 2. We might summarise the groups as follows:

- **Cluster 1 - Regular Website Visiting Local Workers:** generally users mainly visiting the website on a regular or annual basis for personal reasons, including preparing for a visit and seeking museum-related information, mostly intermediate and higher levels of domain and CH knowledge, working, aged 35–64 and local to the Merseyside area (99 users).
- **Cluster 2 - Local Enthusiasts:** also mainly using the site for personal use (and pass time) and preparing for a visit; however, mostly first-time and annual website visitors with intermediate levels of domain and CH knowledge, mostly 55+, retired and from the Northwest and Merseyside (64 users).
- **Cluster 3 - First-time Non-local Workers:** mostly first-time users of the website using the website for personal use and to pass time, mostly in preparation for a visit; generally working with lower levels of domain and CH knowledge, mostly middle-aged 35–64 and from England but outside the Merseyside area (73 users).

The RF classifier is trained, with the target variable being the cluster number from PAM. Using a similar experimental setup as before, we obtain an accuracy of 0.8841 (NIR = 0.4203) on the test data (0.8980 on training data). Again, using impurity to calculate global feature importance, the variables are ranked as follows: employment (100), frequency (68.9), location (62.6), domain knowledge (50.9), age (50.4), CH knowledge (24.4), visit purpose (7.2) and visit reason (0).

5 Discussion

In this section, we summarise our findings and revisit the questions posed in Sect. 1.

[RQ1] How do cluster analysis results compare with the self-assigned groups? The results of the self-assigned groupings differ from the clusters based on the cluster analysis. This is evident from our analysis in that the self-assigned groups (using features collected from the users) tend to overlap. This is most clearly seen in the classification with self-assigned groups as the target feature where the classification accuracy is very low. In comparison, the groups based on clustering are fewer in number (using the simplest solution) and more distinct, resulting in far higher overall classification scores. We deduce three main categories of users from the overall data: online researchers, CH enthusiasts and local visiting workers that may provide much simpler (and more distinct) categories of users for NML to cater for.

[RQ2] Do sub-groups exist within the self-assigned General Public group? Much previous work has analysed the rather mystical 'general public' user that for NML provide a dominant user category. We find this group seems largely homogeneous but distinct and separable from the other groups - this is seen in the far higher classification accuracy for the GP class. However, potential sub-groups within the GP user group are identifiable, which we have labelled as: regular website visiting local workers, local enthusiasts, and first-time non-local workers. The first group may represent off duty teachers from the local area preparing for a personal visit or searching family history in their own time; the second group mainly reflects hobbyists and enthusiasts (e.g. interested in local history and genealogy). Finally, the third group may represent groups such as culture tourists, who are from outside the local area, arrive at the website and only view one or two pages before leaving. There are clearly similarities between the GP sub-groups and clusters obtained using all users (Tables 1 and 2). This may suggest that we do not need to cater for this group separately as they may be implicit within all groups already.

[RQ3] Can we classify the users based on the identified clusters? Overall, we are able to classify the users based on the features derived from the online survey and using the groups derived from cluster analysis. We have shown that the results on the clusters are far higher than the self-assigned groups, although we do find that the General Public user group can be distinguished using classification. This suggests we could automatically identify this group and then apply cluster analysis to further segment the group if desired.

6 Conclusions and Future Work

In this paper, we have extended prior work on studying users of the National Museums Liverpool websites using cluster analysis and classification. Based on a sample of users taken from an online survey, We have shown that a smaller set of more distinct groups exists, which may be easier to cater for than using self-assigned groups that commonly overlap and share characteristics. We also find that the General Public group (often treated as one group) may contain subgroups. However, these reflect clusters from all users and may alleviate the need to model them separately. In future work we plan to experiment with further approaches for automatically profiling users, such as automated persona generation, comparing clustering methods and identifying ways of automating the process to alleviate the need for gathering data from user surveys for categorising online visitors (e.g., using relevant features from transaction logs).

References

1. Hadley, W.: COVID-19 impact museum sector research findings (2020). Accessed 23 Mar 2021
2. Skov, M., Ingwersen, P.: Exploring information seeking behaviour in a digital museum context. In: Proceedings of the Second International Symposium on Information Interaction in Context, IIiX 2008. ACM, New York, pp. 110–115 (2008)
3. Case, D.: Looking for Information: A Survey of Research on Information Seeking, Needs, and Behavior. Library and Information Science (2007)
4. Taylor, R.S.: Value-added processes in the information life cycle. J. Am. Society Inf. Sci. **33**(5), 341–346 (1982)
5. Johnson, A.: Users, use and context: supporting interaction between users and digital archives. In: What Are Archives?: Cultural and Theoretical Perspectives: A Reader, pp. 145–164 (2008)
6. Whitelaw, M.: Generous interfaces for digital cultural collections. Digit. Hum. Q. **9**(1), 38 (2015)
7. Allen, R.B.: Chapter 3 - mental models and user models. In: Helander, M.G., Landauer, T.K., Prabhu, P.V. (eds.) Handbook of Human-Computer Interaction, 2nd edn., pp. 49–63. North-Holland, Amsterdam (1997)
8. Cifter, A.S., Dong, H.: User characteristics: professional vs. lay users (2009)
9. Salminen, J., Jung, S.G., Chowdhury, S., Robillos, D.R., Jansen, B.: The ability of personas: an empirical evaluation of altering incorrect preconceptions about users. Int. J. Hum.-Comput. Stud. 153, 102645 (2021)
10. Walsh, D., Hall, M.: Just looking around: supporting casual users initial encounters with digital cultural heritage. In: Gade, M., et al. (eds.) Proceedings of the First International Workshop on Supporting Complex Search Tasks colocated with the 37th European Conference on Information Retrieval (ECIR 2015), Volume 1338 of CEUR Workshop Proceedings. CEUR-WS.org, March 2015
11. Walsh, D., Hall, M., Clough, P., Foster, J.: The ghost in the museum website: investigating the general public's interactions with museum websites. In: Kamps, J., Tsakonas, G., Manolopoulos, Y., Iliadis, L., Karydis, I. (eds.) TPDL 2017. LNCS, vol. 10450, pp. 434–445. Springer, Cham (2017). https://doi.org/10.1007/978-3-319-67008-9_34
12. Walsh, D., Hall, M.M., Clough, P., Foster, J.: Characterising online museum users: a study of the national museums Liverpool museum website. Int. J. Digit. Libr. **21**(1), 75–87 (2020)
13. Villaespesa, E.: Museum collections and online users: development of a segmentation model for the metropolitan museum of art. Visitor Stud. **22**(2), 233–252 (2019)
14. Walsh, D., Clough, P., Foster, J.: User categories for digital cultural heritage. In: Clough, P., Goodale, P., Agosti, M., Lawless, S., (eds.) Proceedings of the First International Workshop on Accessing Cultural Heritage at Scale co-located with Joint Conference on Digital Libraries 2016 (JCDL 2016), Volume 1611 of CEUR Workshop Proceedings. CEUR-WS.org, June 2016
15. Pantano, E.: Virtual cultural heritage consumption: a 3d learning experience. Int. J. Technol. Enhanced Learn. **3**(5), 482–495 (2011)
16. Marty, P.F.: Meeting user needs in the modern museum: profiles of the new museum information professional. Libr. Inf. Sci. Res. **28**(1), 128–144 (2006)
17. Hogg, C., Williamson, C.: Whose interests do lay people represent? Towards an understanding of the role of lay people as members of committees. Health Expect. **4**(1), 2–9 (2001)

18. Vilar, P., Šauperl, A.: Archival literacy: different users, different information needs, behaviour and skills. In: Kurbanoğlu, S., Špiranec, S., Grassian, E., Mizrachi, D., Catts, R. (eds.) ECIL 2014. CCIS, vol. 492, pp. 149–159. Springer, Cham (2014). https://doi.org/10.1007/978-3-319-14136-7_16

19. Kelly, L.: The interrelationships between adult museum visitors' learning identities and their museum experiences, chap. 3. Methodology, pp. 3–46 (2007)

20. Skov, M.: The reinvented museum: exploring information seeking behaviour in a digital museum context. Ph.D. thesis, Københavns Universitet 'Københavns Universitet', Faculty of Humanities, School of Library and Information Science, Royal School of Library and Information Science (2009, unpublished thesis)

21. Elsweiler, D., Wilson, M.L., Lunn, B.K.: Chapter 9 understanding casual-leisure information behaviour. In: New Directions in Information Behaviour (Library and Information Science, Volume 1) Emerald Group Publishing Limited, vol. 1, pp. 211–241 (2011)

22. Spellerberg, M., Granata, E., Wambold, S.: Visitor-first, mobile-first: designing a visitor-centric mobile experience. In: Museums and the Web (2016)

23. Ardissono, L., Kuflik, T., Petrelli, D.: Personalization in cultural heritage: the road travelled and the one ahead. User Model. User-Adap. Inter. **22**(1–2), 73–99 (2012)

24. Falk, J.H.: Identity and the Museum Visitor Experience. Left Coast Press, Walnut Creek (2009)

25. Booth, B.: Understanding the information needs of visitors to museums. Museum Manage. Curatorsh. **17**(2), 139–157 (1998)

26. Sweetnam, M., Siochru, M., Agosti, M., Manfioletti, M., Orio, N., Ponchia, C.: Stereotype or spectrum: designing for a user continuum. In: The Proceedings of the First Workshop on the Exploration, Navigation and Retrieval of Information in Cultural Heritage, ENRICH (2013)

27. Krantz, A., Korn, R., Menninger, M.: Rethinking museum visitors: using k-means cluster analysis to explore a museum's audience. Curator Museum J. **52**(4), 363–374 (2009)

28. Nyaupane, G.P., White, D.D., Budruk, M.: Motive-based tourist market segmentation: an application to native American cultural heritage sites in Arizona, USA. J. Herit. Tour. **1**(2), 81–99 (2006)

29. Ackerman, M., Ben-David, S., Loker, D.: Towards property-based classification of clustering paradigms. In: Advances in Neural Information Processing Systems, pp. 10–18 (2010)

30. Ackerman, M., Ben-David, S., Loker, D.: Characterization of linkage-based clustering. In: COLT, pp. 270–281 (2010)

31. Ackerman, M., Ben-David, S.: Discerning linkage-based algorithms among hierarchical clustering methods. In: Twenty-Second International Joint Conference on Artificial Intelligence (2011)

32. Ackerman, M., Ben-David, S., Brânzei, S., Loker, D.: Weighted clustering. In: Twenty-Sixth AAAI Conference on Artificial Intelligence (2012)

33. Brida, J.G., Meleddu, M., Pulina, M.: Understanding museum visitors' experience: a comparative study. J. Cult. Herit. Manage. Sustain. Develop. **6**(1), 47–71 (2016)

34. Qiu, W., Joe, H.: Generation of random clusters with specified degree of separation. J. Classif. **23**(2), 315–334 (2006)

35. Brickey, J., Walczak, S., Burgess, T.: A comparative analysis of persona clustering methods. In: AMCIS, p. 217 (2010)

36. Van der Maaten, L., Hinton, G.: Visualizing data using t-SNE. J. Machine Learn. Res. **9**(11) (2008)

37. Adolfsson, A., Ackerman, M., Brownstein, N.C.: To cluster, or not to cluster: an analysis of clusterability methods. Pattern Recogn. **88**, 13–26 (2019)
38. Preud'homme, G., et al.: Head-to-head comparison of clustering methods for heterogeneous data: a simulation-driven benchmark. Sci. Rep. **11**(1), 1–14 (2021)
39. Kaufman, L., Rousseeuw, P.J.: Finding Groups in Data: An Introduction to Cluster Analysis, vol. 344. Wiley, Hoboken (2009)
40. Breiman, L.: Random forests. Mach. Learn. **45**(1), 5–32 (2001)

Humanities Scholars and Digital Humanities Projects: Practice Barriers in Tools Usage

Rui Liu(✉) ⓘ, Dana McKay ⓘ, and George Buchanan ⓘ

The University of Melbourne, Parkville, VIC 3010, Australia
ruiliu2@student.unimelb.edu.au

Abstract. Humanities scholars face many problems when trying to design, build, present, and maintain digital humanities projects. To mitigate these problems and to improve the user experience of digital humanities collections, it is essential to understand the problems in detail. However, we currently have a fragmented and incomplete picture of what these problems actually are. This study presents a wide systematic literature review (SLR) on the problems encountered by humanities scholars when adopting particular software tools in digital humanities projects. As a result of this review, this paper finds problems in different categories of tools used in digital humanities. The practice barriers can be divided into four types: content, technique, interface, and storage. These results draw a full picture of problems in tools usage, suggest digital humanities discipline further improve tools application and offer developers of software designed for humanities scholars some feedback to make them optimize these tools.

Keywords: Practice barriers · Digital humanities · Systematic literature review

1 Introduction

Digital collections on the web sites of libraries, archives, galleries and museums, are proliferating and are an increasingly important means of access. Most simply replace the traditional medium with an electronic version. Keyword search is the primary way to access the collections, in contrast with their paper counterparts [1].

These web sites have several well-established limitations, both with analysis of the content, and the methods available to find content [2]. For example, administrators can find it difficult to provide an effective range of visual presentations of the collection to help users discover useful information. At the same time, users cannot easily find or describe the information that they want, or readily browse casually through the collection [1, 3]. Digital humanities ultimately aims to create rich and detailed collections that enable scholars and the public gain new insights into the collection material. The adoption of digital technology can help make even complex collections easier to present, and even reduce some of these problems, particularly when they reduce the complexity of organising the collection, or improving navigation [4].

Considering the importance of digital humanities research and the complexity of digital humanities researchers, it is important to both improve individual tools and to

© Springer Nature Switzerland AG 2021
G. Berget et al. (Eds.): TPDL 2021, LNCS 12866, pp. 215–226, 2021.
https://doi.org/10.1007/978-3-030-86324-1_25

help developers better select the right tools for digital humanities projects. For example, many digital humanities projects need programming to achieve the desired effect, but often humanities scholars who are key to a project are not familiar with information technology. This hinders the progress and success of projects. Thus, we emphasize the rising importance of evaluating digital humanities tools to know the practice barriers of humanities scholar's using experience. Studies about in-depth evaluation of tools usage in digital humanities projects is not as much as in digital library [5]. Digital library research on usability barriers have helped librarians know individual strengths and weaknesses of different software and give them recommended tools and advises to consider [6, 7]. There is a need for digital humanities tools to do the same work.

This paper focuses on the problems encountered by humanities scholars when adopting digital tools to create a new collection. Humanities scholars are a key stakeholder group in DH projects: they account for a large proportion of digital humanities researchers both in general, and in most DH projects. They also encounter problems more often when using digital tools, as they necessarily have on average fewer technical digital skills than IT experts. They are, perhaps most importantly, the discipline experts and are better placed to make decisions about, and manage, the content. They also are better placed than technologists to understand the likely uses and users of the collection, and thus can help improve the user experience of the final collection. The main research question of this study is what are the practice barriers of humanities scholars in digital humanities projects. This study presents a systematic literature review (SLR) of tools usage problems in digital humanities field, digital library field and institution repertories area, and then produce a framework of practice barriers.

Digital humanities scholarship is facing many challenges with the development that one of them is the invisible and unsystematic infrastructure. By exploring the humanities scholars' practice barriers of using digital humanities tools will make the infrastructure more robust, user-friendly and sophisticated, which is the key to make digital humanities projects and community more useful and impactful.

2 Methods

To comprehensively understand humanities scholars' problems with tools, we performed a Systematic Literature Review (SLR). We adopted an SLR method to avoid repeating existing research, and identify gaps for future empirical work. SLRs aim to produce a comprehensive picture of existing knowledge, and seek to avoid citation and availability biases distorting the picture of the current state of knowledge. We combined the SLR guidelines by Kitchenham and Brereton (2013) [8] with the extensions to it developed by Martin-Rodilla and Sánchez (2020) [9]. Following that approach, the process of the systematic literature review found in this paper contains three stages: first, defining research questions; second, searching appropriate publications; third, data analysis and synthesis.

2.1 Research Questions

Defining the research questions is the first stage in SLR. The choice of specific research questions will inform and direct the search strategy, the selection of publications and the data analysis. We started with the main research question of this paper: what are the practice barriers encountered by humanities scholars in digital humanities projects? Our SLR addresses the following sub-questions:

RQ1: What are the main practice barriers in different categories of tools used in digital humanities projects or research?

RQ2: Are there relevant publications from digital library research discipline that can supplement the experiences with digital humanities specifically?

RQ3: Can we develop a framework for the practice barriers encountered by humanities scholars when using tools in digital humanities projects?

From an initial informal survey of the area, it was clear that there is a modest literature on the problems that digital humanities scholars encounter when building digital humanities collections. Furthermore, there were few developed methods to help evaluate those problems. Hence, we developed RQ2, which aims to broaden the width of information available, but also may provide models of good practice in the tools of closely related fields. RQ3 more informs our analysis of the literature, as we seek to provide a structured account of the problems currently being experienced in digital humanities projects.

2.2 Materials

Searching and selecting high quality publications that match our research aims is critical to gaining reliable and conclusive research results. Following the approach to SLR we adopted, there are four steps in this stage, which are source selection, search strategy, filtered criteria, quality assessment. We will now explain the decisions taken for each of the four steps of our research.

Source Selection: We primarily used Web of Science as the publication source, and getting the full text through their original database. Web of Science contains Social Sciences Citation Index (SSCI), Arts & Humanities Citation Index (A&HCI), Conference Proceedings Citation Index - Social Science & Humanities (CPCI-SSH), which could satisfy our requirements for publications. With its wide coverage of areas related to digital humanities, it is particularly likely to give us comprehensive results.

Search Strategy: Due to there being a limited number of papers directly about the problems scholars experience in practice when developing digital humanities projects, we extend the scope of search terms and added closely related research disciplines. Digital humanities tools evaluation studies will reveal the practice barriers of digital humanities projects. And there are several relevant evaluation studies of tools in the digital library research area. The following Table 1 gives a summary of search queries and the initial number of publications. We provide the full query terms to help reproducibility and for future researchers to identify future changes in the field.

Besides, keywords search as shown above, we also add some publications that we already familiar with about our research questions. David M. Nichols research team wrote 4 papers about tools evaluation in digital libraries, and 1 publication about tools usage in institution repositories. And we add 4 more publications about tools used frequently in digital humanities projects, which are content management systems, visualization tools, and text mining tools. Thus, we had 1974 publications in the beginning.

Table 1. Search queries and the number of resultant publications.

Search queries	Number
Topic = ((digital humanities) AND (tool OR software) AND (problem OR barrier))	105
Topic = ((humanities scholars) AND (tools OR software))	309
Topic = ((evaluate OR assess) AND (digital humanities) AND (software OR tool))	82
Topic = ((evaluate OR assess) AND (digital cultural heritage) AND (software OR tool))	121
Topic = ((evaluation OR assessment) AND (digital library) AND (checklist OR framework OR model))	799
Topic = ((digital humanities) AND (digital library))	548
Total	1964

Filtered Criteria: With the change of technologies since 2000, and the rise of digital repository use and widespread digitisation of humanities materials since then, there is a strong risk that earlier material may provide problems that are now irrelevant, or resolved, or overlook problems that have only emerged since. We chose to focus on the limitations of tools in common use by digital humanities scholars. Tools that are infrequently used, or only on a small number of projects, may have little influence on the general picture of digital humanities practice.

The inclusion criteria are:

The language of this publication is English;

The year of this publication is after 2000 to now (03/2021);

This publication needs to focus on tools usage or refers to tools usage;

These tools are suitable for humanities scholars;

This publication discussed the relationship between digital humanities and digital library.

Applying these criteria, we selected 36 different publications from 1974 publications, referring to evaluation of digital humanities tools and digital library tools, as well as the relationship between digital humanities and digital libraries.

Quality Assessment: In order to gain the most relevant and high-quality publications, quality assessment process is essential. We use the following questions as a checklist to select the final publications for SLR. We adopted the guidance from the original methodology to address these issues.

Q1: Does this publication have a clear research objective and an appropriate research method?

Q2: Does this publication have some tools' problems description or evaluation?

Q3: Does this publication point the practice barriers of humanities scholars or librarians?

Q4: Does this publication address the relationship between digital humanities and digital library?

Q5: Dose this publication refers to specific influencing factors of practice barriers?
Through answering yes (Y) or no (N) of above questions and evaluating the quality of these publications by scores (Y = 1 point, N = 0 point), each publication will have a result of quality assessment. The final publications needed to have a score higher than 3 points (out of 5). And if the publication gets Y in Q4, it can be adopted directly. The SLR final selected material for analysis was 28 publications.

2.3 Data Analysis

By browsing the evaluation criteria and conclusion parts in publications carefully, we extracted the key relevant information about problems of tools usage faced by humanities scholars from each of the 28 selected publications. From these noted we then integrated related ideas and concepts found in different papers to produce a holistic synthesis. Analysis was driven by, but not limited to, the three main research questions. Following the original methodology, there were two stages: general analysis identified the overview of the publications about practice barriers of humanities scholars in tools usage during building digital humanities projects, and research methods of them. Detailed analysis interconnected these insights around the research questions.

3 Results

The results of this study are presented in five parts. The first section is a general analysis of the 28 publications, including which tools they address and the research methods. The next section focuses on practice barriers for each specific tool type, then we turn to the relationship between digital humanities and digital libraries. Then, we begin to develop a framework of practice barriers faced by digital humanities scholars in creating digital collections. The framework consists of content, technique, interface and storage four parts. Finally, we summarized this SLR.

3.1 General Analysis

Overview

The studies focus on the main research question *'What are the practice barriers encoun-tered by humanities scholars in digital humanities projects?'* can be divided into two general groups: first, those that focus on infrastructural problems; second, those that focus on specific tools. We will consider these in turn.

10 studies discussed the practice barriers encountered by humanities scholars in dig-ital humanities projects from the whole infrastructure aspect. Digital humanities infras-tructure means the research environment of technology facilities when digital human-ities scholars engaged in digital humanities projects, which could conclude software, hardware, dataset, institution, investment and people. The current problems of digital humanities infrastructure would refer to following aspects:

Software: Lack of interoperability, the problem of software sustainability [10], Insufficient functionalities [11, 12], long processing time [13].

Hardware: Problems of storage and download [12].

Dataset: Homogeneous metadata [13–16], unsupported data format [12].

Institution: Insufficient assistant support [13, 17, 18], lack of physical space and digital humanities scholars [18], ignore the importance of digital humanities research center [18].

Investment: Lack of funding for tools development and sustainable usage [18], time and labor required [12].

People: Lack of professional technical skills [11–13], ignore the importance of digital humanities tools [19].

11 studies examined the practice barriers in digital humanities projects through the lens of one or more specific tools. The digital humanities tools contain semantic enrichment tools, such as Recogito, Ontotext; content management systems, such as Scalar, DSpace, WordPress; visualization tools, such as OWL-VisMod, Gephi; text analysis tools, such as Voyant, TAPoR; and text mining tools, such as GATE, MONK. In this paper, we divided them into three tool types. The following Table 2 gives a summary of these tools.

Table 2. Types of tools and the number of papers.

Tool types		Papers	Tools
Project-making tools	Semantic enrichment tools	1	Pelagios, Ontotext, BgLinks, VocMatch
	Content management systems	3	Omeka, Scalar
Visualization tools	Visual modeling tools	1	OWL-VisMod
	Network visualization tools	1	Gephi
Content analysis tools	Text analysis tools	2	Voyant, TAPoR
	Text mining tools	3	MOOK, GATE, ATLAS.ti, STING

Research Methods Used

The research methods of the 28 publications can be divided into qualitative and quantitative methods. Most of the qualitative studies use semi-structure interviews to gather data [5, 20, 21]. Researchers can produce in-depth and specific insights from the rich data of face-to-face interviews. Other studies adopted a case study method or a participant-observer method to allow a focus on pre-determined research questions, rather than on themes that emerged from the research data [12, 22]. Case studies can also produce specific recommendations for a particular development problem. Turning to quantitative studies, Ying (2010) examined the patterns of the frequency distribution of problems reported in interviews. They focused on pre-determined criteria and the relative important of a criterion would be indicated by its frequency [7]. A research method that combines quantitative and qualitative analysis is comprehensive checklists [6]. The checklist inspection method is appropriate for systematic evaluation of problems: the checklist formats captures each criterion explicitly so that researchers can check them in sequence, and detail the specific problem accordingly.

3.2 Practice Barriers in Different Categories of Tools

The first research question is *RQ1: What are the main practice barriers in different categories of tools used in digital humanities projects or research?* Following our chosen methodology, we organized results by the three types of digital humanities tools found during our general analysis: project-making tools, visualization tools, and content analysis tools. Reviewing the problems encountered with these three types of tool will allow us to identify similarities and differences between the three categories.

For project-making tools, the problems focus on how well the technology enables effective content creation. For example, semantic enrichment tools have been evaluated comparatively on a sample dataset from Europeana, and the mechanisms for disambiguating data, and quality issues of both technology and datasets are the primary reported problems [23]. In the case of Scalar, a digital humanity publishing platform for media-rich projects, interviews found many usability issues and, critically, a mismatch between users' mental models of creation and the corresponding content creation processes in Scalar [20]. Problems were also found in content management systems commonly used in digital humanities projects: e.g. Omeka cannot have interactive and exploratory items [24], and Omeka needs more user engagement and user education [22].

For visualization tools, the reported problems mostly concern the interface. OWL-VisMod, a visual modeling tool for OWL ontologies, was evaluated from the view of the human-computer interaction. A usability evaluation identified several recurring practice barriers. First, the visualizations can be confusing until the user becomes completely familiar with the domain and visual presentation; Second, the help function should be clearer and enriched with videos and images to help users use this tool [25]. In another study Gephi, a popular network visualization software, was critiqued by researchers investigating how to evaluate tools. They found several criteria, such as the proficiency of researchers, open source or not, and compatibility with hardware [26].

For content analysis tools, the problems mainly refer to specific content management. By evaluation of online text analysis tools including Voyant and TAPoR by interview and task design methods, the practice barriers among using these tools are simple data visualization not satisfying users' dynamic and interactive demands, coordination of different tools, flexibility of changing or updating content, and collaborative practice [5]. Miller (2018) also explore the accessibility limitations of Voyant [27]. GATE, a tool used for sentiment analysis, was improved by adding multiple language plugins, as many practice barriers are languages issues and multilingual text disambiguation [28]. MONK, a web-based text mining software, faces the challenges that its technology is not flexible and granular enough to meet DH needs. Furthermore, MONK is designed for small dataset, so there are some usability problems when facing large volumes of data [29]. ATLAS.ti has restricted visualization and STING is not available via a web interface [30].

A systematic literature review of textual analysis tools offers several influencing factors in their selection and use, which are availability, visualization techniques employed, theoretical framework supported, collaborative editing, and reuse software mechanisms [9].

3.3 Practice Barriers in Relevant Research Discipline

The second research question is *RQ2: Are there any relevant publications in digital library research discipline can offer some references?* Compared with digital library (DL) applications, digital humanities projects focus more on exhibiting specific content and the interpretation of data. So, we cannot just assume the tool application methods of digital libraries that improve usability and utility will work directly in digital humanities. However, the evaluation concepts and criteria can draw from DL experiences, because they have some similarities in institutions and roles.

Digital humanities has similar research institutions to many digital libraries. DLs are deployed in libraries and research in information- and-library-science schools. Digital humanities has potential connection both to libraries and information and library Science. According to the New Companion to Digital Humanities (2016), of 55 digital humanities scholars, ten are affiliated with Information and Library Science programs, five with libraries, and thirteen with digital humanities centers. Information and library Science curricula increasingly include digital humanities content [31].

The research roles of digital humanities and DL are also similar. The DL domain includes librarians and developers. There are also similarities between humanists and librarians, e.g. a lacking of programming expertise, familiarity with humanities research methods, and large volumes of raw data. With the increasing collaboration between digital humanities and digital libraries, the lines separating the humanities scholars, the librarians, the editor, and the information technology expert are blurring [32].

Thus, drawing influential practice barriers found when evaluating digital humanities tools would help expand this literature review. There are several evaluations of digital library tools. Ying (2010) interviewed with DL administrators, developers, and researchers and examined the frequency distribution of digital library evaluation criteria. The important evaluation dimensions: are usefulness and ease of understanding in content, interoperability, effectiveness, and reliability in technology, ease of use, appropriateness, and effectiveness in interface, responsiveness, accessibility, and gaps in service, productivity, successfulness, and learning effects in user, sustainability and integrity in context [7]. Hoe-Lian Goh (2006) used a checklist to evaluate the CERN document server (CDSware), EPrints, Greenstone and Fedora, and the evaluation criteria related to practice barriers are content management, content acquisition, search support, access control and privacy, preservation and maintenance [6]. Gkoumas (2015) evaluated 13 DL tools, proposing two common problems which are poorer language support for less popular languages and usability problems about unexpected actions or some unimplemented options [33].

Digital institution repositories are a specific type of digital library used for scholars. Digital institution repositories have richer metadata schemes than DL, but have less maturity than DLs. These features are shared between repositories and digital humanities. Nichols (2009) interviewed several repository managers who were working with commonly uses systems, including Digital Commons, DSpace, Eprints, and Fedora, and got feedback about influencing factors, which are usefulness, cost of correcting, availability and archiving issues [21].

3.4 The Framework of Practice Barriers

The third research question is *RQ3: Can we develop a framework for practice barriers of humanities scholars using tools in digital humanities projects?* From the SLR, practice barriers faced by humanities scholars in digital humanities projects can be listed as different influencing factors. We summarize them through the sequence of designing, building, presenting and maintaining digital humanities projects, and divide them into four aspects, which are content, technique, interface, sustainability. Table 3 shows the framework of influencing factors of practice barriers which contains sources and meaning of these influencing factors.

3.5 Summary

According to the SLR, the practice barriers faced by humanities scholars in digital humanities projects particularly involve two issues: infrastructure problems and specific tools' problem. The infrastructure problems relate to software, hardware, dataset, institution, investment and people. While the tools' problems can be divided into difficulties around content, technique, interface and storage; the problems emerge from different kinds of tool used across the whole development process of digital humanities projects, including designing, building, presenting and maintaining.

Some practice barriers are both founded in infrastructure problems and tools' problems, which are software problems about interoperability, sustainability, functions and processing time; hardware problems about storage and download; homogenous dataset problems; storage sustainability problems causing by insufficient investment; and problems of people without professional skills. However, the infrastructure problems further indicated that the research institutions and humanities scholars ignored the importance of digital humanities research, and the institutions should put more efforts in digital humanities research centers construction.

Based on the specific practice barriers of tools usage, we found many influencing factors in Table 3 are also mentioned in Usability Evaluation Model and Technology Acceptance Model. The practice barriers about technique are the most related to some variables of these two models: related variables in Usability Evaluation Model are language, technique, efficiency, level of experience and level of complexity [35]; related variables in Technology Acceptance Model are ease of use, compatibility, complexity, accessibility, system quality and prior experience [36]. Usability Evaluation Model also mentioned modeling competence which is the same as matching ability in Table 3. Thus, the special influencing factors of practice barriers faced by digital humanities scholars are flexibility, collaboration, disambiguation, content management and completeness of content; quality, interoperability, assistance and no code of technique; and all influencing factors in interface and storage part.

Table 3. The framework of influencing factors of practice barriers.

Aspect	Influencing factors	Meaning	Sources
Content	Matching ability	Match between users' mental models and system regarding function & interaction	[9, 13, 16, 20, 21, 23]
	Flexibility	Can expand and revise content	[5, 9]
	Collaboration	Collaborative editing	[5, 9]
	Disambiguation	Making complex and heterogeneous resources work together	[23, 28] [13–16]
	Content management	Cost of money, time and labor; Functions of submitting content	[6, 34]
	Completeness	All of the dataset is available and accessible	[13–15, 19, 27, 34]
Technique	Ease of use	Low complexity and intuitive to use	[7, 19, 25]
	Efficiency	Useful and effective support of user goals	[7, 9, 20, 26]
	Proficiency	Required technical skill level(s) of users	[11, 13, 19, 26]
	Quality	Functionality of final system	[11, 23, 33]
	Interoperability	Can share/connect with other systems	[7, 13, 34]
	Assistance	Support of communities, resources and tool	[12, 13, 17]
	No code	Full comprehension of the programming code is not mandatory	[13]
Interface	Visualization	Dynamic and interactive visualization	[5, 9, 24]
	Language	Multi-language support	[28, 33]
	Responsiveness	Response speed of webpage	[7, 13]
	Search support	Varied and effective tools for search and browse	[6, 14, 15]
Storage	Compatibility	Compatibility with hardware	[26]
	Sustainability	Long term use and storage	[7, 34]
	Integrity	Keeps the dataset uncorrupted and unmodified	[7, 14]
	Safety	Privacy protection, preservation of data	[6, 21]
	Funding	Continuous financial support	[34]

4   Conclusion

As it has been shown throughout this paper, the practice of humanities scholars in digital humanities projects presents many problems which hindered the development of digital humanities scholarship. This paper makes value contributions in practice barriers identify and tools improvement. The following steps of this research would be some interview to deeper understand the common problems and reveal some unprecedented problems. In the future, we will do research about digital resource aggregation that can help humanities scholars solve these practice barriers in some extent.

References

1. Whitelaw, M.: Generous interfaces for digital cultural collections. Digit. Humanit. Q. **9**, 16 (2015)
2. Borgman, C.L.: The Digital Future is Now: A Call to Action for the Humanities. eScholarship, University of California (2010)
3. Borgman, C.L.: Why are online catalogs still hard to use? J. Am. Soc. Inf. Sci. **47**, 493–503 (1996)
4. Nyhan, J., Flinn, A.: Computation and the Humanities: Towards an Oral History of Digital Humanities. vol. 285 (2016)
5. Given, L.M., Willson, R.: Information technology and the humanities scholar: documenting digital research practices. J. Am. Soc. Inf. Sci. **69**, 807–819 (2018)
6. Hoe-Lian Goh, D., Chua, A., Anqi Khoo, D., Boon-Hui Khoo, E., Bok-Tong Mak, E., Wen-Min Ng, M.: A checklist for evaluating open source digital library software. Online Inf. Rev. **30**, 360–379 (2006)
7. Ying, Z.: Developing a holistic model for digital library evaluation. J. Am. Soc. Inform. Sci. Technol. **61**, 88–110 (2010)
8. Kitchenham, B., Brereton, P.: A systematic review of systematic review process research in software engineering. Inf. Softw. Technol. **55**, 2049–2075 (2013)
9. Martin-Rodilla, P., Sánchez, M.: Software support for discourse-based textual information analysis: a systematic literature review and software guidelines in practice. Information **11**, 256 (2020)
10. Buddenbohm, S., Matoni, M., Schmunk, S., Thiel, C.: Quality assessment for the sustainable provision of software components and digital research infrastructures for the arts and humanities. Bibliothek Forschung und Praxis **41**(2), 231–241 (2017)
11. Bulatovic, N., Gnadt, T., Romanello, M., Stiller, J., Thoden, K.: Usability in digital humanities - evaluating user interfaces, infrastructural components and the use of mobile devices during research process. In: Fuhr, N., Kovács, L., Risse, T., Nejdl, W. (eds.) TPDL 2016. LNCS, vol. 9819, pp. 335–346. Springer, Cham (2016). https://doi.org/10.1007/978-3-319-43997-6_26
12. Rath, L.L.: Low-barrier-to-entry data tools: creating and sharing humanities data. Libr. Hi Tech **34**, 268–285 (2016)
13. Terras, M., et al.: Enabling complex analysis of large-scale digital collections: humanities research, high-performance computing, and transforming access to British library digital collections. Digital Sch. Humanit. **33**(2), 456–466 (2018)
14. Frosini, L., Bardi, A., Manghi, P., Pagano, P.: An Aggregation framework for digital humanities infrusturatures: the parthenos experience. Sci. Res. Inf. Technol. **8**, 17 (2018)
15. Hyvönen, E.: Using the semantic web in digital humanities: shift from data publishing to data-analysis and serendipitous knowledge discovery. Semant. Web **11**, 187–193 (2020)

16. Martin-Rodilla, P., Gonzalez-Perez, C.: Metainformation scenarios in digital humanities: characterization and conceptual modelling strategies. Inf. Syst. **84**, 29–48 (2019)
17. Kaltenbrunner, W.: Digital infrastructure for the humanities in Europe and the US: governing scholarship through coordinated tool development. Comp. Support. Coop. Work **26**(3), 275–308 (2017)
18. Shanmugapriya, T., Menon, N.: Infrastructure and social interaction: situated research practices in digital humanities in India. Digit. Humanit. Q. **14**, 16 (2020)
19. Juola, P.: Killer applications in digital humanities. Literary Linguist. Comput. **23**, 73–83 (2007)
20. Tracy, D.G.: Assessing digital humanities tools: use of scalar at a research university. Portal-Libr. Acad. **16**, 163–189 (2016)
21. Nichols, D.M., et al.: Experiences in deploying metadata analysis tools for institutional repositories. Cataloging Classif. Q. **47**, 229–248 (2009)
22. Marsh, E.: Chickens, aprons, markets, and cans: how the national agricultural library uses omeka as its content management system for digital exhibits. Digit. Libr. Perspect. **33**, 361–377 (2017)
23. Manguinhas, H., et al.: Exploring comparative evaluation of semantic enrichment tools for cultural heritage metadata. In: Fuhr, N., Kovács, L., Risse, T., Nejdl, W. (eds.) TPDL 2016. LNCS, vol. 9819, pp. 266–278. Springer, Cham (2016). https://doi.org/10.1007/978-3-319-43997-6_21
24. Rath, L.: Omeka.net as a librarian-led digital humanities meeting place. New Lib. World **117**, 158–172 (2016)
25. Garcia, J., Garcia-Penalvo, F.J., Theron, R., de Pablos, P.O.: Usability evaluation of a visual modelling tool for OWL ontologies. J. Univers. Comput. Sci. **17**, 1299–1313 (2011)
26. Van Es, K., Wieringa, M., Schäfer, M.T.: Tool criticism. In: Proceedings of the 2nd International Conference on Web Studies. ACM Press, Paris, France (2018)
27. Miller, A.: Text mining digital humanities projects: assessing content analysis capabilities of voyant tools. J. Web Librariansh. **12**, 169–197 (2018)
28. Amjad, A., Qamar, U.: UAMSA: unified approach for multilingual sentiment analysis using GATE. In: Proceedings of the 6th Conference on the Engineering of Computer Based Systems, Association for Computing Machinery, Bucharest, Romania (2019). pp. Article 25
29. Green, H.E.: Under the workbench: an analysis of the use and preservation of monk text mining research software. Literary Linguist. Comput. **29**, 23–40 (2014)
30. Spinakis, A., Peristera, P.: Text Mining Tools: Evaluation Methods and Criteria. pp. 131–149. Springer Berlin, Heidelberg (2004)
31. Poole, A.: The conceptual ecology of digital humanities. J. Doc. **73**, 91–122 (2017)
32. Zhang, Y., Liu, S., Mathews, E.: Convergence of digital humanities and digital libraries. Libr. Manage. **36**, 362–377 (2015)
33. Gkoumas, G., Lazarinis, F.: Evaluation and usage scenarios of open source digital library and collection management tools. Program-Electron. Libr. Inf. Syst. **49**, 226–241 (2015)
34. Rosenthaler, L., Fornaro, P., Clivaz, C.: DASCH: Data and Service Center for the Humanities. Digital Scholarship in the Humanities fqv051 (2015)
35. Condori-Fernandez, N., Panach, J.I., Baars, A.I., Vos, T., Pastor, O.: An empirical approach for evaluating the usability of model-driven tools. Sci. Comput. Program. **78**, 2245–2258 (2013)
36. Lee, Y., Kozar, K.A., Larsen, K.R.T.: The technology acceptance model: past, present, and future. Commun. Assoc. Inf. Syst. **12**, 752–780 (2003)

Researching Pandemics Through Time: A Covid-19 Inspired Data-Driven Approach to Explore Historical Newspapers

Mirjam Cuper$^{(\boxtimes)}$ (iD)

KB, National Library of the Netherlands, The Hague, The Netherlands
mirjam.cuper@kb.nl
http://www.kb.nl

Abstract. Heritage institutions are exploring new ways to open up their digital collections. In this context, the KB, national library of the Netherlands, has built a data-driven demonstration website based on historical newspapers. This website centers around a currently relevant topic due to the Covid-19 crisis: pandemics. A Toolbox with Notebooks and a sample data set is provided to support students and starting researchers. This paper describes the data selection process, the functionality of the website and corresponding Toolbox, as well as the initial reception.

Keywords: Digital cultural heritage · Digital libraries · User interface · Historical newsarchives · Exploration · Pandemics · Demo website

1 Introduction

Most heritage institutions provide a straight-forward way of searching through their digital collections. Users specify a search query and a list with snippets of results is returned. Such an interface works fine when users know what they are looking for, but is not well suited for exploration of a specific topic. An alternative to searching is browsing, but due to how digital collections are often displayed, browsing is not enticing for users [8,12].

Several studies suggest other ways of displaying digital collections, such as a topic-based search interface, in which results are clustered based on a certain topic [8]. Furthermore, institutions can decide to display their textual search results through visualisations [4]. This can, among others, be used to create summaries of the textual data. A benefit of visualisations is the ease with which users can extract information from them [4,9].

Since heritage institutions started digitizing their collections, the use of these collections has changed. A lot of research shifted from mainly manually researching collections to using computer science techniques [10]. In our experience, it

© Springer Nature Switzerland AG 2021
G. Berget et al. (Eds.): TPDL 2021, LNCS 12866, pp. 227–231, 2021.
https://doi.org/10.1007/978-3-030-86324-1_26

often occurs that students or starting researchers are interested in working with digital collections, but lack the skills needed for analysing large amounts of textual data.

Recently, various heritage institutions started experimenting with new ways of exposing their data and providing tools for researchers querying their collections. This is often done by offering 'Workbenches' that contain Notebooks: open-source web applications consisting of code and documentation [2,3,11].

The KB, national library of the Netherlands, has closely followed these developments, and decided to set up an experimental data-driven demonstration website. The aim of this website is to examine new ways of displaying the historical newspaper collection of the KB. We created a topic-based website (in Dutch) (http://delpher_demo.kbresearch.nl/) [5], with a relevant topic for the year 2020 due to the Covid-19 crisis: pandemics. The website provides four pandemic related categories, from which users can choose to start their exploratory journey through related historical news articles. The results are summarised by using a timeline and various other visualisations. We deliberately used rather basic visualisations, to be able to provide entry-level demonstration code. A Toolbox with example data and Notebooks is provided for those who are interested in performing these analyses themselves (https://github.com/KBNLresearch/delpher_demo) [6].

In this paper we describe the data collection process and the functionality of the website and Toolbox, after which we conclude with the initial reception of the website.

2   Data Collection

The data used for the website is collected from Delpher, a digital heritage archive that provides access to historical books, periodicals and newspapers [7]. For this project, we used the historical newspaper collection.

We started with the selection of pandemic related words by analysing a collection of 295.612 European news articles about Covid-19. These articles were retrieved through the Aylien Coronavirus News dataset [1]. Out of the 50 most commonly used words from these articles, we extracted pandemic related words. This led to the following set: corona, pandemic, outbreak, infection, spread, virus, disease and quarantine. The word 'corona' was excluded because there were less then ten articles about this disease in the Delpher news archive. Instead, we added the words 'flu' and 'influenza' to the set. During the development of the website (November 2020), vaccines and immunity were a hot topic in the Netherlands. Therefore the words 'vaccine' and 'immunity' were included. Finally, we decided to add 'Spanish flu', since this was a noteworthy pandemic in history. The end result was a set of twelve keywords, which we translated to Dutch.

We chose four of these keywords to use as main categories around which the site was built: 'pandemic', 'outbreak', 'immunity' and 'Spanish flu'. We collected all articles from Delpher in which at least one of these four words was present. Then, we prepared the data for further use on the website, and enriched it by adding metadata about which categories and keywords belong to which article. The remaining keywords where used as sub selections for more in-depth analyses on the website.

3   Tool Description

The homepage presents an introduction and four buttons, each containing a category. The buttons navigate to a page dedicated to this category. Each category page shows a timeline. This timeline shows all the years in which at least one news article from this category was found. Furthermore, the page displays some descriptive analyses. The number of total articles is shown and the content of all articles is summarized in a word cloud. This word cloud shows the 20 most common words from these articles based on their frequency. We only altered the results by removing stop words. The font size and frequency of a word are correlated, which means that a word appears bigger when the frequency is higher (see Fig. 2).

The page also displays a line chart showing the number of found articles per year. This can be switched to a bar chart that shows the number of articles per keyword. The user can scroll through the timeline to discover the various years in which articles were found. By selecting a year, the before mentioned descriptive analyses adapt to the selection. The page is also extended with buttons for keywords that were found in the articles corresponding to this selection. Furthermore, a bar chart with the number of articles per keyword is shown (see Fig. 1).

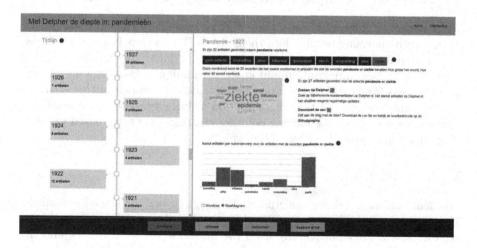

Fig. 1. Overview of the website once a main category and a year are selected.

When a further selection is made by choosing a keyword, a word tree is displayed. The word tree shows the relationship between keywords that are co-occurring in the articles. The bigger the font size, the more frequent the words occur together (see Fig. 2). The word tree is set as default, but the user can switch back to the bar chart.

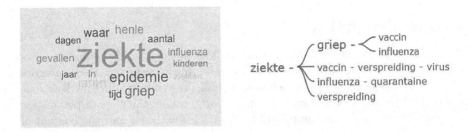

Fig. 2. Examples of a word cloud (left) and a word tree (right) for the category 'pandemic' for the year 1927 and with 'ziekte' (disease) as selected keyword.

The page contains a link to the original scans of the selected articles, to give users the opportunity to explore them on Delpher. Clicking on the words in the word cloud also navigates to Delpher. In that case, the Delpher result is further narrowed down to not only the category, but also to the corresponding word in the word cloud and, if applicable, the earlier selected keyword.

There is an option to download a file with metadata and a 'bag of words' of each article from the current selection. Finally, a link to the Toolbox is provided.

4   Toolbox: Example Data and Jupyter Notebooks

We provided a Toolbox for students or starting researchers to help them getting started with analysing textual data themselves. The Toolbox is a Github repository containing Jupyter Notebooks and example data. The Notebooks guide users through basic preparation and analysis techniques. Users can also download data sets from the demonstration website and use them for further analysis.

The complete code of the demonstration website was also made available. This code can be used as a starting point for creating other topic-based websites or to make an improved version of our website.

5   Conclusion

The demonstration website was promoted through several social media channels. The feedback we received was positive. Users liked the way they where able to explore topics. They particularly liked the timelines and word clouds, and the fact that the website was showcasing a currently relevant topic. Multiple request where made for more information about how to replicate the visualisations, after which we showed them the Toolbox. Thus, a recommendation for further development would be to give the Toolbox a more prominent place on the website. To determine the actual added value of this website, a more comprehensive evaluation is desirable in the near future.

References

1. AYLIEN: Free news intelligence dataset (2020). https://aylien.com/resources/datasets/coronavirus-dataset
2. BVMC labs: GLAM Jupyter notebooks (2020). http://data.cervantesvirtual.com/blog/notebooks/
3. CLARIAH media suite: Jupyter notebooks (2020). https://mediasuite.clariah.nl/documentation/howtos/jupyter-notebooks
4. Conner, C., Samuel, J., Kretinin, A., Samuel, Y., Nadeau, L.: A picture for the words! Textual visualization in big data analytics. arXiv preprint arXiv:2005.07849 (2020). https://doi.org/10.13140/RG.2.2.25351.83360
5. Cuper, M.: Met delpher de diepte. In: pandemieën (2020). http://delpher_demo.kbresearch.nl/
6. Cuper, M.: Toolbox delpher demo site (2020). https://github.com/KBNLresearch/delpher_demo
7. Delpher. https://www.delpher.nl/
8. Grant, C.E., George, C.P., Kanjilal, V., Nirkhiwale, S., Wilson, J.N., Wang, D.Z.: A topic-based search, visualization, and exploration system. In: Proceedings of the 28th International FLAIRS Conference (2015)
9. Heimerl, F., Lohmann, S., Lange, S., Ertl, T.: Word cloud explorer: text analytics based on word clouds. In: 2014 47th Hawaii International Conference on System Sciences, pp. 1833–1842 (2014). https://doi.org/10.1109/HICSS.2014.231
10. Jänicke, S., Franzini, G., Cheema, M.F., Scheuermann, G.: On close and distant reading in digital humanities: a survey and future challenges. In: Borgo, R., Ganovelli, F., Viola, I. (eds.) Eurographics Conference on Visualization (EuroVis) - STARs. The Eurographics Association (2015). https://doi.org/10.2312/eurovisstar.20151113
11. Sherratt, T.: GLAM workbench (2020). https://glam-workbench.net/
12. Whitelaw, M.: Generous interfaces for digital cultural collections. Digit. Hum. Q. **9** (2015)

Author Index

Printed in the United States
by Baker & Taylor Publisher Services

Printed in the United States
by Baker & Taylor Publisher Services